Pictorial Research by Carol M. Martel

"Partners in Progress" by
John Bret-Harte and Dean E. Smith

Produced in cooperation with the Arizona Historical Society

Windsor Publications, Inc.
Northridge, California

ARIZONA

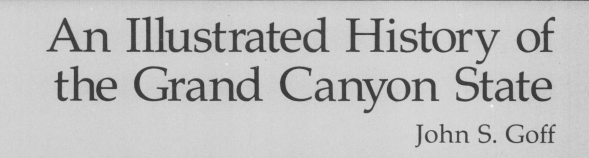

An Illustrated History of the Grand Canyon State

John S. Goff

Windsor Publications, Inc.—History Books Division
Managing Editor: Karen Story
Design Director: Alexander D'Anca

Staff for *Arizona*
Manuscript Editor: Marilyn Horn
Photo Editor: Susan L. Wells
Developmental Editor: Pamela Schroeder
Editor, Corporate Biographies: Judith L. Hunter
Production Editor, Corporate Biographies: Phyllis Gray
Senior Proofreader: Susan J. Muhler
Editorial Assistants: Didier Beauvoir, Thelma Fleischer, Alyson Gould,
    Kim Kievman, Michael Nugwynne, Kathy B. Peyser, Pat Pittman,
    Theresa J. Solis
Sales Representatives, Corporate Biographies: Beverly Cornell, Dick
    Fry, Walker Whitley
Layout Artist, Text: Michael Burg
Layout Artists, Corporate Biographies: Angie Ortiz, Mari Catherine
    Preimesberger
Designer: Ellen Ifrah

Library of Congress Cataloging-in-Publication Data
Goff, John S., 1931-
Arizona, an illustrated history of the Grand Canyon State/by John S.
Goff; pictorial research by Carol M. Martell; Partners in progress by
John Bret Harte and Dean E. Smith; produced in cooperation with
the Arizona Historical Society—1st ed.
Bibliography: p. 220
Includes index.
ISBN 0-89781-230-1
1. Arizona—History. 2. Arizona—Description and travel—Views.
3. Arizona—Industries.
I. Arizona Historical Society. II. Title.
F811.G56 1988
979.1—dc19

James L. Fish, III, Chief Operating Officer
Hal Silverman, Vice-President/Publisher

FRONTISPIECE: This painting depicts a jerk-line mule team pulling freight up the west side of the Black Mountains near Sitgreaves Pass, between Goldroad and Kingman. This stretch later became a segment of the famous Route 66. Many of the highways built prior to the modern freeway were roads with historic pasts. Most were animal trails, then Indian trails, then wagon trails, and finally roads for the early automobile. Courtesy, Jo Proferes

OPPOSITE: Ed Schieffelin, founder of Tombstone, dared to search for silver in the San Pedro Valley, a land frequented by hostile Apaches. Two years after the influx of miners to the silver-rich hills, the miner's camp became a city known as Tombstone, the name of his first claim. Schieffelin left Arizona in 1880 to prospect in Alaska and died in 1897. As requested, he was buried in the desert in the dress of a prospector. Courtesy, Tombstone Courthouse State Historic Park

Contents

The Land and Its Early People

Artist Jo Proferes depicts the Grand Canyon in all its ancient mystery. Courtesy, Jo Proferes

Arizona is both an old and a new place. It is new in the sense that there was no place by that name until a century and a quarter ago, and it is old because some parts of the area, such as the Hopi Reservation, have been continuously inhabited for as long as we have record of human beings in what is now the United States.

The name Arizona, which most likely means "land of few springs," or "land of little springs," was first applied to an area in what is now Sonora, Mexico, and was variously spelled. The name was again unofficially used after the United States acquired the southwestern portion of the nation after the Mexican War. It was first formally used when the Confederate States of America created the Territory of Arizona during the Civil War.

Arizona is a land of diversity. Unlike some states which are similar in geography throughout their boundaries, Arizona is a place of three separate and distinct climatic zones. In the southern portion of Arizona the land is a part of the great Sonoran desert. In the middle there is a chain of mountains running from the northwest to the southeast. These mountains have as their most spectacular feature the Mogollon Rim, which dramatically marks the end of the desert. The northeastern part of Arizona is the high plateau country. It is also a desert, but a cold one, featuring unusual and beautiful land formations.

The low desert lands are a continuation north of the dry areas of Mexico. Ranging in altitude from about 200 to about 2,000 feet, this area is not entirely flat as one usually expects a desert to be, but contains some modest mountain chains and now and then a solitary mountain. The Harquahala and Kofa mountains are examples of the former, while Mount Lemmon near Tucson rises to more than 9,000 feet from the desert floor. Rainfall is very limited; Yuma with about three inches per year and Phoenix with just over seven are typical. Moisture falls during two different seasons. In the winter, storms come out of the Pacific and cross California before reaching the dry land. In the summer, the "monsoons" are provided by thunderstorms. Then the moisture makes its way from the Gulf of Mexico across Mexico to Arizona.

Arizona has very little water. Stoneman Lake, 100 miles north of Phoenix, is the only natural lake; all others are man-made. In the south the Gila is the principal river, and its tributaries, the Salt, the Verde, the Santa Cruz, and the San Pedro, all help to form the major stream.

Unless one has lived through a summer in the Arizona desert, especially without air conditioning, one does not truly know hot weather in the United States. There is an old legend of a man from Yuma who died, went to hell, and promptly sent home for his blankets. Some say that the dry heat makes high temperatures bearable, but when the thermometer reaches above 100 degrees Fahrenheit it really doesn't matter how high the humidity measures. On the other hand, the pleasant, mild winters draw people from many other areas and attract tourists, giving the state one of its major economic benefits.

Almost one-third of Arizona consists of mountains and forested high country, with an average altitude of 5,000 feet. Spruce or pine cover this land and there are high annual levels of rain and snowfall. Humphreys Peak at 12,670 is the highest mountain in the state. An area of beautiful scenery and clean clear air, Humphreys Peak is a lovely place. Not long ago an Eastern humorist was visiting Flagstaff and reported that he realized something was wrong. The atmosphere was so pure and unspoiled he had to stand behind an automobile to breathe normally.

The plateau province or the high plateau country is largely another desert, although in some areas there is sufficient moisture for forests to exist. Mountains keep out rain and snow which is why it is a cold, dry desert. The average altitude is over 5,000 feet and the landscape is characterized by unusual formations, almost otherworldly in appearance. Canyons are cut by rivers; there are cliffs and mesas and evidence of past volcano activity. The great river, the Colorado, once called the "Nile of the West," is supplemented by the Little Colorado and other streams.

The Colorado River plays a major role in the history of Arizona. It runs through the Grand Canyon, which was supposedly "discovered" by the Spanish in the 1500s, although the Indians who had lived there for centuries must have had some inkling of the presence of one of the most spectacular natural wonders of the world. It is almost impossible to describe the beauty and grandeur of the gorges cut by the passage of the river.

A visiting British writer once described Arizona as "geology by day and astronomy by night." The geological story of the state is a colorful one. At the bottom of the Grand Canyon one can find the granite which formed the original crust of the earth. For many millions of years Arizona was covered by seas. Limestone found in many places was at one time the shells of living creatures. Mountains have appeared and been worn down. It is believed that about 20 million years ago volcanic activity was pronounced in the mountain region. Some of that activity continued for many, many years, and it is believed that the last eruption in the Flagstaff area took place a little more than 1,000 years ago.

One of the important effects of the involved geological history is that rich mineral deposits were found within Arizona. A single gold mine, the Vulture, is estimated to have produced $8 million worth of bullion, and that was in nineteenth-century dollars. The Tombstone mines in southeastern Arizona and others in central Arizona produced rich silver ore. Even so, copper mining overshadowed all other mineral extractions.

Although the mineral ores have now been seemingly exhausted, the nonmetallic resources are almost endless. A modern wit has described Arizona as being 10,000 square miles of "kitty litter." The sand and gravel are quite marketable, as are cement, gypsum, and lime. Coal deposits exist in northeastern Arizona, but thus far little petroleum or natural gas has been located. The soils of the state are among the richest in the world. If enough water was available, more than eight million acres of land in Arizona could be farmed.

There are over 3,000 species of plant life found in Arizona, an amazing diversity caused by both the size of the area and its different climate zones. In the mountains there are the impressive pine trees, gently bending in the wind and beautifully scenting the pure mountain air. Harvesting these giants has

provided a livelihood for generations. Mesquite is commonly found near streambeds and on lower mountain slopes, where its amazingly extensive root system allows it to survive. The state tree, the palo verde or green stick, is seemingly leafless, but its

ABOVE: Projectile points and point fragments depicted here were taken from a site in Sulphur Springs Valley in southeastern Arizona and date from the late Cochise-culture Indians. The Cochise people were hunters, gatherers, and grinders of foods found in the wild. Courtesy, Arizona State Museum, University of Arizona, Helga Teiwes, photographer

LEFT: Human effigy figures had a long history among the Hohokam peoples, but examples as fine as these jars are rarely found. These two delightful vessels came from the 1964-1965 excavations at Snaketown. Both have painted faces and pierced ears, but the more robust nature of the jar on the right suggests it is male, and the diminutive one on the left suggests a female portrayal. Courtesy, Arizona State Museum, University of Arizona, Helga Teiwes, photographer

These pottery bowls and jars are Mogollon Brown Ware. Classified as red-on-brown types, they date from around A.D. 650 to 1400. The bowls in the back were found in Graham County, Arizona; the center left jar is from Gila Pueblo, Gila County; and the Mogollon red-on-brown bowls in the center and right front are from the Harris Village site in New Mexico. Courtesy, Arizona State Museum, University of Arizona

yellow flowers bring beauty in the spring.

Wildflowers abound in springtime as well. Relatives of the California poppy cover fields not far from Wickenburg. They turn the ground copper-colored for miles. In many places lupine turns the landscape blue.

The giant saguaro, with its small white blossom, is the most remarkable of all of Arizona's cacti. When a decade old, the plant is little more than six inches in height, but when it reaches a mature 150 years old it stands about 35 feet in height. Its blossom is the Arizona state flower.

The cholla, or jumping cactus, is plentiful in the desert. Contrary to rumor, it does not "jump," but the slightest touch will result in a most unpleasant experience.

The prickly pear cactus is also very plentiful, and from its dark red fruit a jelly can be made, provided one is careful to avoid the tiny spines. The barrel cactus (also called the compass cactus, since it always grows toward the southwest) is a source of water in the desert. In southern Arizona, along the Mexican border, the organ pipe cactus is a tourist attraction and reaches a height of 10 to 15 feet. The ocotillo, or the Devil's coachwhip, is not actually a

cactus but is often considered to be one. It can be grown to form a living fence, dotted with small red blossoms.

Long ago trilobites, animals resembling salamanders, strange flying reptile birds, and even dinosaurs roamed Arizona. When humans first arrived there were mammoths, camels, and horses; all of which had disappeared by the time the first Europeans saw the land. In more modern times elk were present until around 1900, and were then reintroduced from Wyoming as a conservation measure. The grizzly bear was last seen around 1916. An animal now found—in one variety or another—throughout Arizona is the deer. Deer are plentiful, so much so that on occasion they have damaged the ground cover. The old enemy of the deer, variously known as the mountain lion, puma, or cougar, is now found in fewer and fewer numbers.

The desert bighorn or mountain sheep is not plentiful either, but always impressive when seen. Then there is the coyote, which always seems to survive. The javelina, which people mistake for a relative of the pig, is characteristic of the desert. Foxes, rabbits, and squirrels are also often found in Arizona. One of the latter is the Kaibab squirrel, considered a

This group of Hopi Indian arts shows the variety of Hopi designs. The prize-winning blanket, left front, is a diamond twill with a black border and stripes. The coiled plaque, left back, is made of thin coiled loops with a winged Kachina design in the center. The polychrome jar, left center, is polished red inside and painted red and black, perhaps representing a stylized bird figure. Among the most famous of the Hopi crafts are the ceremonial Kachina dolls; this one is an eagle Kachina. The belt is woven Navajo-style, edged in white next to inner red. The sash is similar to those worn in the antelope dance. Courtesy, Arizona State Museum, University of Arizona, Helga Teiwes, photographer

Kiet Siel, which means "broken pottery" in the Navajo language, is a thirteenth-century cliff dwelling of the Pueblo culture. With 350 rooms, it was the largest cliff city in Arizona. The ruins, photographed here in 1929, can be seen at Navajo National Monument near Kayenta. The ruins lie in a long cave, roofed by a cliff still blackened from prehistoric fires. Courtesy, Arizona State Museum, University of Arizona

separate species from other squirrels, and found only at the Grand Canyon.

Arizona bird life is of great variety. Some of the better known residents are the roadrunner, the cactus wren, which is the state bird, and Gambel's quail, with its curious topknot. In addition there are many doves, woodpeckers, sparrows, and hummingbirds.

Reptile life is also very plentiful. The Gila monster is a notorious desert dweller. Though very poisonous, it is not really terribly dangerous because it cannot open its mouth wide enough to bite its victim and inject its venom. The rattlesnake and the sidewinder continue to inhabit land recently taken over by humans. Another less-than-friendly Arizona resident is the scorpion; the infamous black widow spider fits into the same category.

At some point in the dim, distant past, human beings began to appear on the Arizona scene. Just when this took place is not known, but most archaeologists believe it was at least 20,000 years ago when inhabitants of Asia crossed on an ancient land bridge into Alaska, and their descendants populated both

North and South America. There is much evidence to support the theory that the ancestors of the American Indians came originally from China. The story of people without a written history, however, is largely conjecture, and from time to time old theories are discarded and new ones accepted.

Archaeologists' methods of dating ancient objects have considerable margin for error. In the early 1900s an Arizonan, Andrew E. Douglass, an astronomer at the Lowell Observatory in Flagstaff, noticed that pine trees produced rings of varying width within their trunks each year according to the amount of moisture they received. Narrow rings meant drought. It is possible, using this observation, to determine approximately when a given tree stopped growing. The science is called dendrochronology, and while it is not exact, due to varying amounts of rain or snow from area to area, it is nevertheless a useful tool for dating the story of the last 2,000 years in the Southwest.

Artifacts left by humans can likewise be used to uncover prehistory. Pottery is especially useful; so,

too, are baskets and clothing. Since humans tend often to live in the same area generation after generation, digging down through layers of soil exposes different cultures. Emil Haury, a distinguished contemporary anthropologist, has done much important work with places such as Ventana Cave on the Papago Indian Reservation.

Unfortunately, material items do not tell us much about governments, religions, and other abstract aspects of life. In such matters there is much room for debate and disagreement, and often controversy arises.

It is currently believed that human beings lived in Arizona at least 12,000 years before the present. We of course have no idea what ancient people called themselves; in more recent times they have been given names by others. For example, the great

Apache leader Cochise who lived in the nineteenth century has had his name given to a group of people who lived from about 5,000 years ago until close to the start of the Christian era. Originally these people were hunters and gatherers, as were those who lived in the area before them, but later they became the first farmers in Arizona. They grew corn or maize and later beans and squash. They were prosperous, and their material wealth increased.

The inhabitants of the high plateau country are today called the Anasazi, a word derived from the Navajo language which means the "old ones," or "those who lived before." Anthropologists have divided the periods of these people into what they call the several Basket Maker and Pueblo stages. It was no easy matter to win a living from the rather poor soil of this area, but these once nomadic people settled down and began farming. Water was always in short supply. Originally their homes were simple, circular, single-room dwellings, but gradually they became more elaborate. Masonry walls were used, and often homes were developed in part through the

people of the Cochise culture but they had a more complex life-style. Houses were clustered around a large pit structure and dwellings were partially underground. Game was plentiful and corn was planted using sharp rocks to till the soil. The Mogollon knew

This display of Indian turquoise and silver jewelry is part of the collection of the Heard Museum in Phoenix. Dwight and Maie Bartlett Heard collected American Indian artifacts which eventually became the basis for the museum at their Phoenix home, Casa Blanca. Courtesy, Heard Museum

use of natural caves. Even later great pueblos or cities were developed—some of which survive to the present. They were the first urban dwellers of Arizona, who by concentrating families in a small area enabled everyone to share the better living areas. It is believed that Oraibi was occupied by about 1200 A.D., and as such it is probably the oldest continuously inhabited settlement in the United States.

This society was an advanced one. Several foods were plentiful and means were discovered to store a surplus. Impressive baskets were made, and pottery featured colorful decoration. After about 1100 A.D. the Anasazi were numerous enough to move into new areas. There are a number of Anasazi ruins which have survived to intrigue the visitor to the high plateaus. Probably the best known is in Canyon de Chelly, which has the impressive White House ruins.

A derivative culture also developed from the main one. These people are now called the Sinagua, "without water," and there was some merging of their culture with the people of the mountains and the desert.

The people of the mountains are called the Mogollon. They probably were the descendants of the

how to make pipe out of stone and seem to have fashioned gaming pieces out of bone. By about 700 A.D. they were trading with their neighbors to the south and obtained cotton, which was woven into cloth. Much of their pottery was brown or red, and while some was rough and poorly formed, they also produced a better quality than did others of the ancient Southwest.

A typical Mogollon settlement is Kinishba Ruin, which was first excavated in the 1880s but more extensively studied in the 1930s. There are two large structures and six smaller ones, dating from at least the thirteenth century; about 700 rooms once housed the inhabitants. Since only hunting weapons were found it may be assumed that the people were peaceful. There is good evidence that the Mogollon carried on trade to the north with the Anasazi and also to the south with the people of the desert, the Hohokam.

The word Hohokam is from the Pima language, and like Anasazi means "the ancient ones." These were the master farmers of the Southwest, and by perhaps as early as 500 A.D. they had laid the foundations for a remarkable canal system which pro-

vided irrigation for their fertile but dry soil, with which they raised corn, cotton, squash, and beans. Over the centuries the canals were expanded. After the canals had been abandoned for almost 500 years, the new pioneers of the nineteenth century were able in some situations to simply clean out the debris and run water through the channels once again.

Most famous of the Hohokam buildings to survive is Casa Grande. A modern city takes its name from the ancient structure. Once considered "Arizona's first apartment house," it is now thought to have been an observatory and religious center. An important Hohokam settlement is Snaketown near Phoenix, which has been excavated twice and then covered with soil. One of the areas explored was either a giant barbecue pit or a crematorium. These people, unlike other early Arizonans, did not bury their dead.

The Hohokam lived in pit houses, which were good for keeping the temperature relatively stable in both winter and summer. Ball courts have been found, where games were played with rubber balls. These rubber balls may well have been obtained in trade from people in the south, where parrot feath-

ers were similarly obtained. The Hohokam manufactured cloth with the qualities of tapestry. Their pottery had the characteristic "red-on-buff" coloring, and is considered more advanced artistically than technically. However, these people did know how to cast copper bells using the lost wax process, and could etch designs on seashells, obtained through trade. Some time before 1100 A.D. a new group called the Salado lived in the Hohokam area, but appears to have been a distinct cultural society.

About 1400 something happened in Arizona which caused many long-inhabited sites to be abandoned. The population declined, and the Anasazi, Mogollon, and Hohokam were no more. No single explanation seems to entirely explain the great changes. There was a drought in the 1200s, but it was not that severe. On the other hand, it is entirely possible that the soil of the Gila Valley became waterlogged and was thus unproductive. The people do not seem to have been warlike, and so a great conflict seems unlikely. There is no evidence that a plague swept the land. Not only do we not know much about the story of Arizona from about 1000 A.D. to 1539, but we will probably never learn much

The Navajos make colorful and symbolic sand paintings as part of some ceremonies. This is a reproduction of **Male Shooting Chant** *by artist Robert Spray. Represented in the painting are Father Sky and Mother Earth. Courtesy, Arizona State Museum, University of Arizona*

ABOVE: The most famous pre-historic ruin in Arizona is probably Casa Grande, or the great house, located on the Gila River near Coolidge and Florence. The ruins are shown here between the 1880s and 1890s. Today they have been roofed to protect the ruins from further deterioration. Casa Grande became a national monument in 1918. The builders of this tall, window-less, pueblo-like structure are unknown, and there is some question whether they were related to the ancient Hohokam peoples. Courtesy, Arizona Historical Society Library, Tucson

more.

Those ancient Arizonans, whatever happened to them, left behind many of their living sites. One of the most popular is Montezuma Castle in the central part of the state. The name comes from the myth that the Emperor Montezuma escaped from the Spanish and later lived there. The "castle" is a group of houses built into limestone cliffs. Nearby is a well, which is also visited by many.

Tuzigoot, which in Apache means "crooked water," is another ancient settlement which was excavated in the 1930s and then preserved. Once it housed perhaps 100 families, and due to its strategic location was easily defended.

To the east and near the Salt River is another national monument, Tonto, a fortress with more than 100 rooms. The people who once lived there were farmers who tilled the nearby fields, but who came in for protection at night.

By the time the recorded history of Arizona began in 1539 the Indian tribal structures as we know them today were in existence, although the evidence tends to indicate that some of the groups had only recently arrived. The "Indians"—misnamed by Columbus—were the descendants of the original humans who inhabited North America.

Anthropologists generally group Indian tribes by the language they speak, and on that basis Arizona has three main divisions: the Uto-Aztecan, Athapascan, and Yuman peoples. In addition to those tribes considered native to Arizona there are those who have from time to time moved here. In the Arizona strip country, north of the Colorado River, there are the Paiutes who came south from Utah, and in southern Arizona there are the Yaquis who came from Mexico little more than 100 years ago.

The Hopi of northeastern Arizona, among the Uto-Aztecans, are called the "peaceful ones." They are best known for having kept their traditional culture intact, probably made possible by the remote

LEFT: Archaeologists worked with mule-drawn plows in the 1930s. They are shown here excavating a house at the Hohokam ruins at Snaketown, on the Gila River Indian Reservation a few miles from Chandler. Courtesy, Arizona State Museum, University of Arizona, Gila Pueblo Staff

LEFT: Pueblo Grande, a Hohokam site in Phoenix, covered more than 1,000 acres, its large compound enclosures spreading in all directions from the central mound. Ball courts, agricultural fields, and irrigation ditches framed this important village. The ruins of the "big house" in the foreground date from the classic Hohokam period, circa A.D. 1100-1450. After 1450, no clear record exists of the Hohokam, a Pima Indian word meaning "all-used-up" or the "ancient ones." In the background is Pueblo Grande Museum, constructed in 1973. Courtesy, Pueblo Grande Museum, Division of the City of Phoenix Parks, Recreation, and Library Department

A Hopi woman sits on the east side of Walpi, First Mesa, in 1922. The Hopi live today on three mesas in northeastern Arizona as a close-knit village society, much as they did when first visited by Spanish conquistadores and Franciscan padres. The villages were moved from the foot of the mesas to the summits after a revolt against the Spanish in 1680. Courtesy, Arizona State Museum, University of Arizona, Forman Hanna, photographer

area in which they live. Called the Moquis in the early days of contact with the Spaniards, they are the only pueblo Indians now living in Arizona.

When the Europeans arrived the Hopi were living and farming on their sacred mesas. Attempts to bring Christianity to them were not very successful, and in 1680 the pueblo people of Arizona and New Mexico drove out the Europeans. When they returned a dozen years later, part of the pacification program included gifts of sheep, cattle, and horses. At the start of the eighteenth century there were about 3,000 Hopi, and a century later about 2,000.

In the early 1800s the Hopi and the Navajo came into conflict, but when aid was requested from Spanish authorities none was forthcoming. Similar results arose when the Hopi again sought help from the new Territory of Arizona a half-century later. When the transcontinental railroad was built across northern Arizona in the early 1880s the builders were unwelcome, and now and then in the 1900s an anthropologist was asked to leave. Despite many

missionary attempts, including those of the noted Mormon pioneer Jacob Hamlin in the late 1850s, it is estimated that less than 2 percent of the Hopi were converted.

Traditional Hopi religion centers around the Kiva, and the people believe in direct contact with the spirit world. Religious festivals take place all during the year, but to the outside world the most famous is the awesome Snake Dance, a nine-day ritual held in August.

Hopis are introduced to the Kachina cult early in life. A Kachina figure is not only a religious object but an ancestor as well.

Today the Hopi Reservation is entirely surrounded by land belonging to the Navajo, and for over a century there have been land disputes. Congress has attempted to solve the problem, with the result that in the mid-1980s some Navajo, who have lived all their lives in one place, must now move and make way for the return of the Hopi. Today there are approximately 6,000 members of the Hopi tribe.

The other two groups who speak a Uto-Aztecan language are the Pima and the Papago, who live in southern Arizona. Just as the Hopi traditions indicate a long residence in the area, so do the Pima's and Papago's. It is believed that the Pima and Papago are descendants of ancient Arizonans, probably the Hohokam. The Pima have legends of once having occupied the Casa Grande ruins.

They probably had their first contact with Europeans in 1694, and the visitors reported them as friendly. The Pima were a farming society who called themselves "river people," indicating their association with the Gila. Since the Pima were enemies of the Apaches the Spaniards counted on them as a line of defense against the other group. Missionaries worked among them until the Pima Revolt in 1751, at which time the Europeans were temporarily expelled from the region. At that time there were probably about 4,000 members of the tribe.

When the United States Army crossed southern Arizona in 1846 they were furnished with food by the Pima, and later other groups found them willing to sell their agricultural surplus. If needed, they would always give supplies to those in trouble and unable to pay. Unfortunately, some who ventured into the area of the "Pima villages," as they were long called, did not treat the residents well. Water and land were taken without justification and the people suffered.

During the nineteenth century the Pima were led first by Cielo Azul and later by his son Anton or Antonio who lived until 1909. Antonio was much respected for his knowledge and wisdom. A Pima, Matthew Juan of Sacaton, was the first Arizonan to be killed in World War I, and in World War II a well-known Pima hero was Ira H. Hayes, who helped to raise the United States flag on Mt. Suribachi during the Battle of Iwo Jima.

Although in the 1870s it was proposed to move the Pima to Indian territory, which later became Oklahoma, they were instead given reservation lands, and remained where they were. Coolidge Dam, built in the 1920s, was said to have been constructed at least partly to provide water for these Arizonans.

In 1870 a young man named Charles H. Cook arrived, having read that Anton Azul had asked for a missionary. Though Cook was never an ordained minister, he—with the financial support of the Presbyterian Church—was a teacher, counselor, and champion of the Pima and the Maricopas who had joined them on their lands.

The word Papago means "the bean people," and in 1986 the members of the group took the name Tohono O'odham, which means "the people of the

A Pima Indian stands by his roundhouse at Snaketown in Pinal County, which he built about 20 years before this photograph was taken in 1935. The lattice resting against the wall serves as a door. The walls were built of brush and wire, with a covering of dirt over the roof. The construction of this roundhouse helped archeologists interpret their excavations of ruins with similar details at Snaketown. Courtesy, Arizona State Museum, University of Arizona, Gila Pueblo Staff

RIGHT: Ida Redbird was a master potter of the Maricopa Indian tribe who spent nearly all her life in Laveen on the Gila River Reservation. She was prominent in the artistic revival of Maricopa pottery and in marketing it and raising the prices paid to the potters and was selected for the Arizona Women's Hall of Fame. She preferred to work outside, and is shown here in the early 1940s shaping the sides of a bowl. Courtesy, Arizona State Museum, University of Arizona, E.B. Sayles, photographer

BELOW: For centuries the Havasupai or Supai Indians have made their home deep in the Grand Canyon. Their name, which means "people of the blue-green water," comes from the beautiful turquoise-colored pools of Havasu Creek. Courtesy, Arizona State Museum, University of Arizona, Helga Teiwes, photographer

desert." They, too, had early contact with the Europeans, and the Spanish built missions in their territory. Living south of the Gila River and numbering about 6,000 at the start of the eighteenth century, this group used flash-flood farming methods, in which the water was allowed to pour over the land when it was available in quantity. Cactus fruit was traditionally harvested and transformed into jelly; when travelers came through this was the only sweet available between El Paso and California. In the fall after the crops were gathered, the Papago would move to winter quarters in the Baboquivari Mountains where a good water supply was available.

The Papago also had trouble with new arrivals taking their land and water. It was not until the early twentieth century that they were given a substantial permanent reservation on which to live. The Papago are famous for the baskets they make, fashioned from yucca and various other plants and grasses, which are among the finest found anywhere in the world.

The Yuman peoples were misnamed in a manner fairly typical of the confusion of the Europeans encountering these tribes. The Spanish thought they were receiving an answer to the question, "What do you call yourselves?" and the Indians thought they were being asked the name of a particular person, who happened to be the son of the chief. It was rather like some visitors from another planet who happened on a garden party at a royal palace in England and concluded that the inhabitants of the area were called "Prince of Wales."

One of the largest of the Yuman tribes was the Mohave, who numbered about 3,000 at the start of the eighteenth century, but who shrunk to one-third that number a century later. The name comes from a word meaning "three mountains," and the reference is to the terrain near Needles, California. The Spanish first encountered the Mohave in the early 1600s and noted that they were athletic, strong, and well developed. The women were attractively tattooed.

The Mohave used rafts to negotiate the Colorado River. Corn, pumpkins, melons, and beans were grown in the bottomlands of the great river. There was some fishing but little hunting. Fighting was a means of achieving status in the tribe. Hereditary chiefs ruled, and a system of family names, similar to ours, was used.

The great leader of the Mohave in historical times was Irataba, a giant of a man well over six feet in height, and an intelligent, highly skilled peacemaker. He was a guide for the United States Army in the 1850s, and a decade later he visited President Lincoln in the White House. When the Colorado River Indian Reservation was created, Irataba settled there, and his people remain to this day although they are now few in number.

Today they share the reservation with the Chemehuevi people, who are not Yumans but of Shoshonean ancestry, perhaps near-relatives of the Paiutes. They lived in early times near the Colorado River and west into California. Nomadic hunters, they dressed in the style of the plains Indians and wore a cap like a headdress adorned with roadrunner feathers. They, too, were noted to be swift runners.

To the south of the Mohave were the traditional lands of the Yuma tribe, or as they called themselves, the Quechans. When the Spanish first encountered these people they numbered about 3,000 and lived in nine villages along the Colorado River and south of the Gila. They were farmers who lived in simple houses which did not have to protect them from the cold. The heat was another matter, and during the summer they lived outdoors, with only a roof supported by poles to shelter them from the sun.

The important leader of the Yumas in early historic times was Olleyquotequiebe, whose name translates as the "Wheezer," or "one who had trouble breathing." In the 1770s he took the name Salvador Palma, and the Spanish confirmed him in his office, giving him clothing that included a cape of blue trimmed with gold braid and a cap of black velvet trimmed with imitation jewels and a crest. He visited Mexico City but was probably a ringleader in the revolt of 1781, which resulted in the death of Father Garces. Somewhat less than 100 years later the tribe was led by Pasqual, sometimes called the last of the great war chiefs.

Near neighbors of the Quechans were the Cocopahs, who were originally from Mexico. They were less inclined to fight than either the Yumas or the Mohave. However, their life-style and customs made it difficult to distinguish them from the Yumas.

Other "cousins" were the Maricopas. Numbering about 2,000 in Spanish times and under 500 by 1900, they traditionally lived in villages along the Gila River. For the most part they did not get along well with the Yumas and for a time did battle with the Pima. In the late 1850s the Yumas attacked the Maricopas and the fighting lasted for several years. When it was over the Maricopas moved in with their allies the Pima, and thereafter lived amicably. The Maricopas are noted for their pottery, and one of the most noted practitioners of this art was Ida Redbird, who lived in the first half of the twentieth century.

For some time the members of the Yavapai group were mistakenly called Apaches, which they were

At Peridot, on the San Carlos Apache Indian Reservation, Cecilia Henry is shown in 1984 holding a burden basket which she has been weaving. Courtesy, Arizona State Museum, University of Arizona, Helga Teiwes, photographer

On the San Carlos Indian Reservation in 1981, an ancient Apache puberty ceremony, "Changing Woman," is being held for Linette Anderson, kneeling. Her sponsor is standing behind the girl. Courtesy, Arizona State Museum, University of Arizona, Helga Teiwes, photographer

not. They were known as the "people of the sun," although some say it is more correctly the "people of the crooked mouth," meaning "those who disagree." The Spanish called them "Cruciferos" because, to the astonishment of the Europeans, they wore small crosses as ornaments. Never numerous, they numbered not much over 600 in Spanish times and half that number around 1900. The U.S. Army put all members of the tribe on land near Camp Verde in 1875 and then moved them to the San Carlos Apache Reservation, although their traditional home was near Prescott and ranging into the mountains of the eastern part of the state. In 1903 old Fort McDowell was turned into a reservation for them.

By far the most famous Yavapai of recorded time was Carlos Montezuma. Born "Wassaja," when he was a small boy his people raided the Pima Villages in 1872 and he was captured. Sold in Florence for $30 he was taken to Illinois by a traveling photographer who raised him. A graduate of the University of Illinois and a physician, he worked for a while for the Indian bureau but did not get along with the officials. An internist of great ability, "Dr. Monty," as his patients called him, practiced in Chicago. When in 1922 his health failed due to tuberculosis he retired to the home of an uncle at Fort McDowell.

The Hualapai or Walapai people are the "pine tree folk." One of the Yuman tribes, they have never numbered more than about 750. They were traditionally hunters and root gatherers who lived in the same area as the Mohave but often did not get along with them. Only about half the original number of members were living when in the mid-1870s Indian agents attempted to move the group from the Peach Springs area in the northwestern part of the territory to the Colorado Reservation. A few years later a separate reservation was established in an area to the north and east of Kingman. Today the Hualapai Reservation is home to over 1,000 people.

One of the better-known Arizona Indian tribes is the Havasupai, or "the people of the blue-green water." They are now residents of the Grand Canyon and take their name from the color of the water which runs through the area where, until the 1890s, they lived part of the year. They also had homes on the south rim of the canyon. Probably once a part of the Hualapai group, they adopted a pueblo lifestyle and lived in homes built in caves. They were skillful at irrigating land and making deerskin clothing. They painted their faces and tattooed their bodies. Total membership has probably never been over 500.

The Athapascan people, in Arizona consisting of the Apaches and the Navajo, are far and away the most numerous group of Indians in the state and also the most recent arrivals. They were once plains residents and arrived in the Southwest before 1500 A.D. Some may have arrived as early as 1100 when they were pushed out of their original homes by the Comanches. Both the Apaches and the Navajo call themselves the "dine," meaning the "people who are completely human." In the early days the two groups were often confused with one another.

The word Apache comes from a Zuni word meaning "enemy." They are not a single tribe, but are subdivided into several groups. In modern terms the bands include the Chiricahua, Mescalero, San Carlos, Cibecue, and White Mountain Apaches. It is estimated that there were about 5,000 Apache people during the Spanish era, and that number had grown by 1,000 at the start of this century.

The groups led a largely nomadic life, and while they occasionally grew crops they were not tied for long to the same land. Their image was not always a good one and they were sometimes labeled treacherous, ruthless, and cunning. It is true that warfare and raiding were a part of their way of life, but such labels are a vast oversimplification of a distinctive culture.

The Apache culture was greatly admired by some who at one time fought them. Thomas J. Jeffords

Navajo men and women at the Northern Arizona State Fair in the 1930s display their beautiful hand-woven rugs and a stunning display of hand-crafted turquoise and silver jewelry and concho belts. Courtesy, Arizona Historical Foundation

Henry Chee Dodge, Navajo states-man, interpreter, and media-tor, is depicted here circa 1880. He was appointed act-ing chief of the Navajo tribe by Indian agent Denis Riordan in 1884, and gained great prestige as a leader. In 1922, when the Tribal Council was organized, Chee Dodge was elected as its first chairman. He fought for Indian educa-tion and mediated between the federal government and the Navajo. Courtesy, Special Collections Library, Northern Arizona University, Flagstaff

and John P. Clum, mediators between the cultures in the nineteenth century, saw the Apaches as brave, honest, and devoted to family and friends. General George Crook came to have much sympathy for them and opposed the treatment they often re-ceived.

One of the great difficulties between the Apaches and first the Europeans and then the Americans was that instead of having a single hereditary leader, as many groups did, they had several chiefs who did not feel bound by what their colleagues had done or said.

Those who shared the land with the Apaches also found it difficult to adjust to their nomadic ways. Un-til about 1750 the Spanish had hopes of changing the Apache life-style, but as the empire became weak and the Apache nation grew in strength it was rec-ognized that this was impossible.

Only when the Indians settled down and stopped

raiding would the colonial authorities provide food, and several bands of Apaches did begin to settle down. Unfortunately, when Mexico achieved its in-dependence an attempt was made to exterminate the group and this created more hatred.

Cochise was one of the most remarkable of the great Apache figures, and he dominated the scene until his death in 1874. Later Victorio, Nana, and Geronimo were important. It was not until the mid-1880s that the Apaches at last stopped fighting. They then settled down on reservations, except for those who were taken as prisoners of war and even-tually settled in Oklahoma.

In the early Spanish period the Navajo had little contact with the Europeans. The Navajo were a no-madic people living west of the pueblo tribes of New Mexico. In time some of them settled down to farm, and they obtained both horses and sheep. They did not participate, as did the Apaches, in the Hopi revolt of the late 1600s. There was some intermarriage with the pueblo people although, in time, animosity began to develop between the two. It is estimated that there were about 8,000 Navajo at the start of the eighteenth century. Their culture was complex, with an elaborate religion, skill in pottery making, and an emphasis on raising sheep. The Navajo lan-guage is a difficult one, so much so that during World War II the Navajo "code talkers" became famous in the Pacific.

In the early 1800s the Spanish began to send raid-ing parties into Navajo country to capture slaves to become household servants. Naturally the Navajo be-gan to retaliate. Mexico paid little attention to these people, they were so distant; but when the United States took control at Santa Fe, New Mexico, the pueblo groups told the authorities of their troubles with the Navajo, and the United States achieved a degree of peace between some of the groups. How-ever, when the Civil War started the Navajo in-creased their raiding, and when Colonel James H. Carleton reasserted United States authority he dis-patched Kit Carson to bring the Navajo under con-trol. This he did, and in 1864 those who did not es-cape were forced to take up residence at Bosque Redondo. Twelve thousand Navajo surrendered and made the long walk to a place they would come to hate when a smallpox epidemic killed over 2,000 in 1865.

Barboncito was recognized as head chief of the Navajo, and went to Washington where a treaty was signed by the leaders including Manuelito, the last of the war chiefs. If the people forever renounced war they could return to their homes, and in 1868 they did. A second long walk took place as the Navajo left Bosque Redondo.

In 1876 Juan Lorenzo Hubbell began to operate a trading post at a place he named for his friend Ganado Mucho, a chief of the western Navajo. It was Hubbell who brought silversmiths from Mexico to teach that craft to the native Americans, at which the Navajo excelled. In time Navajo weaving also became world famous.

Over the years the population increased and more land was added to the reservation, only a part of which is in Arizona. Today about 70,000 people make their homes on the reservation in this state. In 1923 the group elected its first tribal chairman, Henry Chee Dodge, long recognized as a major leader. The Navajo nation is very much like a state within a state.

For the most part, throughout the Spanish period of Arizona history the Indians were largely allowed to go their own way, and there were relatively few clashes with the intruders. The Spanish were not entirely without impact, however. Once they realized they had not found their way to the Indies, the Spanish decided that the residents of the New World were possessed of minds and souls and they set out to control both. It became the duty of those serving the king to help bring Christianity to the Indians. Their success rate was not always high. For example, when they brought the people in close contact with one another they often caused plagues of disease. To the European, chickenpox was a minor annoyance; to the Indian it was often fatal. Indians have also always been especially susceptible to tuberculosis. Syphilis, which the Spanish called the "French disease" (the French called it the "Spanish disease"), was unknown in the New World prior to the coming of the Europeans, but did not remain unknown for long.

Spain was underpopulated and had great difficulty in finding enough people to operate the empire. Therefore there was no objection to intermarriage with the natives, although the elaborate caste system of the Spanish placed the progeny in an inferior social position.

The Mexican period was similarly unintrusive, as the new republic was too busy attempting to achieve internal stability to be bothered by some people living far to the north. A notable exception was the infamous scalp hunting allowed. Failing in various attempts to control the Apaches, Mexican authorities began to offer bounties on Apache scalps. This grizzly practice continued through the 1830s.

Conditions largely changed with the coming of

people from the United States. For one thing there were so many more of them. Also it is probably fair to say that they were not as tolerant of the original inhabitants of the land as had been the Latins. Many new controllers of the land believed that Indians were inferior and that the only good one was a dead one.

A goal of the United States government was to place the Indians on specific grants of land, the reservations. This worked for the sedentary tribes but not for the nomadic. In addition there was the chronic problem of the dishonest Indian agent. One secretary of the interior was heard to complain that he was certain he had sent at least one competent and honest agent west but now he could not find him. People made money selling supplies to the reservations, but often the food which arrived was unfit to eat and chronic shortages beset the system.

In 1887 Congress enacted the Dawes Act, which attempted to end the Indian tribal system. The land would henceforth be divided into individual allotments. In some places this was accomplished, but mostly it was not. For years the old system continued and was ignored by the federal government. Indians were repeatedly promised citizenship but this was not granted until 1924. In Arizona Indians living on the reservation were not allowed to vote until after a state supreme court ruling in 1948.

In 1933 the United States government again reversed its policy toward the Indians and placed renewed emphasis on the tribal system. Henceforth the reservations would be like states or cities within the larger governmental framework. Tribal councils governed, codes of laws were created and approved by the secretary of the interior, and police forces executed many of the laws. For the most part that system applied only to those who lived on the reservation, but now and then, as in hunting and fishing matters, those who visited were also liable.

Tribes have been compensated for the loss of their land in the past, yet today there are still unanswered questions regarding the future of Arizona's tribes. Has the time come for the Bureau of Indian Affairs to cease operating the administrative affairs of native Americans? At the moment that is an open question.

Often American Indians are caught between two cultures—their traditional way and the mainstream. Social problems are many and complex. Above all else it must be remembered that the heritage of the native Americans is a rich one, and one of which all may be proud.

Spanish and Mexican Arizona

San Xavier del Bac Mission, near Tucson, is said to be the finest of all the old Spanish missions. It was founded in 1692 by Father Kino at a site nearby and is still being used. The present structure, called "the white dove in the desert," was completed by Franciscans in 1797 with the aid of the Indians. Courtesy, Arizona Department of Library, Archives, and Public Records

This is how a sixteenth-century Spanish conquistador might have looked in Coronado's expedition through Arizona. Courtesy, Arizona Historical Society Museum

Once Spain had the mightiest, richest, and most colorful and romantic of all the New World empires and Arizona was, in theory at least, a part of it. As a practical matter it took time to reach and explore the land called the "northern mystery."

Spain was one of those nations which in the fifteenth century became interested in new trade routes. Christopher Columbus sailed to unknown lands for King Ferdinand and Queen Isabella, and although he probably never realized that he had found new lands, others did. The West Indies became the empire's early base of operations and from there in 1519 Cortez began his conquest of Mexico. Two years later Mexico City fell and it then became the hub from which the explorers and conquerors fanned out in all directions in the New World.

The Europeans were interested in gold, silver, and precious stones. Ponce de Leon wandered about Florida looking for the fountain of youth, but we may safely assume that the material riches he found were a reasonable compensation for the onset of old age. Tons of valuable materials were transported back to Spain.

There were those who looked for another type of wealth: souls to be saved. "His Catholic Majesty," the king of Spain, wanted to bring his faith to all the heathens of the New World. Two servants of the church may have been the first white men to see Arizona.

Juan de la Asuncion and Pedro Nadal were Franciscan friars who left Mexico City in January 1538 on a trek to see what lay to the north. As they passed through Culiacan they were joined by others seeking wealth. It has been said that the group traveled north along the San Pedro or Santa Cruz River and perhaps reached the Gila. They may have seen Casa Grande, according to Nadal, a mathematician who was calculating their position along the way.

At this time the great viceroy Antonio de Mendoza was in office in Mexico City, and he had considerable interest in the north. There had been reports of the land of Cibola with its seven golden cities, and stories of another land called Grand Quivira, a place also supposed to be rich and interesting. Spanish navigators had long sought the Strait of Anian beyond which lay great treasure. In 1536 Spaniards who were slave hunting north of Culiacan unexpectedly came upon four men. The leader of the quartet was Alvar Nunez Cabeza de Vaca, who had been a part of a Florida expedition, and he told of being shipwrecked off the Texas coast.

Cabeza de Vaca and his companions, one of whom was a Moorish slave, Esteban, had convinced the Indians they met that they were medicine men and had moved across the terrain from tribe to tribe. Taken to Mexico City by the Spaniards, they told fantastic stories which generated much interest in the "northern mystery." Although he would have been the ideal man to lead a new expedition, Cabeza de Vaca was still more interested in Florida. The viceroy instead selected Frenchman Marcos de Niza, who had been a prominent Franciscan in Mexico for several years. Esteban would go along as a guide. Mendoza told the "walking friar," who had a reputation of being the champion of the Indians, to treat them well, study them and their ways, and to learn everything about the terrain. Anything of value was to be reported and of course the party should take possession of the lands in the name of the Crown.

The instructions were issued in September of 1538 and the journey began from Culiacan on March 7, 1539. Another friar was to go on the journey but he became ill and returned, leaving Fray Marcos, Esteban, and a party of Indians. The group was well received and the leader became much interested in what he heard about the coastal area of the Pacific. While he waited to send messengers to the coast, Esteban went ahead to the north. He was to cover only about 150 miles and was to use crosses to signal his discoveries. The Moor was to send back crosses the size of a human hand if the news was of some significance and a larger one if something was more important. A "great cross" would tell of something of the greatest and most unusual nature.

Esteban was evidently having a very good time, and instead of stopping he pressed on ahead. The crosses he sent back became larger and larger, some as tall as a man.

Fray Marcos followed Esteban and along the way met a man who had been exiled from Cibola. As the priest reached the San Pedro Valley he was told that he was about to enter desert country, immediately beyond which was his goal. Exactly where he was is uncertain, but he may well have been in the general area of the modern highway known as the Coronado Trail.

Meanwhile, Esteban had in all probability reached the Zuni pueblo of Hawikuh, near the Arizona-New Mexico border, and assumed his medicine man role to impress the residents. It did not go well. For some reason, the visiting dignitaries were not well received, and Esteban and most of his party were killed. Only one, who happened to be drinking water from an irrigation ditch away from the others, escaped unhurt and reported to Fray Marcos.

The "walking friar" was doubtless uncertain of what to do next but he did not turn back. It took some bribing to get his companions to go on, and a few days later they encountered the other two wounded survivors of Esteban's party. The Indians again rebelled, and exactly what happened from this point on is unclear. Marcos de Niza later claimed to have viewed one of the cities of Cibola—from a safe distance, of course. If he did it was Hawikuh. Then he beat a hasty retreat and probably retraced his steps to reach Culiacan in late July and continued on to Mexico City.

To this day Fray Marcos remains a controversial character. It has been said that he was a plain liar who made up much of what he told. A slightly more charitable view is that, as a good bureaucrat, he saw what he knew his superiors wanted him to see. The kindest view of him is that he observed Hawikuh from a considerable distance and was honestly mistaken as to what he was seeing. After all, an adobe pueblo in the late afternoon light, with the sun making everything golden, could play tricks on a man. At any rate the news traveled quickly and created a great stir.

Plans were already underway for a larger exploring party to go north, and it was headed by a 30-year-old well-to-do man named Francisco Vasquez de Coronado. The viceroy's purpose for the exploring party was to not only search for wealth but to provide employment for adventurers who were idling in Mex-

The Coronado Expedition *depicts the exploring party of Spanish soldiers, Indians, and padres led by Francisco Coronado in 1540. The group started from Mexico City in February 1540 and went north near Tucson along what is now called the Coronado trail. The artist is Frederic Remington, whose scenes of Western military and Indian life made him a popular and successful illustrator. Courtesy, Arizona Historical Society, Tucson*

ico City. In February 1540 the group, composed of 200 horsemen, 100 foot soldiers, and 1,000 Indians, passed in review before Mendoza and headed toward the unknown. Coronado wore gold-plated armor and rode at the head of the men and their 1,000 horses, not to mention the herds of cattle, sheep, and pigs which were taken along for food. The viceroy himself went along for the first two days and then turned back.

Early in April when the party was near Culiacan, Melchoir Diaz and Juan de Saldivar, who had been sent ahead the previous autumn—and had reached perhaps as far north as the Gila River—returned and reported seeing nothing of value. This was not good news, but it was a mere indication of what was to come. Other difficulties came about because Fray Marcos had reported that the land was flat and good for traveling, but in reality, while some of it was level and quite barren, the rugged Sierra Madre were not easy going at all. Fray Marcos' popularity began to wane.

Coronado divided his party and pushed north at the head of the smaller advance group—about 100 Spaniards and perhaps an equal number of Indians. Although there are differences of opinion as to the exact route followed, there is general agreement that the group entered Arizona in the general vicinity of present-day Bisbee and traversed roughly the Coronado Trail.

When they reached Hawikuh, which they took with force, on July 7, 1540, one of those who wrote an account of the adventure noted "such were the curses that some hurled at Fray Marcos that I pray God to protect him from them." The "walking friar" was sent home to Mexico in disgrace. The explorers were not, however, easily discouraged, and every effort was made to search out anything of value anywhere in the area. The main part of the band reached Hawikuh and a reunited group set about this task.

Hernando de Alarcon had been sent north by ship on the orders of the viceroy to take supplies to the main expedition. On August 26, 1540, the *San Pedro,* the *Santa Catalina,* and the *San Gabriel* reached the mouth of the Colorado. The currents were so strong they could make no further progress. Leaving the ships the Spaniards went north in smaller boats. Alarcon, described as dressed elaborately and always accompanied by his dog, fifer, and drummer, made quite an entrance into Arizona, but how far north he went is disputed. That he reached the mouth of the Gila River seems likely, but stories that he reached as far as present-day Lake Mead are now generally dismissed as fiction.

Unable to deliver the supplies he had for Coronado, he returned home. Coronado in the meantime sent Melchior Diaz in search of Alarcon. He and his group reached near where Yuma is now and found letters left by Alarcon, but did not rendezvous with him. Traveling what became the infamous "Devil's Highway," along the United States-Mexico border, Diaz accidentally fell on a spear in December 1540 and died days later.

From his headquarters at Hawikuh, renamed Granada because it reminded him of Spain, Coronado continued to hear stories of cities and of potential riches. A group of Indians, in actuality the Hopi, was reported, and on July 15 Don Pedro de Tovar, a friar, and 20 soldiers were dispatched. When the Spaniards arrived at Awatovi the Indians decided to fight. The priest led an attack which, because of the Spaniards' superior weapons, ended almost as soon as it had begun. Afterward relations were friendly and Tovar was told of a great river which lay beyond. Not having any orders to proceed, he and his party returned and reported to their leader. Coronado then sent Garcia Lopez de Cardenas and two dozen men to investigate and report back. Guided by the Hopi, they became the first Europeans to see the Grand Canyon. They were unable to descend to the river below and on their return reported that they had seen some very strange cows. The American bison had been "discovered."

In the autumn of 1540 the main party of explorers moved their headquarters to Tiguex, not far from modern-day Albuquerque, where they wintered and listened to stories of Grand Quivira. A character called El Turco, a Florida Indian, was the source of many of the tales. In the spring of 1541 the expedition crossed the Texas panhandle and pushed into Kansas.

Grand Quivira turned out to be a collection of poor miserable villages and El Turco was executed for his errors. In August a council decided that the group should return to New Mexico. The beleaguered party returned to Tiguex on October 21, 1541. Real trouble then followed. Coronado was nearly killed and his health remained poor.

In the spring of 1542 they all started home. Details of the return are not as well reported as the outward journey. The explorers disbanded at Culiacan and the leader faced the viceroy in August 1542. By then it was realized that the "northern mystery" did not hold the great wealth of which they had all dreamed. It was 40 years before another Spaniard would enter the land, except perhaps for an occasional wandering priest.

When Sir Francis Drake, an Englishman, started on what became the second recorded circumnavigation of the globe in the late 1570s the Spanish were alarmed. This was considered an intrusion into the Spanish New World. When Drake did not return south the Spanish authorities feared he might have found the fabled Strait of Anian, or the Northwest Passage, as some then called it. The Spaniards decided that more exploration would be necessary. King Philip II also decided that some areas would have to be settled to keep them from falling into rival hands. The latter became the famous policy of "defensive expansion" which would characterize the Spanish Empire for the next 200 years.

When volunteers were needed to conduct explorations of the northern lands the Franciscans offered their services. Three priests led a party north into the Rio Grande Valley in 1581. Soldiers went along and upon arrival at the pueblos things went well until the Indians tired of the visitors. Then there was trouble. One padre made it back to Mexico and soon the Franciscans demanded that an expedition be sent to rescue the stranded missionaries. Antonio de Espejo, a wealthy mine owner, offered to finance the venture and a group was organized. Upon reaching the area where Albuquerque now is the group found that the priests had been killed by the Indians.

Espejo reasoned that as long as he was there it would be a good idea to search for something of value. Looking to the east he decided the plains did not seem a likely prospect and so started west. At Hawikuh he talked with people who remembered Coronado. Very likely the expedition saw the Verde River and may well have been in the area where one day the city of Prescott would stand. There were reports of finding rich silver ore, but the member of the party who wrote the chronicle of the trek said the ore was not silver but copper, and of rather poor quality.

The Royal Patent gave the right to establish colonies in the lands to the north of Mexico, and it went in 1595 not to Espejo, as he had hoped, but to Juan Oñate, now called the founder of New Mexico. Oñate started north with a party of settlers to establish the new colony. Within a few months after their arrival a party was sent westward to relocate the mines Espejo had found earlier. In the fall of 1604 Oñate, 30 soldiers, two priests, and a number of Indians started west. They reached the Bill Williams Fork and followed it to the main Colorado River.

Down the great river went the party and in time they passed the point where the Gila joined the Col-

orado. In the latter part of January 1605 they were at the mouth of the Colorado and took possession of it in the name of King Philip II. Slowly the unknown was becoming the known. However, from this point on, military and government authorities became secondary to the work of the Catholic Church in exploring the New World.

Tenacious, dedicated, and hardworking priests of all nationalities continued to toil in New Spain. New Mexico was the domain of the Franciscans, while the Jesuits were assigned to Mexico proper.

Although not well remembered, the first attempts at establishing missions in what is now Arizona occurred in Hopi country. Many records have been lost, but it seems likely that during the summer of 1629 three priests established the mission of San Bernardino near the town of Awatovi. The new arrivals were not welcomed and supposedly one of the fathers was poisoned in 1633. Still the work went on, and in time four other missions were started in the area.

Father Kino, who first visited Arizona in 1691, traveled many thousands of miles on horseback on his missions to Indians in the Southwestern desert. He was also an important explorer and cartographer of Primeria Alta, which extended from Mexico to the Gila River, and from the Gulf of California to the Colorado River and the San Pedro River. Courtesy, Arizona Historical Foundation

The ruins of San Jose de Tuma-cacori, seen here in 1972, are now a national monument. Situated on the Santa Cruz River north of Nogales, Tuma-cacori was first built by the Spanish padres and their Indian converts after Father Kino visited it on his first trip to Arizona. Courtesy, Arizona Historical Society, Tucson

In 1680 the great revolt of the Hopi forced out the missionaries. A dozen years later a Spanish army reestablished European rule over New Mexico and the surrounding territory but no further attempts were made to maintain churches in the north. Instead, future missionary activity would be in what is now southern Arizona.

By the middle 1600s there were approximately 35 missions in operation in the region of Sonora in the northern part of Mexico. The cost to the king of Spain was small as the church attempted to bring European civilization to the natives. Today, except for a few well-remembered names, the several hundred men who labored on the frontiers of the Spanish Empire are forgotten. Probably the best known is the "first Arizonan," Eusebio Francisco Kino.

Father Kino, who variously spelled his name Chino, Chini, and Quino, was an Italian who at the age of 18 fell ill and promised God he would serve as a missionary if he recovered. Accordingly he entered the Jesuit order at age 20 in 1665. He wanted to spend his life in China, but when he drew lots with another to see who would go there he lost, and instead journeyed to Mexico City. In 1687 Kino was appointed missionary to the Pima Indians and for nearly the next quarter of a century, the life span remaining to him, he worked in what was by then

called Pimeria Alta. Before his first year of work was over he had founded Nuestra Senora de los Delores, located about 75 miles southeast of modern-day Nogales. This was to be his headquarters. Father Kino first entered what is now Arizona in January 1691 in response to a request from a group of Indians who wanted him to visit their villages in the Tucson area.

Impressed with what he saw, Kino returned the next year and again in 1694 when he recorded the first visit of a European to the ruins of Casa Grande. The priest journeyed along the Santa Cruz and Gila valleys, traversing the latter almost to its junction with the Colorado. Then, beset with problems in Sonora, Kino did not return to Arizona until 1697. The general thinking of the time was that lower California was an island, and Kino, interested in sending help to a fellow priest trying to establish missions in Baja, busied himself trying to find a convenient land route to California. Between 1698 and 1702 he made a series of visits in which he explored the valley of the San Pedro River and traveled to the junction of the Gila and the Colorado. Kino proved that California is not an island, and he saw more of Arizona than any European since Oñate's exploration nearly a century earlier.

The term "mission" was sometimes used to designate even temporary camping places or settlements. However, as a result of Father Kino's life and work, three reasonably permanent missions were established, one of which survives with its original purpose to this day. Another is now a historical monument, while the third has fallen into ruin and vanished. The latter is the unfortunate Guevavi, meaning "large spring" or "well," and it was called the Mission of Sorrows. The spot, about 50 miles south of Tucson, was visited by Father Kino on his first trip to Arizona, but the mission was probably founded in 1692. The first resident priest arrived in 1701 and for nearly seven decades attempts were made to keep the place in operation. Subject to Indian raids, Guevavi had more than its share of misfortune. Frequently the priests there had to report more deaths than baptisms, and ultimately the mission was abandoned. Some walls stood into the 1890s but are now gone.

Tumacacori, located between Tucson and Nogales, was visited by Father Kino on his first trip to Arizona and a few years later a mission was established. A resident priest watched over the building, which was destroyed in an Apache raid in 1730. Other buildings replaced it and the present structure was not dedicated until 1822. By that time the new Republic of Mexico was about to secularize and sell its missions. Tumacacori declined. In 1898 it was designated as a national monument.

Time has been kinder to San Xavier del Bac, which is located not far from Tucson. The beautiful "White Dove of the Desert" has been in its present-day form since the early 1900s. On an early trip Kino visited the people who lived at Bac, and was with them again before work started on a church in the spring of 1700. Meanwhile cattle, sheep, and horses had been delivered as gifts to the residents. The first building, built in Kino's time, lasted until the 1750s, when it was replaced by another.

The resident priest left in 1831 and for a time the old mission seemed destined to fall into ruin. However, under the direction of the famous Bishop Lamy of Santa Fe, some reconstruction was undertaken, and in 1866 Father John Baptiste Salpointe, later the first bishop of Arizona, arrived on the scene. The church was reactivated, a school opened in 1873, and in 1906 and 1907 much more work was done on the old building.

Father Kino was a remarkable man. A devout Christian, he labored hard and lived a life of strict virtue. He defended his Indian friends and did all

ABOVE: In the late eighteenth century, the Franciscans built a new church at San Xavier Mission on the site of the old Jesuit mission founded by Father Kino. This is the high altar of San Xavier del Bac in 1968, after it was cleaned and restored. It is still in active use as a church for the Papagos, who are now known as Tohono O'odham, meaning "the people of the desert." Courtesy, Arizona State Museum, University of Arizona, Helga Teiwes, photographer

LEFT: This sketch of Tubac shows the town as it appeared to J. Ross Browne, who wrote about his 1869 tour of Arizona in Adventures in the Apache Country. *Tubac had been established as a Spanish presidio in 1752 in order to protect nearby missions and Spanish settlers. Courtesy, Arizona Historical Society Library, Tucson*

he could for them. It is estimated that he covered about 75,000 miles in his travels throughout the land. The only criticism ever leveled against this great missionary was that he sometimes painted too attractive a picture of the land when he was trying to encourage others to take up labors in Pimeria Alta.

At 66, Kino was worn out by toil and died on March 15, 1711, at Magdelina in Sonora. He was buried in the chapel of his mission there. Not until 1966 was his gravesite marked. The year before, the State of Arizona placed a statue of the "first Arizonan" in the statuary hall of Washington, D.C. The likeness is based on imagination, for no portrait of him exists.

After Kino came others who attempted to carry on his work. They had dreams of bringing Christianity to the Hopi, the Navajo, and the Apache, but however well-intentioned, Kino's successors for the time being were barely able to hold on to the system that existed. Spain was deeply involved in European politics and neglected its New World colonies. In the 1730s a new group of priests arrived who hoped to revitalize the missions. Father Ignacio Keller visited the Gila Valley in 1736 and 1737 and Father Jacobo Sedelmayr journeyed up the Colorado River hoping to extend missions to what is now northern Arizona.

The Spanish Empire was marked by two separate lines of command. The Catholic Church was responsible to the king, and so too were the soldiers and government authorities, who did not always get along well with the clerics. Each side blamed the other for the Pima revolt of 1751. To better defend the area the Spanish created two new forts or presidios. One was in present-day Sonora, and the other, Tubac, founded in 1752, was located south of present-day Tucson. It was the first of its kind in Arizona.

By this time the land had a new name. An official government report mentioned finding silver ore between the mission of Guevavi and the rancheria of Arissona. That was in 1737, causing a brief but unfortunately unprofitable silver rush. The mines proved to be unproductive and were closed within a few years but there was now a place, vague and yet undefined, called Arizona.

Tubac, located on the Santa Cruz River, had been settled first as an outpost of the operations of Guevavi, and then was staffed by a few soldiers. Within the walls of the adobe military base lived the soldiers and their families, and occasionally someone who sold supplies to the presidio. At first there were few inhabitants apart from those in the army, but gradually more arrived. The men often intermarried with the Indians.

In 1763, following the end of the French and Indian War, Spain took control of the Louisiana Territory which had belonged to France. France had been the great rival of Spain, and now Spain was able to concentrate its defense efforts in other areas. The Russians were moving down the Pacific Coast and the British were in the habit of raiding Spanish coastal settlements. In 1765 the royal inspector-general of New Spain, Jose de Galvez, visited Mexico, including the northern provinces such as Sonora, and made recommendations for the improvement of defense. One of these was the settlement of Alta (or upper) California.

King Charles III, an able and energetic man, came to the Spanish throne in 1759. He was determined to breathe new life into colonial administration. For various reasons, but mainly because he did not trust their loyalty, in the spring of 1767 the king expelled the Jesuits from all Spanish lands. The removal of the "black robes" was an often tragic story accompanied by great suffering. To this day there are rumors of "Jesuit gold" left behind and riches buried somewhere in the American Southwest.

In 1769 an extensive report was made regarding the revitalization of the empire. At this point in history the Spanish Empire was in its late middle age, tending toward creakiness, and troubled with approaching old age. It had always been an overly organized and highly centralized system. Everything

This is artist Cal Peters' conception of the Royal Presidio of San Agustin del Tucson as it might have appeared in the 1790s after the wall and chapel were completed. The open gate is at the spot where modern-day Main Avenue intersects with Alameda Street. The Tucson presidio was established in 1776 when the Spanish garrison was moved from Tubac. Courtesy, Arizona Historical Society, Tucson

had to be approved by the king, and authority to act was extremely limited. The Spanish invented the term "red tape," which refers to the ribbons the Spaniards used to tie up reports in government offices.

In addition to the plan to settle Alta California, there was also a proposal to work more closely with the various Indian groups to ensure their loyalty to Spain. Both of these plans would affect the land called Arizona.

One of the major players in this act arrived at San Xavier del Bac in the summer of 1768. He was 30-year-old Father Francisco Tomas Hermengildo Garces, a native of Aragon who had taken holy orders at the age of 16 and was ordained in 1763. The first Franciscan on the scene, Garces was the equal of Kino in all respects. Within six months of his arrival he had visited all of southwestern Arizona and was developing plans to expand church activities. The Indians called him the Old Man, despite his relative youth, and he had that same zest for living which had characterized Kino. He also lived simply and was devoted to his God.

Garces made another fairly extensive journey in 1770 and the next year went down the Gila to its mouth, where he became acquainted with the Yuma Indians. Another remarkable Arizonan of this time was the military counterpart of Garces, Juan Bautista de Anza, two years older than the priest and the son and grandson of frontier army officers of the same name. In 1760 Anza was made the commander of Tubac and he energetically carried out his duties.

In 1772 Anza proposed to lead an exploring party to upper California at his own expense. He planned to mark a trail from Sonora to the West Coast and the new viceroy was interested in the project. Typical of the way in which things were done, it took two years to get the king's approval of the idea. By that time Anza and Father Garces were already on their way. Starting from Tubac in January 1774 they traveled the Devil's Highway to Mission San Gabriel, near Los Angeles, and then went north to the presidio of Monterey.

On his return home Father Garces left the main party and visited the Yavapai Indians before returning to San Xavier on July 10, 1774. As a result of the trip the viceroy decided to send Anza with a party of colonists to found a new settlement in California, which was ultimately named San Francisco. The group, numbering about 250, came north out of Sonora and stopped at Tubac. There in October 1775 Father Garces joined them and everyone

journeyed to the Colorado River. It was late November when they reached the Colorado River, and Garces continued with the group a while longer before turning east when in the area of Needles. He went on to the land of the Hopi, returning by way of the Colorado River until he reached the Gila. By the time the priest returned to San Xavier he had marked important trails for future use.

For the most part Spanish interest in what is now Arizona was concentrated in the southern part of the land, but because of a desire to create a trail from the New Mexico settlements to Upper California, a Franciscan, Father Silvestre Velez de Escalante, undertook travels in 1775 from the Zuni pueblos to the Grand Canyon. Unable to find a way over that barrier he returned to New Mexico and reported what he had seen. In July 1776 he started another trek from Santa Fe, and this time he went north to where Provo, Utah, would later be, and then moved southwest for about 200 miles before abandoning the idea of visiting Monterey in California. On its return the Escalante expedition passed through areas of northern Arizona.

Meanwhile Father Garces at San Xavier was dreaming of building missions where the Gila and Colorado joined, and at the same time the military considered erecting a presidio there. In 1779 Garces was placed in charge of the proposed missions, and without waiting for the promised full military escort he went to the area with another priest and about 10 soldiers. Two settlements were planned and both would serve a religious and a military function. One was to be located where the city of Yuma is now, and the other was placed a dozen miles down the river. Garces and his coworkers set about their tasks.

The Indians had expected gifts which did not arrive, and Chief Palma was having trouble controlling his people. Food supplies ran low. A party of soldiers and about 200 civilians and 1,000 horses and mules arrived, and while some went on to California, others remained in the area. On July 17 the Quechans killed all at the southern mission and then turned against the northern settlement. Garces was killed the next day. The death of this great man altered the future of Arizona. Within weeks a party of Spanish soldiers arrived in the area, but no one could take the place of the Old Man of Bac. The idea of new missions was forgotten.

A Dublin-born, red-haired captain in the Spanish Army, born Hugh O'Connor but known as Hugo Oconor by the time he reached the New World, was ordered by the viceroy in the spring of 1772

to reorganize the military on the northern frontier. The Apache menace was of considerable worry and there was talk of moving the garrison at Tubac to a new spot west of the existing presidio. Instead, by the end of the year 1775, Oconor had brought about the founding of a new settlement called San Agustín del Tucson. The Tubac presidio was abandoned and the garrison moved to Tucson.

Tucson had been an Indian village but "Captain Red" and Father Garces had looked it over and both agreed it was a good site for not only a fort but a pueblo as well. In time walls 10 to 12 feet high were built in a square that was 750 feet long on each side, with only one gate. The church and a cantina were inside the pueblo walls, but three stores were outside. For years when an attack came everyone ran inside. Three hundred and fifty Apaches raided Tucson in 1779, and in the spring of 1782 there was another raid. The walls held.

There were two other presidios aside from Tubac, but they did not last long. It was necessary for Spain to cut back on its expenditures. The mission and the presidio were of great importance to the Spanish Empire, but toward the end the pueblo or town became more significant. A law issued by the king in 1791 authorized and encouraged settlement in northern Mexico. People in small numbers moved north from Mexico and began to settle around Tubac and Tucson.

Not everyone lived in pueblos; a few people lived out in the open on ranches and some others were engaged in mining. The success of both ranching and mining depended largely upon keeping the Apaches friendly. In the 1790s groups of Apaches actually settled near Tucson, but many more clung to the old culture with its raiding practices.

At the start of the nineteenth century, supplies for the frontier provinces were growing short, taxes continued to rise, and restrictions on life were great. Trade was very limited and various areas had to be self-sufficient. Some English colonists had been involved in a revolution and won their independence from Britain in 1776, and the French Revolution of 1789 had an even greater influence on Europe. In September 1810 Father Miguel Hidalgo y Costilla first raised the issue of independence for Mexico, and although he was executed his ideas lived on. The Indians, sensing the Spanish were weak, asserted their power. It is estimated that by 1820 about one-fourth of the ranches, mines, and small settlements of northern Mexico, including

Arizona, had been abandoned.

While the Spanish Empire was strong, trade by colonists had been strictly controlled. All trade was to be carried on with Spain alone. In time, however, the colonists began to smuggle goods with the British and the Americans. These ventures were especially important to upper California and New Mexico, but those few items which reached Arizona were brought in indirectly.

Under the Treaty of Cordoba on August 24, 1821, Spain recognized the independence of Mexico. The last viceroy gave over his powers to the revolutionary leader Agustin de Iturbide, who not long afterward declared himself emperor of Mexico. His empire fell in 1823 and the Republic of Mexico was reestablished.

These events took place far away from Arizona. At Tucson the changes meant only that the officers and soldiers swore allegiance to the republic rather than to the king of Spain.

In 1824 the congress of the republic joined Sonora and Sinaloa into a new state, called Occidente, and its northern boundary may have extended as far as the Gila River; certainly it included Tucson. There was friction and rivalry among the leaders of the area and problems in selecting a capital city. In 1830 the action was rescinded and the next year the two old states came back into being. All of this had little or no effect upon Arizona.

By the middle 1820s there were but five officers and 29 men stationed at Tucson. Mexico would continue to technically hold the area until the Mexican War and the later Gadsden Purchase, but for all practical purposes there was little effective government.

What government policy there was included a bounty for Apache scalps, beginning after the failure of an 1831 treaty with the Apaches. One hundred pesos were paid for the scalp of a man over the age of 14, 50 pesos for a woman's scalp, and 25 pesos for that of a child. Several notorious men, among them James Kirker, recently arrived from Ireland by way of the United States, hunted scalps. Kirker and his associates were not very careful who they killed, and anyone with reasonably dark hair was a potential victim. Needless to say this inflamed Indian hatred of both Latins and Anglos.

Arizona still feels the influence of the long-gone Spanish Empire. Nearly 20 percent of Arizona's population is of Spanish descent, and Spanish styles, traditions, and customs enrich all aspects of Arizonans' lives.

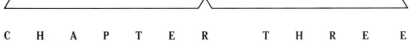
Mountain Men and the Mexican War

In the Arizona Territory of 1908, trapping and hunting continued to be a way of life for a few individuals, such as these trappers in the rugged Four Peaks area of the Matzatzal Mountains in northwest Maricopa County. Courtesy, Phoenix Public Library

Almost a century after Spain established its first New World colonies, Great Britain did likewise on the Atlantic Coast. From that moment on a westward movement started in America. The China trade began in the 1780s, Lewis and Clark went overland to the Pacific in 1803, and in 1807 Lieutenant Zebulon Pike was in Santa Fe. Although that gentleman was arrested by Spanish authorities, that did not stop others from following his path. After 1810 visitors from the East began to appear in the Southwest. Trade developed in time, but it was illegal as long as Spain controlled the area.

The key to the development of relations between citizens of the Southwest and the new nation on the East Coast was the fur trapper, the mountain man. Fur trappers always had to keep one jump ahead of civilization, for as soon as settlement took place the animal population declined.

It took a certain type of person to be a trapper. These truly rugged individualists were often described as being half-men and half-animals. They lived as they pleased and accorded that same standard to others.

After a year or so of trapping these men would gather together to trade animal skins, to obtain supplies, and generally to have a good time for a few days. Liquor was not unknown on these occasions. Taos, New Mexico, was the scene of these sessions after 1820.

Trade moved over the Santa Fe Trail; furs went east, and cloth, hardware, mirrors, and luxury items came west. Some trappers drifted south into Mexico and others went west. By 1830 the Old Spanish Trail wound up through Colorado, Utah, Nevada, and into California. Since the mountain men ranged over the whole terrain of the West they naturally found their way into what is now Arizona. It is generally believed that Arizona's first visitors from the United States were trappers who worked the upper Gila River in the early 1820s.

Often the stories told by early Southwestern travelers are vague and contradictory, and at times they stretch the truth beyond the breaking point. Yet if even a portion of the narratives are true they tell of remarkable adventures. In 1831 a book titled *The Personal Narrative of James Ohio Pattie* was published. It related the adventures of James and his father Sylvester Pattie between 1824 and 1830. They supposedly won the right to trap beaver on the Helay River by rescuing the beautiful daughter of a former governor of New Mexico from the Comanches. Together with about a dozen other men they followed the river west, perhaps to the point where it joins the Salt, and then returned to New Mexico. Later James Ohio Pattie claimed he was with a group which retraced the earlier trip and continued down the Gila to the Colorado and then followed it north to about where Lake Mead is now. The travelers then moved east until they reached Santa Fe.

Kit Carson is the best remembered of the mountain men, and one of the most likeable, even if he did later turn against his old way of life, going so far as to learn to read and write. For years he ranged over the West as a trapper and buffalo hunter. He knew Arizona well—well enough to later guide the Army of the West across the area during the Mexican War. In 1829 Ewing Young took a party through the Verde Valley, with Carson along, and they went to California after completing some exploring.

One of the most colorful of the mountain men was "Old Bill" Williams, who started life as a Baptist missionary to the Indians but later converted to their religion. He first visited Arizona in 1826 with a party which traveled the Gila River. A mountain, a town, and a fork of the Colorado River now bear Williams' name.

All in all the mountain men were great characters. They later served another important function: they were the guides for those who came later. The

The Old Trapper, *an 1888 print by Frederic Remington, depicts the unique garb and rugged individualism of the early trappers and mountain men who ranged Arizona in the early nineteenth century. Courtesy, Arizona Historical Society, Tucson*

fur trade declined around 1840, partly due to changing fashion styles, but also because many of the areas had been overtrapped. As another phase of the western movement unfolded, the old trappers were the only ones who knew the terrain through which the new arrivals had to travel.

While a few citizens of the United States came to Arizona in the second and third decades of the nineteenth century, many more went to California and Texas. Mexico allowed immigration and thousands of new arrivals came from the East to settle in Texas. In order to live there one had to do two things: become a Mexican citizen and join the Catholic Church.

Before long there was trouble because the new arrivals wanted things to be as they had been in the United States. They backed a new leader in Mexico, Juan Antonio Lopez de Santa Anna, and in return they were to receive, they thought, autonomy. Soon they discovered, as would Mexico, that Santa Anna was not reliable. Following the battle at San Jacinto in 1836, Texas became an independent nation.

After nine years the United States annexed Texas, and then a question arose over the western boundary of the new state. Texas claimed all the territory west to the Rio Grande, while Mexico claimed that the Nueces River was the true boundary. President Polk attempted to buy the disputed

Trapper, hunter, mountain man, guide, and legendary hero Christopher (Kit) Carson piloted General Stephen Kearny across Arizona in 1848. He later settled in New Mexico and led a troop of Union volunteers from that state in the Civil War. In 1863 Carson commanded an expedition against the Navajos in their Canyon de Chelly stronghold. Courtesy, Arizona Historical Society, Tucson

territory plus upper California, but the Mexican government was not interested in selling.

Alta California had a history somewhat parallel to Texas. United States citizens arrived there in the 1820s and 1830s and, while not as vocal as the Texans, they were also not content with rule by Mexico. By the early 1840s it was clear that California would

Colorful stories about Arizona mountain men include that of "Bear" Howard, center, with the rifle, shown here in a Flagstaff street scene, circa 1890. After his partner had been killed by a bear in 1880, Howard made it his life's work to hunt bear. Howard ranged around the San Francisco and Bill Williams mountains area and Oak Creek Canyon. Courtesy, Arizona Historical Society, Pioneer Museum

Colonel Philip St. George Cooke was appointed by General Stephen Kearny in 1846 to lead the Mormon Battalion from Santa Fe to California, and establish a wagon road through Arizona. The battalion was hastily assembled with untrained volunteer Mormon soldiers and their families. Courtesy, Sharlot Hall Museum

soon belong to someone else; the only question was to whom. The United States was interested and so were France and Great Britain. Arizona was between the two fought-over areas, Texas and California, and was about to enter a new era.

The United States insisted that Mexico had shed "American blood upon American soil," referring to some shooting which took place on the eastern bank of the Rio Grande, and declared war upon Mexico. Although the resulting conflict was not particularly popular in the North, the South and West joined in it wholeheartedly.

When the war began, Colonel Stephen W. Kearny began assembling the Army of the West at Fort Leavenworth, Kansas. Starting in June 1846 small detachments of men, mostly volunteers, pushed west and south. Colonel Alexander W. Doniphan arrived from Missouri with 800 mounted troops. Eventually, nearly 2,500 men assembled at Bent's Fort in southeastern Colorado. On July 31 a Santa Fe trader, James W. Magoffin, went ahead to pave the way for the troops. The Army of the West escorted 400 wagons which contained one million dollars worth of goods over the Santa Fe Trail. The Americans arrived in Santa Fe and displaced the Mexican authorities without bloodshed.

In a ceremony held in the old Palace of the Governors on August 18, the colonel asserted the authority of the United States over the Southwest. On September 22 another proclamation was issued establishing a government for New Mexico, which then included Arizona.

On September 25 Kearny and 300 mounted dragoons started south down the Rio Grande River, leaving the other troops in Santa Fe. On October 6, near modern-day Socorro, New Mexico, the Army of the West encountered Kit Carson and a dozen or so men heading east. As Kearny's guides were not very experienced, Carson, who was heading for Washington, D.C., with war news, was persuaded to turn around and guide the army west to California. Thinking that the war was nearly over, Kearny sent 200 of the dragoons back to Santa Fe.

On the way through Arizona the soldiers met Magnas Coloradas, who was so angry at the Mexicans that he offered to help Kearny invade Mexico. Instead Kearny traded for some mules and continued westward.

Over the Gila Trail went the army. They viewed Casa Grande, they were given food by the Pima Indians, who declined to take any money for it, and they deliberately bypassed Tucson, a Mexican stronghold. Not far from the Colorado River in the latter part of November the army encountered a party of Mexicans driving 500 horses to California. Since they were under orders not to disturb civilians they did not stop them.

Kearny found that, fortunately, the river was no deeper than four feet, and he and his men marched into California. They participated in the surrender of General Andres Pico to American forces near modern-day Hollywood in January 1847.

Close on the heels of the Army of the West came another military group, the Mormon Battalion. It had been organized by Brigham Young of the Church of Jesus Christ of Latter-day Saints and was mustered into service at Council Bluffs, Iowa, in mid-July of 1846. The battalion was divided into five companies, and when it reached Santa Fe it had nearly 500 men, 25 women, and several children. There had been some trouble with the group's commanding officers, and orders came from Kearny to place Colonel Philip St. George Cooke in command. He took charge on October 13 and culled out more than 80 men and most of the women and children as being physically unable to make the trek to California.

On October 19 those remaining in the battalion started slowly down the Rio Grande, guided by Pauline Weaver and Antoine Leroux. The only action the Mormon Battalion saw occurred on December 11 when the "Battle of the Bulls" took place. Animals living wild at an abandoned cattle ranch between modern-day Bisbee and Benson objected to intruders, and a bull tossed a private high into the air. Colonel Cooke was prepared to run for his life but someone shot the charging animal and it died at the officer's feet.

Tucson lay ahead and there was some worry over what to do about the settlement. Cooke lectured his men on military tactics while Leroux went ahead to scout the situation. A small party of Mexicans came to talk under a flag of truce.

The commander at Tucson, Captain Comaduran, sent word that he had orders not to allow the enemy into Tucson but he would not molest the troops if they bypassed the pueblo. Cooke rejected this notion and demanded surrender. He was prepared to fight, but upon reaching the settlement it was found that Comaduran and his men had fled.

Tucson was declared an open city; the colonel ordered the public stores opened and the men gorged themselves until they were sick. The Mormon Battalion raised the first American flag over Tucson.

Suddenly fear swept the battalion that the Mexicans would return and attack, and Cooke had great difficulty in maintaining order. These comic-opera military operations came to a halt after Cooke issued a proclamation saying he made war only on military men, not on civilians, and wrote a letter to the governor of Sonora urging that residents of the area come to the support of the United States.

The troops then marched north until they reached the Gila, whereupon they turned west. The Pima greeted the battalion with gifts of saguaro jelly. On January 7 and 8 the soldiers reached the junction of the Gila and Colorado and then crossed into California. By the end of January they had reached San Diego, but with the fighting over they were mustered out in Los Angeles on July 16, 1847. On their trek west, Cooke and the battalion had achieved their primary goal: to mark what became known as "Cooke's Wagon Road."

The Treaty of Guadalupe Hidalgo was signed by the U.S. and Mexico in February 1848. In return for a payment of $15 million Mexico transferred to the United States the disputed area of Texas, upper California, and the territory in between, south to the Gila River. Tucson and Tubac remained part of Mexico.

The Disturnell map on which the boundary lines were based was inaccurate, which would lead to serious disputes later. Another matter which would prove to be of concern was that, under the Guadalupe Hidalgo treaty, the United States was responsible for damage done to Mexican holdings by Indian raids. Nevertheless, the Senate approved the treaty and in September of 1850 created a new political subdivision called the Territory of New Mexico. With its capital in Santa Fe, the area encompassed the modern-day state of Arizona with two differences: what is now southern Nevada was a part of the territory, but the land south of the Gila River was not.

At almost the same time the peace treaty ending the Mexican War was signed, gold was discovered in California. Thousands of people rushed toward the source of the wealth. Those who could afford it went by way of Cape Horn or across the Isthmus of Panama, but those who were poor came overland, and many went through Arizona.

It has been estimated that as many as 50,000 individuals followed the Gila Trail west in the years 1849 to 1851. Most went to the goldfields but some remained along the way. The population of Arizona grew modestly as people reasoned that if there was gold in California there might well be some in Arizona, too.

In 1849 Camp Calhoun was founded in California at the Yuma crossing on the site of the mission established by Father Garces over a half century before. Its purpose was to aid travelers, scientists, and the Indians of the area. It ultimately became Fort Yuma.

An important task after the Mexican War was the running of the boundary line between the two former enemies. President Polk appointed a boundary commissioner, John B. Weller, who had no sooner begun his task than he was out of office due to a change in national administrations. The new president, Zachary Taylor, appointed John Russell Bartlett to the post. Bartlett made some unfortunate choices in selecting his assistants, and despite the fact that he had inadequate supplies and equipment, he set to work. In December 1850 Bartlett met his Mexican counterpart. By then it was obvious to all that the map on which the peace treaty had been based had El Paso 34 miles too far north and nearly 100 miles too far east. The result was the disputed "Mesilla strip" of uncertain ownership, which threatened to renew hostilities. The two commissioners made a compromise, but the whole matter was still unsettled when there was another change in national administration in the United States.

This time the new president not only sent out a new boundary commissioner but also dispatched James Gadsden as the new United States minister

While surveying for the Gadsden Purchase, the U.S. Boundary Commission, led by John Russell Bartlett, was attacked by stampeding wild horses on December 3, 1852. This sketch is from Bartlett's own narrative of the explorations. Courtesy, Arizona Historical Foundation

to Mexico. By this time it was the dream of those who wanted to develop the economy of the Southern states to see a railroad built from New Orleans to Los Angeles. Its logical route would be in the vicinity of Cooke's Wagon Road and that land was still held by Mexico. Although called "General" Gadsden, a title stemming from service in the South Carolina militia, the new minister was basically a railroad promoter and enthusiast. His instructions were to secure the railroad site, to settle the dispute over the "Mesilla strip," and to free the United States from responsibility for the Indian raids. Unfortunately for Mexico the dictator Santa Anna was once more in power and again in need of funds.

Santa Anna felt that money paid for any additional territory belonged to him personally; he was also fearful that someone would seize control of the territory, anyway, and it would thus be lost to Mexico. The result was that on December 30, 1853, a treaty was signed. A few Senate members opposed the transaction, which promised to pay $15 million for the land. A Virginian rewrote the treaty to offer $10 million instead. Santa Anna accepted and the Gadsden Purchase went into effect June 30, 1854.

The international boundary ran west 50 miles from El Paso and then south 30 miles before it continued west to a point just west of where Nogales would later be founded. Then it moved west to a point eight miles north of the mouth of the Colorado River. With the boundary survey in 1855 began one of the great myths of Arizona history. The story

goes that the boundary line was supposed to go directly west from Nogales until it touched the Gulf of California, but that the surveyors were either drunk, or wanted to get drunk, so they hurried toward Fort Yuma.

Everyone now recognizes how valuable a seaport would have been for Arizona, but at the time the United States got exactly what it wanted. Kit Carson said the land was so hopeless that "a wolf could not make a living upon it," and who would want to buy more of that?

Actually Mexico, which soon ousted Santa Anna once and for all, probably would not have released any more land. To move the boundary straight west from Nogales would have meant there would have been no land bridge between Baja California and the rest of the republic. By the time the matter was again discussed in the 1870s there was definitely no interest in such a sale.

Mexican troops were withdrawn from Tucson and Tubac in March 1856, much to the unhappiness of the settlers in the area, who were without protection until the arrival of Major Enoch Steen and his United States Dragoons in late November.

The new territory was incorporated into New Mexico, which had seven counties that ran across its entire area east to west. All of the additional land was in Doña Ana County, the southernmost county. It is estimated that there were about 2,500 non-Indian inhabitants there at the time.

Policing the land was a major problem. Even more basic was the need to explore the region. In an age before the camera was in general use, a drawing was the only way to record what an area looked like. That was the specialty of the United States Army Corps of Topographical Engineers. Until the corps was formally disbanded during the Civil War, these engineers roamed the West and faithfully recorded on paper what they saw.

In September 1850 the United States government made the first grant of land to a railroad, and thus started a system which for years helped to promote this new form of transportation. Soon there was not only the dream of the New Orleans-to-Los Angeles line but several other routes as well. The government sent explorers to determine possible routes west along the 35th parallel.

In September of 1851 Captain Lorenzo Sitgreaves, guided by Antoine Leroux, started west from the Zuni villages. With them were Lieutenant John G. Parke, physician and naturalist Dr. S.W. Woodhouse, about 15 civilians, and a military escort commanded by Major H.L. Hendrick of the Second

Artillery. They endured considerable hardships, and after reaching the Mohave villages on the Colorado River they followed that stream south to Fort Yuma. In 1853 the government published their report as the first mapping of the area.

Another expedition traveled roughly the same route from west to east during the summer of 1853. Francois Xavier Aubrey, "the Skimmer of the Plains," and about 18 men left Tejon Pass in California, and in September reached the Zuni villages. As was the case on several of these expeditions, the going was difficult—mule meat was standard dining fare—but Aubrey went on to Albuquerque and drove a flock of sheep back to California.

In the summer of 1853 the Skimmer and 60 men again traveled the 35th parallel, this time pulling a wagon to show the practicality of the route. Unfortunately for Aubrey, on the day he arrived in Santa Fe, August 15, 1854, he was knifed to death by a disgruntled newspaper owner into whose face Aubrey had thrown liquor. In time railroad tracks would be built on almost exactly the trail traced by Aubrey.

In March of 1853 Congress appropriated a sizable sum of money to determine the best possible railroad route from the Mississippi River to the Pacific Ocean. Lieutenant Amiel W. Whipple of the Topographical Corps was placed in charge of the expedition organized to trace the route, and Lieutenant Joseph C. Ives was his assistant. The party assembled at Fort Smith, Arkansas, and it was November 1853 when they reached Albuquerque. From that locale

Francois Xavier Aubrey, sometimes called "the Skimmer of the Plains," led exploring expeditions from New Mexico to California in 1853. His demonstration of the practicality of the route along the 35th parallel would soon be put to good use; the railroad across northern Arizona traced Aubrey's route almost exactly. Courtesy, Arizona Historical Society, Tucson

This lithograph depicts the **Valley of the Gila and Sierra de las Estrellas from the Maricopa Wells,** *circa 1847. It was done by A.H. Campbell for the general report on the exploration and survey of the 32nd parallel route to California. Maricopa Wells, at the foot of the Estrella Mountains, later became the most important stop on the San Antonio and San Diego Mail Line, commonly known as "Jackass Mail," which began in 1857. Courtesy, Arizona Historical Society, Yuma*

This is the only known photograph of the camels brought to Arizona by Lieutenant Edward F. Beale in 1857. The camels came from Syria and carrried three times the load a mule could handle, but Beale failed to convince people they were ideal for pioneer transportation. Some were turned loose on the plains, some sent to zoos, and a few became mail carriers, like this camel in 1863 standing before a military headquarters building. Mail carrier Thomas Keaveney loads the camel. Courtesy, Title Insurance and Trust Company, Los Angeles, Collection of Historical Photographs

they moved west approximately the same way Sitgreaves had gone earlier. Moving to the south they followed the Santa Maria River and Bill Williams Fork until the latter emptied into the Colorado. That point was reached on February 20, 1854, and Whipple and Ives then went north to the area of modern-day Needles and moved into California. The result was a report, and this one quite elaborate, favoring the 35th parallel.

Not all attention was given to this area, however. In 1854 Lieutenant Parke, with Lieutenant George Stoneman in charge of the military escort, traveled over Cooke's Wagon Road. Surveying east from the Pima villages, they went through Tucson and continued east to the Rio Grande. This route was used almost immediately, with a few modifications, by the Butterfield stage line.

Another party of 19 men was led west through the area by Andrew B. Gray. Sponsored by the Texas Western Railroad Company, Gray's group went on to San Diego and reported that the 32nd parallel offered good opportunities for construction.

Without doubt the most colorful of all the groups to cross Arizona in the 1850s was that led by Lieutenant Edward F. Beale in 1857. Beale, who had made several trips across the country, once with the news that gold had been discovered in California, was assigned the task of surveying a wagon road from Fort Defiance to the Colorado River. What was unusual about the party were the camels it had. The War Department purchased the animals in the Middle East, and the first group landed in Texas in 1856 and the second a year later. With the animals came drivers, who bore such colorful names as Hadji Ali, Greek George, Long Tom, and Short Tom.

The expedition left the Zuni pueblos in August 1857. Beale daily grew more enthusiastic about the camels. At one point he rode more than 25 miles on a single animal just to see how it would behave. In January of 1858 the group reached the Colorado River. It was thought that camels were afraid of rivers, but the animals willingly swam the Colorado on their way to Fort Tejon.

There was, however, one thing which made the great camel experiment a failure. Horses and mules were afraid of them, and since there was no chance of replacing all the horses and mules owned by the army, the camels had to go. It might also be noted that most men who had to work with the camels were not overly fond of them either. The camels were auctioned off by the government as the Civil War started and

some of them came back to Arizona.

The most famous of the camel drivers, Hadji Ali, or Philip Tedro, as he was also known, continued to live in the territory until his death at Quartzsite in 1902.

Camels for a while roamed wild in Arizona; occasionally a traveling circus would round up a few. One of the animals, called the Red Ghost, was driven mad by having a person strapped to its back, and trampled at least one person to death before it was shot. The last known survivor of the original band of imported camels died peacefully in the Los Angeles Zoo in 1934.

Camels were rather exotic in the land now called Arizona, but the 1850s also saw the appearance of another strange new form of transportation. It was the steamboat, and the first of these, the *Uncle Sam,* reached Yuma in December of 1852. The Indians took one look and decided

This 1883 team of oxen transported military supplies in the Arizona Territory. Courtesy, Phoenix Public Library

RIGHT: The confluence of the Gila and Colorado rivers made Yuma a strategic hub of transportation. Fort Yuma guarded the crossing from the Indians, but it was not until 1877 that the crossing was bridged by the Southern Pacific Railroad. In 1915 the Ocean to Ocean highway was completed with the construction of this bridge. Showing the bridge halfway built, this view looks west to the California side of the Colorado, with Fort Yuma buildings on the right, now an Indian hospital. Courtesy, Arizona Historical Society, Yuma

OPPOSITE BOTTOM: The Butterfield Overland Mail was a legendary institution of the Southwest. Its southern route through Arizona tested the courage of drivers who guided galloping horses and swaying coaches while encountering deserts, mountains, and Indians. In 1857 John Butterfield and his associates signed a contract with the Post Office Department to provide semiweekly service between St. Louis and San Francisco, but the coaches also carried passengers. The stage line ended in 1869 when the Union Pacific Railroad linked east and west. Courtesy, Arizona Historical Society Museum

Yuma on the first of October 1855 and soon became active in mining. Owner of the Patagonia Silver Mine, a champion of the idea of separate territorial status for Arizona, and a Confederate supporter who was jailed at Fort Yuma when the Union took control, Mowry died before he was 40 in London, England, with Poston at his bedside. Later, it is said, Poston brought his body home in a barrel of brandy.

Michel Goldwater, patriarch of a noted Arizona family, got his start as a merchant in the gold camps along the Colorado at this time. His counterpart in Tucson, Solomon Warner, was the first man to open a store there, and later spent his life experimenting with a perpetual motion machine.

Another early settler, Pete Kitchen, managed to survive on his ranch near modern-day Nogales, on which he raised cattle and hogs. He also sold grain, potatoes, and fruit. His wife's many relatives and several others worked on the ranch. The house was extremely well fortified and Kitchen was known as a crack shot. The devout Doña Rosa Kitchen tended a cemetery where those outlaws who attempted to kill or rob her husband were buried.

People like these came from all over the world to join those already living in Arizona. Among them was Estevan Ochoa, a native of Mexico, who became an important merchant, freighter, and civil leader. These early Arizonans were colorful and strong characters.

Except for Tucson and Tubac most other settlements in the western part of New Mexico Territory were just getting started in the 1850s. Some survived but did not grow to any degree; Ajo and Patagonia are examples. Some did not survive at all. Gila City, 20 miles east of Fort Yuma, produced two million dollars in gold bullion and then vanished. To the north, La Paz suffered the same fate.

No matter where the early residents lived, one of the major problems they faced was the lack of government. Not only was there no law and order, but there was also no system of land registration. Theoretically the government at Santa Fe should have met these needs, but it was far away and busy with local problems.

In August of 1856 a meeting was held in Tucson with Mayor Mark Aldrich presiding, resulting in a petition signed by 260 men who asked that the separate Territory of Arizona be created by Congress. Nathan P. Cook, a road builder, was sent as the delegate to Washington, and Granville H. Oury went to Santa Fe to present the message. Both were ignored. More meetings and petitions followed. In September of 1857 the people of Tucson elected Sylvester Mowry as their delegate to Congress but he was denied admission, although he spent some time lobbying on behalf of his homeland. Other bills were introduced in Congress on behalf of Arizona but they all failed to be adopted.

In December of 1857 President James Buchanan recommended separate territorial status for Arizona, and the following February a senator from California introduced a proposal to carry the idea into effect. But nothing happened.

FAR LEFT: Pioneering merchants such as Michel Goldwater helped settle the Arizona frontier while establishing mercantile dynasties. Michel and his brother Joseph were Polish immigrants who moved from the California gold-rush country to sell boots and whiskey to miners in La Paz and Ehrenburg when gold was discovered in those Colorado River towns in the 1860s. The company moved to Prescott in 1864 and a chain of Goldwater stores spread across the territory. Courtesy, Arizona Historical Society, Tucson

LEFT: Estevan Ochoa, the "freight king," was a successful Tucson businessman with close ties to the Spanish-American community. With his partner Pinckney Randolph Tully, he operated one of the strongest mercantile and freighting firms in the territory in the 1860s until competition from the railroad caused the business to fail by the time Ochoa died in 1888. Noted for his philanthropy and support of community causes, Ochoa also exerted a powerful influence in Arizona politics during the 1870s. Courtesy, Arizona Historical Society, Tucson

The problem was that creating Arizona would reactivate the slavery controversy. Technically slavery was legal in New Mexico, although there is no evidence that any slaves of African ancestry were ever brought into Arizona. Northerners were opposed to the further extension of slavery, and many wanted to end it in the territories altogether.

The president, in a message to Congress in December 1858, noted that the people of Arizona were "practically without a government, without laws, and without any regular administration of justice. Murder and other crimes are committed with impunity."

On the first of February 1860 the New Mexico legislature created Arizona County, with Tucson as the county seat, but never put it into operation. The people of southern Arizona and southern New Mexico then attempted to create a territorial government for themselves. At a convention held in Tucson in April they wrote a constitution which was to be in effect until Congress acted. The resulting published document plus the proceedings of the meeting was the first book published in Arizona.

On the fourth of April, Dr. Lewis S. Owings of Mesilla was inaugurated as governor. An unpracticing physician, Owings was a land speculator and mining man. In his inaugural address he again called for Congress to act on separate territorial status and also called for all-out war against the Apaches.

For more than 300 years, the land now called Arizona was a part of the Spanish Empire. Because of events in the early nineteenth century, however, Arizona's destiny would change radically. Lying between Texas and California—both of which were desired by the United States—Arizona saw its Latin-American heritage infiltrated by the Anglo-American culture. Although both the Indian and Latin influence would continue to be felt, the economic, political, and social life of Arizona would be heavily influenced by newcomers from the East.

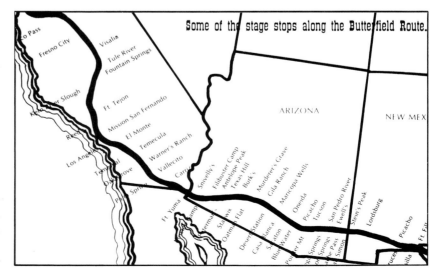

Some of the stage stops along the Butterfield Route.

Civil War and the Creation of Arizona Territory

One of the frontier army posts established in Arizona during the late nineteenth century was Fort Huachuca, deep in Apache country in southeastern Arizona. Troops I, H, and L of the 6th Cavalry and Company C of the First Infantry parade in dress uniform and helmet before the barracks at Fort Huachuca in 1884, seven years after the post was established. Courtesy, Fort Huachuca Military Museum

During the winter of 1860 something happened far from Arizona which would directly influence the Southwest. After years of trying to avoid such a calamity, the Union of states seemed to collapse.

The area soon to be officially named Arizona was one of the reasons for the final collapse. The Southern states would probably not have seceded if the Crittenden Compromise could have been agreed upon. A line would have been drawn at 36°30′ across the nation, and south of that line slavery would have been forever guaranteed. President-elect Abraham Lincoln did not agree to the proposal because it meant that New Mexico and Arizona might have the "peculiar institution." The issue would be settled on the battlefield.

The Butterfield stages stopped running across Arizona and with them stopped communication. Forts Buchanan, Breckenridge, and Defiance were abandoned, as was the camp at Tucson. In May of 1861 the troops at Fort Mojave burned their buildings and returned to Los Angeles. The Indians did not clearly understand the situation and concluded that something they had done caused the intruders to depart. They therefore reasserted their authority.

The forts were abandoned because traditionally the South had furnished the officer class of the United States Army and many were now leaving to show their loyalty to their states. Before it all ended there was only one loyal commander in New Mexico and none in Arizona.

Those who favored the Confederacy took control of Tucson. At a meeting held in Mesilla on March 16, 1861, attended by delegates from Arizona, it was decided that the Southwest should be a part of the Southern republic. This action was taken, some said later, in the hope of gaining some protection and law and order. Another gathering held in Tucson in August not only declared Arizona to be in support of the South but selected Granville H. Oury as delegate to the Richmond government.

The Confederacy was interested in Arizona for at least two major reasons. There were valuable minerals to be found there, and the area provided a land bridge into California. The rebels hoped that enough people in the southern part of the state would join them in their fight for independence to cause at least part of California to leave the Union.

Groups of Texas volunteers moved west. One such party, numbering about 300, mounted and armed, was led by Lieutenant Colonel John R. Baylor, a former Indian fighter. While he was at Mesilla, on the first of August 1861, Baylor proclaimed the existence of the Territory of Arizona. That action was confirmed by an act of the Confederate Congress in February 1862. This Arizona was the southern part of the modern-day states of Arizona and New Mexico. The northern boundary was the 34th parallel, although more land might later be claimed. Colonel Baylor was made governor of the new area and its capital was at Mesilla.

A military unit, the Arizona Rangers, was created to defend the land. Captain Sherod Hunter, under Baylor's command, arrived in Tucson with his men on the last day of February 1862 and raised the "Stars and Bars" over the town. They were warmly greeted by the residents, for some of the loyalists had already left town. Hunter sent some men to the Pima villages and even beyond to the west, but as they went down the Gila River they learned that forces loyal to the Union were being assembled at Fort Yuma. Confederate control would not last long.

Governor Baylor got into trouble by issuing an order in March 1862 telling subordinates to "Use all means to persuade the Apaches or any tribe to come in for the purpose of making peace, and when you get them together kill all the grown Indians and take the children prisoners and sell them to defray the expense of killing the Indians." Jefferson Davis disagreed strongly with Baylor, and he was removed from office.

Union Colonel James H. Carleton assembled his

Colonel John Robert Baylor was Confederate governor of Arizona after an August 1861 proclamation in which he took possession of the Territory of Arizona in the name of the Confederacy. Tucsonians enthusiastically approved his actions, especially since the withdrawal of Union troops had left the area open to Apache and Mexican bandits. Baylor proved to be a tempestuous governor and he was removed in 1862 when he issued instructions to volunteer troops to lure Indians in under a flag of truce, only to slaughter them. Courtesy, Arizona Historical Society, Tucson

California volunteers, popularly known as the "California Column," in March and April of 1862. The advance party started into Arizona and at the abandoned Stanwix stagecoach station some shooting took place, which should probably be called the westernmost battle of the Civil War. Instead that title is generally bestowed on the fight which took place at Picacho Pass on April 15, 1862, when a few Union cavalrymen had been captured by the rebels and a party was sent to free them. Lieutenant James Barrett of the California Column and two of his men lost their lives in the resulting battle, while the Confederates suffered two men killed and three captured. Exactly who won seems uncertain, but more importantly Captain Hunter and his men saw what was about to happen and abandoned Tucson.

The first of the California volunteers arrived in the "Old Pueblo" on May 20, and soon Colonel Carleton was on the scene and declared martial law. Sylvester Mowry, who had vigorously championed the rebels, was confined at the Fort Yuma stockade, and some others had their property confiscated. Taxes were levied on behalf of the United States and those loyal to the Union returned from hiding.

Carleton and his men pushed east. Later, in July 1862, the Battle of Apache Pass marked the largest engagement between soldiers and the Apaches. The Indians were led by Mangas Coloradas and Cochise. They suffered a loss of more than 60 men, while the army suffered two killed and three wounded. The colonel gave orders to place a military camp, Fort Bowie, in the area to aid travelers through the land and to hold on to what had been won.

Colonel Carleton also issued an order which commanded that all Apache men "are to be killed whenever and wherever you can find them; the women and children will not be harmed, but you will take them prisoners." Carleton told Kit Carson to treat the Navajo in the same manner. The venerable mountain man began a series of attacks during the summer of 1863. Despite his orders to kill, he took many prisoners. By the following spring 8,000 Navajo were being held at Bosque Redondo near Fort Sumner, New Mexico. Mangas Coloradas was taken prisoner by a ruse and moved to Fort McLane, New Mexico. He died there the night of January 18, 1863, reportedly as he tried to escape.

Despite the turmoil of the Civil War and the Indian conflicts, some people managed to go on living their normal lives. New groups and individuals arrived in Arizona, and one of the most important was the Walker Party. Led by the mountain man

LEFT: Colonel, later general, James Henry Carleton led volunteers from California into Tucson in 1862 to regain southern Arizona after John Baylor had claimed the area for the Confederacy. The controversial Carleton set up military courts, tried supposed rebels, and set himself up as governor of the Territory of Arizona. He also established Fort Bowie at Apache Pass after his troops had run into trouble at that strategic point. Courtesy, Arizona Department of Library, Archives, and Public Records

and explorer Joseph Reddeford Walker, the party's original idea in the spring of 1861 was to search for gold on the Little Colorado River. Things did not go well and the men reorganized in Santa Fe.

Down the Rio Grande they went, exploring southern Arizona and stopping at Tucson and the Pima villages. The seekers after riches were joined along the way by new arrivals, while others left the party along the way. Walker, a wise and careful man, went as far west as near the mouth of the Hassayampa River before turning north and following that streambed, where they soon found gold. In the final analysis the Walker Party was largely re-

BELOW: On April 15, 1862, the only Civil War battle in Arizona was fought at Picacho Pass, 45 miles northwest of Tucson. The monument in the foreground was dedicated in 1928 to commemorate the three Union soldiers and Lieutenant James Barrett from the First Cavalry of California Volunteers, who were killed during the battle. Courtesy, Arizona Historical Society, Tucson

BELOW RIGHT: Joseph Reddeford Walker, who spent most of
his life trapping, guiding, and
exploring, was chosen when
he was between 60 and 70 to
lead a party of gold seekers
through central Arizona.
Between 1862 and 1864,
Walker's party opened the
area for settlement as they
made surface strikes on the
Hassayampa River, five miles
from present-day Prescott.
Other discoveries near Big
Bug, Lynx, and Weaver creeks
came to be known as the
Walker Mining District. The
party camped near a site
where Henry Wickenburg
would soon open the fabulous
Vulture Mine. Courtesy,
California State Library

BELOW: Lynx Creek was the
site of gold mining claims
along its entire 18-mile course,
after Joseph Reddeford
Walker's party had explored
north-central Arizona in 1863.
Most of the gold had played
out by 1897, but young men
and women like these still
hoped to find some gold by
panning in Lynx Creek. Courtesy, Sharlot Hall Museum

sponsible for the opening of central Arizona to settlement by non-Indians.

In the early 1860s the United States government
had little time to pay attention to events in the far
Southwest. But in February 1862 Representative
James M. Ashley of Ohio, whose friends were stockholders in the Sonora Exploring and Mining Company of Arizona, introduced a bill to divide New Mexico at approximately the 109th meridian and rename
the western portion Arizona. There was some opposition in Congress to the proposal on the grounds
that the area was under Confederate control, but
the bill nevertheless passed in the House of Representatives on May 8, 1862.

President Lincoln felt the proposal would win approval despite the opposition of Senator Lyman Trumbull of Illinois and others. Another Ohio politician,
Senator Benjamin F. Wade, supported the plan, and
the Senate voted in favor by 25 to 12 on February
20, 1863. Four days later the president signed the
Organic Act, which formally created the Territory of
Arizona.

For many years, starting in the 1880s, a fine story
of the creation of the territory was told by Charles
D. Poston. In it he was the "Father of Arizona Territory," and his version of what happened was that
he almost single-handedly brought about the creation of the new political subdivision. He said he gave
an "oyster supper," a term used to describe a cocktail
party and dinner in the 1860s, to which he invited
a group of lame-duck members of Congress. Poston
supposedly told those assembled that if Arizona was
created there would be all sorts of lucrative jobs available. The offices were accordingly parceled out
among the party guests. Near the end of the evening
Poston inquired, "But what is to become of me?" He
was told he could be superintendent of Indian affairs, and was so named by appointment of the president.

There is no doubt that Charles D. Poston labored
hard to bring Arizona into being, but the "Prince of
Pioneers" neglected to mention the others who
worked equally hard. In fact, General Heintzelman
paid the bill for the "oyster supper" which Poston
claimed he hosted. In actuality only two lame-duck
members of Congress, John A. Gurley and John N.
Goodwin, were interested in or received appoint-
ments in Arizona.

On the fourth of March 1863 President Lincoln
named the first officials for the Territory of Arizona.
Gurley of Ohio was made the first governor but he
died in mid-August before everyone started west. In
his place was John N. Goodwin of Maine, who was
originally to have been chief justice. Richard C.
McCormick, a 30-year-old newspaperman from New
York, became the first territorial secretary, while William F. Turner of Iowa, whose wife started the first
Sunday school in Arizona, was the first chief justice.

It took a while for the officials to assemble, but
they left Fort Leavenworth, Kansas, in late September and arrived in Santa Fe a month later. With
a military escort provided by General Carleton, the
group started west from Albuquerque. The Organic
Act did not specify where the capital should be located, but most assumed it would be in Tucson. Instead the officials decided that they would go to a
new military installation, Fort Whipple, then under

construction in central Arizona. Two days after Christmas in 1863 the governor's party calculated that they had crossed the Arizona-New Mexico boundary line and were thus in their jurisdiction.

On December 29 the group stopped so that the officials could take their oaths of office, make speeches—largely to one another—and begin receiving their salaries, as Congress had provided they were not to be paid until they were in office on Arizona soil. The Reverend Hiram W. Reed offered prayer and translated some of the proceedings into Spanish. For a long time it was believed that this took place in the midst of a snowstorm, but a letter was found from Secretary McCormick to General Carleton in which he stated that the snow had stopped and the weather was clear and cold. To help alleviate the suffering caused by the temperature, one of the party, Henry W. Fleury, informed Governor Goodwin that he had brewed a vat of his "Oh Be Joyful Juice" in the communal washtub.

Originally Fort Whipple was located in the Chino Valley to the north of its later site, and there the provisional capital was established on January 22, 1864. Governor Goodwin set out to visit some of his new domain while others went to work establishing government. A census was taken which revealed a population of 4,573 persons.

It was realized at once that the location of the fort had been poorly chosen, and so in May it was decided to move to a new site. There the town of Prescott was founded and named for the American historian, William H. Prescott. The judges were dispatched to different areas and began to hold court. Elections were held to choose the members of the first legislature. Those lawmakers gathered in September, ready to enact the first laws under which Arizona would be governed.

A shortage of buildings existed in early Prescott. On the town square a log structure was erected and rented to the territory to house the sessions of the legislature. Justice William T. Howell, formerly of Michigan, was responsible for drafting the first code, which was named in his honor. Four counties —Mohave, Pima, Yavapai, and Yuma—were created. A company of rangers was authorized, and some money appropriated for schools. Secretary McCormick had already created a territorial seal, but someone claimed that it was taken from a baking powder can and so a new one was authorized. It featured a deer, a saguaro, and a pine tree, plus mountains in the background, and it would be used until 1912 when a new state seal was adopted.

A log-cabin governor's mansion was built near the

Charles D. Poston, sometimes called the "Father of Arizona Territory," and the founder of the Arizona Historical Society, posed, on the right, with Lee H. Chalmers on the left and J.H. Tevis, standing. The photograph was taken in Phoenix at the time of the 16th territorial legislature, about 1891. Courtesy, Arizona Historical Society, Tucson

Prescott town square and Governor Goodwin, Secretary McCormick, and others had their offices in the building. Soon Goodwin was elected as the delegate to Congress and was succeeded as chief executive by McCormick. That man had a fiancée in New Jersey and he journeyed east to be married in the fall of 1865.

Margaret Hunt McCormick thus became the first First Lady of Arizona actually in residence (Goodwin's wife and three small children did not come to Arizona). Unfortunately her story is a sad one. She came to Arizona with her husband and was warmly welcomed. The ladies of Prescott refurbished the gov-

ernor's mansion and made it ready for her. While expecting her first baby in the spring of 1867 she made the trek from Tucson to Prescott. Her baby was stillborn, and a few days later, on April 30, 1867, she, too, died. Mother and child were buried in the pine forest near the mansion on the day before the First Lady's 24th birthday. Mrs. McCormick had brought rose cuttings from the East with her, and for years the plants grew around the old house as a memorial to her.

The location of the capital was one of the major political controversies in Arizona for many years. Great rivalry existed among cities and towns, some

of which no longer exist. La Paz on the Colorado was once a contender, but lost not only the race but finally its existence. In 1867, amid great bickering, Prescott lost the seat of government to Tucson.

For 10 years the government operated in rented quarters and then Prescott was again victorious. This time the offices were located on the second floor of a newly completed school building. Other spaces were rented as needed.

With each session of the legislature other attempts were made to again select a new location, but not until 1889 did it actually occur. In that year Phoenix was chosen, with Tucson lawmakers supporting the idea on the grounds that the new city was in the south. Though attempts were later made to move the capital back to Tucson, Phoenix held on to the prize. The lawmakers traveled from Prescott to Phoenix by way of Los Angeles, as there was no direct rail service between the Arizona cities. The speaker of the house of representatives had with him the legislative body's mascot, the "Legislative Brown Pup," supposedly the first canine to travel in a Pullman car.

There was, of course, no capitol building waiting in Phoenix when everyone arrived in 1889, so space was rented in the Phoenix City Hall, then located on East Washington Street. Finally in 1900 the Arizona Territory capitol (later the state capitol), with its shining copper dome topped by a statue of the goddess of liberty, often mistakenly called "the angel," was ready for occupancy. Over the years it has been expanded and many other government buildings have been added in the area.

In the 1940s the great architect Frank Lloyd Wright designed a new capitol to be located in Papago Park near Phoenix. One state senator looked at the plans and told Wright the new building looked like a "Siamese house of ill repute," to which the architect retorted he was certain the lawmaker would know more about that than he did. There matters remained, and the proposal never became a reality. Part of the original capitol has been restored as it was in 1901 and functions today as a museum.

Between December of 1863, when the first party of officials arrived, and February of 1912, when Arizona was admitted into the Union, the area was an "organized territory" of the United States. Basically it was an arrangement for an area which was not yet ready for statehood. The federal government had supervisory powers over the territories. The president of the United States appointed the principal officials. Congress had financial jurisdiction and could limit the amount of money spent as well as the debt of the territory. It could also veto any law passed by the territorial legislature. The courts were federal institutions. Until the Indian wars ended in 1886 the War Department was responsible for maintaining peace in Arizona. The Department of the Interior operated land offices to sell the real estate the government owned. The Post Office Department opened mail routes and kept them running, despite the difficulties of the frontier.

The governor of the territory was the highest official in residence and he had greater powers than later state governors would have. Until the 1880s the governors were appointed from outside the territory—they were called "carpetbaggers"—and the residents did not appreciate this.

The governor's mansion was a two-story log house built in 1864 in Prescott for the first territorial governor, John N. Goodwin, and Secretary Richard McCormick. It was considered a mansion because most Prescott residents were then living in tents, wagons, or crude shacks. It is depicted here in the 1870s. Courtesy, Sharlot Hall Museum

When Governor McCormick was elected to Congress and left in 1868 he was succeeded the following spring by Anson P.K. Safford, perhaps the most important of the territorial governors. Prior to his arrival from Nevada, Safford had lived in Illinois, and was born in Vermont. A very efficient and capable governor who was thoroughly devoted to developing Arizona during his eight years in office, Safford also played a large role in establishing public schools, helped to open the first bank in the territory, brought sheep and cattle to the Southwest, and was the first to interest Eastern capital in investing in the mines.

Safford also has another distinction, a unique one. He is the only governor in the history of the nation to grant himself a divorce. The legislature passed the divorce bill, and it was said that the governor signed that one faster than any other proposal which came across his desk.

The most famous of the territorial governors was John C. Frémont, the "Pathfinder of the West," who had been the first Republican nominee for president of the United States in 1856. Once an explorer and colorful character in the winning of the West, the old general in 1878 was 65 years of age and financially down on his luck. He had lost his fortune in land, and railroad promotion had not enriched him, so he needed a salary.

At first he was very warmly welcomed in Arizona, but Arizonans grew angry at his inability to remain in the area. Some grumbled that he thought the territorial capital was New York City. Although techni-

cally in office until 1882, he was rarely on duty. His wife, Jessie Benton Frémont, claimed that she ran the store while he tried to make money from mining. Fortunately other governors, while less well known, were more content to pay attention to their office.

When appointed governor in 1885, C. Meyer Zulick had to be freed from a Mexican jail, but the incident did not discredit him. A lawyer, he represented some mining companies who operated in Mexico and had not paid their employees. The attorney was held for ransom until his clients paid. A United States marshal helped him escape and brought him back to the United States.

Colonel Alexander O. Brodie, governor from 1902 to 1905, was a West Pointer who had been a Rough Rider and was a personal friend of Theodore Roosevelt. Joseph H. Kibbey was an expert on water law and was the chief legal architect of the Salt River Project. The last of the territorial governors, Richard E. Sloan, had earlier been a distinguished judge.

There were 16 territorial governors; 13 were Republicans and three were Democrats. Several of them had some sort of college education and a majority were lawyers by profession while others were journalists, surveyors, and businessmen. One or two of them were reasonably wealthy but most were not. None of them were involved in major public scandals, and by and large they served Arizona well.

As a territory Arizona had neither United States senators nor representatives. Instead there was a delegate to Congress, elected by the people every

The Arizona capitol building has a copper dome, topped by a statue of the goddess of liberty. The original building was finished by 1900, but it is shown here about 1910 as the front gardens and landscaping were being done. New wings have been added on both sides and the back for the senate, house, and state offices. Courtesy, Arizona Historical Foundation

two years, who sat in the House of Representatives, but did not vote. Over the years, Charles D. Poston, John N. Goodwin, and Richard C. McCormick served as delegates. Granville H. Oury was a delegate to both the Confederate and United States congresses. One of the most interesting and colorful of these men was Marcus Aurelius Smith, who served frequently between 1887 and 1909, and who was called by his friends "Mark the Idol," and by his opponents "Mark the Idle."

The territorial legislature met once a year until 1871, and thereafter every other year. The voters chose the members of the council, as the upper chamber was called, and the house of representatives. For a very small amount of pay, citizens were willing to serve in the lawmaking bodies. Some sessions were colorful. Once a representative lost heavily at the races and the next day promptly introduced a bill to outlaw horse racing. Each of his colleagues asked that his particular county or district be exempted until the proposed bill would apply only to the loser's ranch.

Another time someone got mad at a newspaper and introduced a bill to make it a felony punishable by a term in the Yuma prison to publish, edit, or even work on a newspaper anywhere in Arizona. Fortunately wiser heads realized that such a bill would violate freedom of the press and it was not seriously considered.

Sometimes the numbered legislatures had nicknames. There was much talk of the "Thieving 13th," but actually there was little graft in that 1885 session. The next meeting was called the "Measly 14th," due to the fact that it did not do much and also because many of the members caught measles from one another. In the early days when there were fights over the location of the capital some members of the legislature would refuse to attend whole sessions in the hope that they could prevent the bodies from securing enough of a quorum to transact business.

The territorial court system featured a supreme court with first three, then four, and finally five justices. One was designated by the president of the United States to be chief justice. These men also functioned as trial court judges presiding over districts. Some were outstanding office holders. Charles G.W. French, as chief justice, really built the court system during the years 1876 to 1884. Edward Kent, the last of the territorial chief justices (1902-1912), was a first-rate jurist by any standard. The main problem in keeping the courts functioning at first was the tendency of the judges, who were

Judge Joseph H. Kibbey was a county and state chairman of the Republican party, Phoenix city attorney, attorney general, and governor of the Territory of Arizona, but his greatest impact was in water law. Courtesy, Arizona Department of Library, Archives, and Public Record

from the Midwest and East, to return home for long visits.

Justices of the peace, chosen from among the citizenry and not expected to be trained in the law, were also a part of the legal picture, handling minor legal problems. Probably the most colorful of these was Charles H. Meyer of Tucson, who held office for over 30 years. One day Judge Meyer was rushing to work in his buggy when he suddenly stopped his horse, realizing that he had been speeding. In a conversation which took place in the middle of the street "Judge Meyer" gave "Charley Meyer" a firm lecture for not setting a better example in the community and fined himself $10.

To many people the mention of government in the Old West brings to mind two other often famous officeholders, the marshal and the sheriff. Western movies and television have made these standard characters. When Arizona came into being President Lincoln named Milton B. Duffield to the office of marshal.

There was only one marshal at a time and he was responsible for carrying out court orders, although he did at times have to arrest people. Marshal Duffield was a man noted for his bad temper, and was finally killed in a dispute over the ownership of a mine. He seems to have left two widows; a third wife died just before he did. Wyatt Earp was once a deputy for Marshal Crawley P. Dake. A few cities and towns named their chiefs of police "marshal," and that use of the word has caused some

Sheriff Bucky O'Neill, third from right, stands with other Yavapai County peace officers, circa 1880s. William "Bucky" O'Neill was a prospector, poet, Indian fighter, sheriff, land developer, and publisher, and became mayor of Prescott in 1898. Bucky organized and captained Troop A of the Arizona Rough Riders and offered his volunteers to President William McKinley to help fight the Spanish-American War. Courtesy, Arizona Department of Library, Archives, and Public Record

confusion because of there being "town marshals" and "federal marshals."

The sheriff was, and still is, a county official. In territorial times he was most often elected by the people every two years, although in some instances the governor appointed him. He too was responsible for enforcing court orders and had deputies to help him. William O. ("Bucky") O'Neill was one of the most noted and best of the Arizona sheriffs. He also was a court stenographer, cattleman, canal builder, and short-story writer. Commodore Perry Owens of Apache County, who wore his blond hair shoulder length, was even more colorful but somewhat controversial, owing to his part in the Pleasant Valley War, in which a number of people were killed, injured, or disappeared. (This feud—which may have been between cattlemen and sheepmen, property owners and rustlers, or simply based on personal animosities—featured the Graham and Tewskury

families and their allies and enemies.)

The Old West was not really as boisterous as most think, and sheriffs had many dull and occasionally even embarrassing days at work. In the 1870s a sheriff of Yavapai County was robbed returning home from escorting a mentally ill person to the hospital in California. Someone took the unarmed sheriff's prized gold watch.

In 1901 the legislature created the Arizona Rangers, consisting of a captain, a sergeant, and 12 privates, and charged it with ridding the territory of criminals wherever they were found. The first captain, Burton C. Mossman, was quiet, softspoken, and a very effective lawman. During their first year of existence the rangers were credited with putting 125 criminals behind bars. Mossman quit in a political dispute and his successor, Thomas H. Rynning, reorganized the expanded group. With a total strength of 26 the headquarters was moved from Bisbee to Douglas. Rynning was succeeded in 1907 by Harry C. Wheeler. The legislature abolished the Arizona Rangers two years later.

There were other governmental offices and office holders—attorneys general, treasurers, auditors, and the like. County and city government came into being. All in all the territorial system worked fairly well in Arizona. The area was for the most part free of the corruption and inefficiency which characterized some of the other Western territories.

One of the aspects of territorial government appreciated by Arizonans was that the federal government paid many of the expenses of operating the system. When statehood was finally achieved the cost of running the new Arizona government came as a shock. There were taxes levied, and most people resented them. One of the long-running controversies of the territorial period was whether the mines were paying their fair share of the costs of operating the government.

The relationship between the Indians and the settlers was the major problem for both federal and territorial governments immediately after the founding of Arizona. An army officer on duty in the 1860s remarked that the settlers actually lived on reservations while the Indians roamed free.

The United States Army, with few troops in Arizona, was hard-pressed to police the area for which it was responsible. The men worked hard for low pay and were little appreciated. A substantial number of the Western soldiers were blacks—the "buffalo soldiers," as the Indians called them.

The job of frontier duty was simply not as glamorous as later generations would believe. The well-known memoirs of an army wife, Martha Summerhayes, demonstrate that fact. She described in very honest detail what it was like to live in Arizona in those days.

Mrs. Summerhays found herself in Ehrenberg on the Colorado River—during the summer, this was not an especially nice place to be.

In the late afternoon of each day, a hot steam would collect over the face of the river, then slowly rise, and floating over the length and breadth of this wretched hamlet of Ehrenberg, descend upon and envelop us. Thus we wilted and perspired, and had one part of the vapor bath without its bracing concomitant of the cool shower. In a half hour it was gone.

Nor were matters any better at night:

The paraphernalia by the side of our cots at night

Commodore Perry Owens, the sheriff of Apache County, is shown as he appeared at the time of his battle with the Cooper-Blevans Gang at Holbrook, Arizona, on September 4, 1887. Courtesy, Arizona Historical Society, Tucson

The troops of Company A, 10th U.S. Cavalry, often called "buffalo soldiers," line up for inspection at Fort Apache in 1887. During the generation following the Civil War, the 9th and 10th cavalry, two regiments of black soldiers, served continuously on the western frontier. Courtesy, Special Collections, University of Arizona Library

consisted of a pitcher of cold tea, a lantern, matches, a revolver, and a shotgun. Enormous yellow cats, which lived in and around the freight-house, darted to and fro inside and outside the house, along the ceiling beams, emitting loud cries, and that alone was enough to prevent sleep.

Rats infested the premises and they were chased by the felines with the result that there was "squeaking, meowing and clattering all the night through."

A fair number of those who accomplished the task of bringing the Indians under control lost their lives in the process. Some who survived would later wonder about the treatment accorded those who had been vanquished.

When officials were unable to maintain law and order on the frontier, often individuals alone or in groups took control. One of these in Arizona was an interesting character named King S. Woolsey. A native of Alabama and a former gold seeker in California, he acquired two ranches. One was at Agua Caliente in what is now the southeastern corner of Maricopa County, and the other, the Agua Fria property, was in Yavapai County, not far from Prescott. Unfortunately both were located on major Apache "plunder trails." In January 1864 Woolsey and about 40 men who had suffered from the raids set out to punish the Apaches.

On the morning of January 24 there occurred the Battle of Bloody Tanks, in which one settler and about two dozen Apaches died. Whether it was a peace conference which turned into a deliberate massacre, or a situation in which the settlers had to fight their way out of a well-planned ambush cannot be determined with certainty. Even the exact spot where the battle took place is uncertain.

It is positively not true that Woolsey attempted to poison the Indians. That myth stems from another adventure of his in which the Apaches had him trapped and planned to finish him off the next morning. Woolsey carried strychnine for his heart condition and he laced the bread he had with him with the medicine. The bread was carried by his burro to where his enemies could get at it. They perished and he walked away.

Colonel Woolsey, as he became when appointed the governor's military aide, led two other major expeditions against the Apaches and was involved in several other battles. He did not battle all Indians, and indeed one of his closest friends was Juan Chivaria, chief of the Maricopas.

Woolsey lived less than 50 years, but at his death he was the largest landowner in Maricopa County. It cannot be determined whether he traded six sacks of flour with the husband for the young redheaded woman who became his widow, or whether he gave the husband six sacks of flour as compensation and told him to keep moving toward California. At any rate, Mary Woolsey survived the colonel by nearly 50 years, outliving at least two other husbands.

After the Navajo were resettled on their reservation in 1868, only the Apaches remained to be controlled. Various army officers were placed in charge of operations. General John S. Mason said that about all he could do was hold the forts and escort travelers between them. General Edward O.C. Ord came in 1868 and took the offensive but with only limited success. General George Stoneman, who had been an explorer in the 1850s, tried in

1870 to pacify everyone and angered nearly everyone with his policies. President Grant sent a peace emissary, Vincent Colyer, a Quaker who was also an artist, but he accomplished little. Colyer came to Arizona partly as a reaction to the infamous Camp Grant massacre.

In April of 1871 William S. Oury and Juan N. Elias led about 150 Anglos, Latins, and Papago Indians in a daybreak raid against a native settlement, and in the process killed about 100 Apaches, mostly women and children. Oury later defended his actions as "work well done" in retaliation for the Apache raids against the settlers. When the federal government insisted upon trying the ringleaders for murder, a Tucson jury refused to convict.

In June General George Crook, the most respected of the army commanders, arrived on the scene. General O.O. Howard also came as a special peace commissioner, and with the help of Thomas J. Jeffords a truce was arranged with the followers of Cochise.

Crook, who had great respect for his adversaries, always took the position that he did not make the rules but he enforced them. So long as the natives remained on their reservations and at peace all would be well; if they broke the peace he would

Routes across the desert were established by the position of rare waterholes. The water was just as important to the Indians as it was to the white military, and Indians often attacked caravans and cavalry when they halted to rest and replenish their water supply. Famed Western artist Frederic Remington depicted this in his drawing Water in Arizona. *Courtesy, Arizona Historical Society, Tucson*

During the Apache Indian Wars in the 1870s, the military signaled from station to station by heliographs, using the sun's rays thrown from a mirror. This station is at Fort Bowie, which was the first station on General Nelson Miles' signaling system. Courtesy, Special Collections, University of Arizona Library

RIGHT: General George Crook twice commanded the Arizona military. The Indians called him "Nantan Lupan," meaning Gray Wolf. He was the first to use Apaches as scouts, to employ mule trains to carry provisions, and to train his men in close, mobile tactical fighting. Courtesy, Arizona Historical Society Library, Tucson

OPPOSITE LEFT: Lieutenant Charles B. Gatewood, 6th Cavalry, shown here in 1895, induced Geronimo to surrender to General Nelson Miles, although he is often overlooked for his part in bringing the Apache Wars to an end. Courtesy, Arizona Historical Society, Tucson

BELOW: Company B, 19th Infantry, crosses the Gila River in buckboard wagons near San Carlos, an Apache reservation, in 1885. Courtesy, Phoenix Public Library

punish them and force them back onto the reservations. Even with the death of Cochise in June 1874 Arizona was quiet, and in March of 1876 General Crook was transferred elsewhere.

When General Howard was in the Southwest he persuaded Victorio, another of the great Apache leaders, to settle on land in south-central New Mexico. In the spring of 1877 government officials decided to remove Victorio and his people to the San Carlos reservation in Arizona but that did not work well, and on the first of September Victorio and his people left. Once again they were persuaded to return, but once more they left, and by the fall of 1879 hostilities

had been resumed. Victorio died in battle, or killed himself to keep from being taken prisoner, as one version goes, in October 1880, but that did not end the fighting. It is estimated that about 1,000 people lost their lives. The two generals in command at that time, August V. Kautz, who had served on the court-martial of the Lincoln conspirators, and Orlando B. Willcox, who wrote military novels in his spare time, could not control the situation. In September of 1882 General Crook was again in command.

There were several Apache leaders with whom the army had to deal. Alchesay, who had earlier been a scout for Crook, had been living quietly on the land since the death of Cochise; he tried later to negotiate with the runaway group. Naiche, sometimes called Nachez, was the son of Cochise, and he had his followers. So too did Loco, Juh, and old arthritic Nana, who may well have been about 80 at this time. Chato, a young chief, raided Arizona from Mexico in the spring of 1883 and was taken prisoner.

The last real fighting took place on July 17, 1882, when the Battle of Big Dry Wash was fought in the southeastern corner of Coconino County. Na-ti-o-tish, leader of the Indians, and about 20 of his warriors died in the fight, while the army lost one soldier.

The best known of the Apache figures of this time is Geronimo, who was born sometime in the 1820s, and who was not born into the Chiricahua group but became its leader. Naiche was usually with him to give authority. Geronimo first attracted attention when the move was made to the San Carlos reservation. Although about 400 men declined to make the move Geronimo had about 100 who followed him and fled to Mexico. They surrendered in the spring of 1877 and settled down as peaceful farmers. In the fall of 1881 Geronimo broke out from the reservation, and after attacking Fort Apache he and his followers escaped into Mexico. General Crook went after them and by January of 1884 Geronimo and his men were back on the reservation.

Conditions were not good at San Carlos and on May 17, 1885, nearly 100 Chiricahuas, led by Geronimo, Nana, and Naiche, again made the dash for Mexico. There followed some skirmishes and one surrender by the Indians, which did not last. General Crook resigned in a dispute with the authorities in Washington over what should be done with the "renegades."

He was succeeded by General Nelson A. Miles, a very different kind of general, who loved publicity and very much wanted to be president of the United States. Miles sent Lieutenant Charles B. Gatewood,

"Big Nose," as the Indians affectionately called him, after Geronimo. This heroic and brave officer, who got very little credit for what he did, arranged the final surrender in September of 1886.

The lieutenant and two scouts found the group and faced them alone when Miles and his 5,000 troops had no idea where they were. The grateful people of Arizona gave the general a ceremonial sword made by Tiffany's for this achievement.

The escapes had greatly inflamed public opinion against the Apaches. At Fort Bowie nearly 500 Chiricahua Apaches, including many who had given no trouble at all, and even some who had helped to capture the renegades, were put on a train which was bound for Florida. It stopped in Texas while President Cleveland considered a petition which demanded that Geronimo be brought back to trial. General Crook interceded and the unhappy band went to Florida, then to Alabama, and finally in 1894 to Fort Sill, Oklahoma, where most of them lived the rest of their lives. In old age Geronimo dictated the story of his life, became a skilled poker player, and rode in the inaugural parade for Theodore Roosevelt in 1905. He lived until 1909.

Thus it was that just a century ago Arizona saw an end to the Indian wars. Despite those troubled decades, year after year more people moved into the territory from all over the United States and from many foreign lands. When the census of 1870 was taken, the population was still under 10,000, but by 1880 that number had increased to more than 40,000. That figure more than doubled in the next decade, and in 1890 there were 88,243 Arizonans. Growth continued, and by the end of the century there were nearly 125,000 people in residence, and by the end of the territorial period an additional 75,000 had arrived.

ABOVE: Geronimo was the most famous of the Apache renegade leaders. This 1886 photograph was taken after his surrender to General Nelson Miles. It was the last photograph taken of Geronimo in the field. Courtesy, Arizona Historical Society Library, Tucson

The Territorial Period

Sierra Bonita Ranch, started in 1872 by Henry Hooker, became one of the largest and most successful in the territory. Hooker introduced new breeds of cattle to the 800 square miles he controlled. Here is a Sierra Bonita herd with 200 Hereford bulls and 1,000 Hereford cows in the background. Courtesy, Arizona Historical Society, Tucson

Those who came to Arizona Territory had to face the hard fact that water was in short supply. In ancient times residents learned how to conserve and transport water. The pioneers' response to the challenge was to organize canal companies to provide irrigation. In November of 1867 the Swilling Irrigation and Canal Company, Inc., was launched by Jack Swilling—a stage driver, Confederate sympathizer, and rancher who in 1878 was charged with stagecoach robbery and died in jail before a trial could be held. Before his unfortunate end, Swilling helped to organize the Tempe Canal Company in 1871. These private, profit-making water companies required that those who received water had to own shares of stock in the company. They were important in the early development of the desert but the "Kibbey decision" of 1892 ruled against them.

This decision held that water was owned by all the people and not just by those who supplied the water. The first person in a place to use water beneficially had the first right to it. The canal companies lost their control over this all-important resource. The story of Arizona water law would take a long time to unfold but this was the beginning.

One of the most beautiful illusions of the 1860s and early 1870s was that artesian wells abounded in Arizona and all that people had to do was dig beneath the surface and water would flow from the wells. Sadly this was not true.

Trapping and holding what water was available was a serious problem. Several earthen dams were built, and some caused disasters. The Walnut Grove dam on the Hassayampa north of Wickenburg burst

The Porter Building at the southwest corner of Central and Washington in Phoenix housed Jim Montano's pioneer wine vault on the first floor, while the Arizona Improvement Company and the Arizona Canal Company occupied the second floor. Courtesy, Arizona Historical Society Library, Tucson

in 1890, killing people and destroying property. Other earthen dams, especially some built on the Gila, simply were not strong enough to hold during spring floods. The technology of the time made it possible to build with stronger materials, but there was not adequate capital in Arizona to finance such projects. The people turned to the federal government for help, but for many years it was not considered proper for public funds to be used for such a purpose.

Water was and is essential for all aspects of life. It became a fundamental principle of Arizona law that "land and water are inseparable." Water was essential to make the land productive.

Both the Treaty of Guadalupe Hidalgo and the Gadsden Purchase treaty held that although ownership of land in private hands would be protected,

LEFT: Phoenix founder Jack Swilling poses for the camera. Courtesy, Arizona Historical Society Museum

all unoccupied land, including the Indians' land, would become the property of the United States government. Thus almost all of Arizona was at one time publicly owned. For many years the Department of the Interior sold land at $1.25 per acre. During the Civil War the Homestead Act offered to give land to settlers, and later acts of Congress supplemented this. Upon the founding of Arizona, land offices were opened in Florence and Prescott, and by either pur-

BELOW: Irrigation was vital to the development of the Salt River Valley. Pumping plants, like this one in Mesa in the 1910s, directed water through valley-wide canals of the Salt River Project. Courtesy, Special Collections, University of Arizona Library

chase or simply living on the land thousands of Arizonans came to own real estate. Some land speculators bought large tracts from the government and then resold smaller plots, often on credit, which the government did not do.

The land had to be surveyed in keeping with practices started in 1785. Most of Arizona was surveyed from an arbitrary point selected near the junction of the Salt and Gila rivers, somewhat to the southwest of modern-day Phoenix. With mathematical precision the land was divided into townships measuring six miles by six miles and then further divided into sections one mile square which contained 640 acres. Those who were to do this work, under a contract from the government, were supposed to go out into the field and check every bit of land. Sometimes they did not and the result was called "saloon surveying" when problems developed due to inaccurate work.

Occasionally disputes arose over land ownership; some problems were caused by fraud. The most famous example of attempted land fraud to be found in Arizona was the work of a former St. Louis streetcar conductor, James Addison Reavis, the infamous "Baron of Arizona." Through purchase and marriage he claimed an 11-million-acre tract of land: a rectangle with a southeastern corner at Silver City, New Mexico, and a northwestern corner near modern-day Sun City, Arizona, not far from Phoenix. A tall, fast-talking, red-haired, gray-eyed confidence man, Reavis bought a questionable land claim and expanded upon it.

Reavis claimed that his wife was the descendant

of the first and second "Barons of Arizona," wealthy landowners who had lived in the Southwest since the 1700s. Despite all sorts of documents and even portraits of Reavis' noble in-laws, shown by the new "Baron," a title he assumed upon marriage to the "Baroness," none of these people ever existed. They were all created by Reavis out of his imagination. For a time the Baron, his wife, and two sons lived in truly royal style compared to the modest life-styles of most citizens of the territory.

Intimidated land owners, including, it was rumored, the Southern Pacific Railroad, gave Reavis considerable amounts of money for land usage. Others went to court to disprove his claim. The evidence

against the Baron proved decisive. Some writing supposedly done in Spain in the 1700s was accomplished with a steel pen not invented until 1880, and some type supposedly used in 1784 was not actually in use until 1875. Reavis was hard-pressed to explain the Wisconsin watermark on another of his "ancient" pieces of paper.

It was not until June 1895 that the Court of Land Claims meeting in Santa Fe held that the whole claim was a fraud. The "Baron," as many people called him, went to prison; later he lived a year in a county poor farm and finally died in Denver, Colorado, in 1914. Oddly enough he appears not to have been a complete scoundrel. He actually had dreams of developing his portion of Arizona with great irrigation projects.

Irrigation was not the only concern of early Arizona residents. Communication and transportation were also of special interest to settlers in the late nineteenth century. The military had to get messages to and from Washington. People needed to communicate with relatives and business associates in other parts of the nation. Everyone wanted to hear the news of the outside world.

The first telegraph in the territory appeared in the early 1870s and was a part of the Mormons' means of communication with their church members. The station was at Pipe Springs in the far north. In 1873 construction was started on a military telegraph which connected the line from San Diego to Yuma on to Prescott and then later Tucson. At first the Congressional appropriation to build the system was insufficient to provide enough telegraph poles, and so saguaros and other natural growth was used whenever possible to keep the wires from touching the ground. Later the telegraph was sold to private companies.

Samuel D. Lount, who in June 1879 operated the first ice-making machine in Arizona, also invented a telephone which he used for messages between his home and office. He saw no particular value to the contraption, however, and never tried to sell it. The first telephone system in Arizona was installed in Tucson in 1881 and at first it had under 100 customers.

During this period, as communication continued to improve, the railroad would revolutionize transportation in Arizona. Arizona participated in the great period of railroad building from 1850 to 1900. The first railroad in the territory was a short narrow-gauge line which ran from a mine to the town of Clifton and was completed in 1873. But it was the two transcontinental lines—in Arizona, the Santa Fe in the north and the Southern Pacific in the south —that were the most important.

The railroad from New Orleans to Los Angeles, which was the dream of the Gadsden Purchase, became a reality in the form of the Southern Pacific line. Congress chartered the Texas and Pacific Railroad to build from Marshall, Texas, to San Diego,

Pipe Springs, eight miles south of the Utah line, was the site of the first telegraph station in Arizona, built to connect Mormon settlements. In 1887 or 1888, the Woolley and Chamberlain families stand before the substantial stone building usually known as Windsor Castle. Presumably a safe refuge from invaders, portholes dotted the walls. The building is now a historic site. Courtesy, Arizona Historical Society, Tucson

ABOVE: Mining executives and their families pose with the engine that ran on the 20-inch gauge line that connected the Longfellow mine and Morenci. The entrance to the Longfellow tunnel is in the background. Courtesy, Special Collections, University of Arizona Library

ABOVE RIGHT: This group of railroad workers and their mules are laying track along the Atchison, Topeka, and Santa Fe railroad at the extreme front of Prescott. The construction, about 1895-1898, came south from the main Santa Fe line that went across the 35th parallel from Albuquerque through Williams, Ash Fork, and Kingman to Needles. Courtesy, National Archives

but it experienced financial troubles and by 1877 it was bankrupt. In the meanwhile the Southern Pacific had built as far east as Yuma and persuaded Congress and the legislatures of Arizona and New Mexico to allow them to build toward El Paso, Texas. By the spring of 1879 the tracks were down as far as Maricopa. On March 20, 1880, the first Southern Pacific engine arrived in Tucson.

There was a great celebration, and telegrams were sent to officials all over the world informing them that the "Old Pueblo" was now connected to the outside world by rail. One went to the Pope in Rome but there was no reply. A local official with a sense of humor created an imaginary reply in which the secretary to the Holy Father reported that the Pope was very pleased to learn this but had one question: Just where in hell was Tucson? Eastward went the line, through Benson and Bowie and into New Mexico, until finally it connected with Texas.

In 1866 Congress chartered the Atlantic and Pacific to build across the 35th parallel route. During the panic of 1873 the line became bankrupt but was acquired by the Atchison, Topeka and Santa Fe line. In May 1880 construction started west from Albuquerque and by late 1881 the Santa Fe, as it was informally called, reached Winslow. Then it was on to Williams, Ash Fork, Seligman, and Kingman before the track finally connected to the California lines at Needles in August of 1883.

The building of railroads caused a great rivalry among cities and towns to be on the routes of this new all-important form of transportation. Whether a town was on a line would often mean the differ-

ence between growth and stagnation. A notable exception was Phoenix, which was not on the main line of the Southern Pacific until 1926. A branch line was built to Phoenix in 1887, and yet another branch was built south from the Santa Fe at Ash Fork to Prescott and Phoenix and was completed in 1895. The latter was the work of Frank M. Murphy, a Prescott businessman. Epes Randolph, another important Arizona railroad man, directed the "Randolph lines" which were actually a part of the Southern Pacific system serving the eastern part of the territory.

Passengers and freight traveled wherever the railroad ran. If, around 1900, one wanted to go from Phoenix to Globe, one first went to Tucson and then north to Globe because the railroad did not run between Globe and Phoenix.

By 1912, the end of the territorial period, Arizona had nearly 1,700 miles of railroad track in operation. Since then that figure has steadily declined. Until 1923, for example, the Santa Fe ran a branch line to Crown King. Other so-called trunk lines took ore from the mines, moved it to smelters, and then transported it to all parts of the nation.

In the economic development of the Arizona Territory nothing was more important than mining. Following the Civil War the old mines were reopened and new ones discovered. Gold is the most glamorous ore, even if it is not the most valuable item in the Southwest. Around Prescott in the 1860s there was placer mining, in which water was used to wash away rock and dirt to yield the pure metal. The most valuable of the underground mines was the Vulture,

discovered near Wickenburg by the man whose name was given to the town. Henry Wickenburg's mine yielded $8 million worth of bullion before finally being turned into a tourist attraction years later.

In the 1870s silver mining became the dominant form of mining in Arizona. After the Civil War the metal was worth more than $1.25 per ounce and strikes were made in several areas of the territory. The Bradshaw Mountains near Prescott had a number of mines, and the great Silver King Mine near Superior yielded ore for many years. However, the area around Tombstone was the most important locale for silver mining. As early as 1857 the Brunckow Mine was opened there, but it was not worked for 20 years. Prospector Ed Schieffelin planned to go into the area, and the soldiers told him that if he did the only thing he would find would

BELOW: Once the center of a rich gold mining area in Mohave County, Oatman now has only a few hundred residents. The town was named for a family massacred by Indians near the site in 1851. Located in the scenic Ute Mountains near Sitgreaves Pass, Oatman is seen in this early 1920s view looking south on Main Street. The Arizona Stores Company general merchandise store and the Oatman Drug Company are on the left, and the Oasis Cafe is in the center. Courtesy, Phoenix Public Library

The Silver King mine was located in 1875 near the present town of Superior. These long ore trains carried more than $6 million in silver produced by the mine during the 1880s, although it was later overshadowed by the Tombstone silver strike. After the Silver King mine ran out, it was acquired by Magma Copper Company, which found rich copper ore there. Courtesy, Special Collections, University of Arizona Library

be his tombstone. After making a strike, he enlisted the aid of his brother and others, including Governor Safford, who wisely invested, and the great boom was on.

The fabulous era at Tombstone is one of the celebrated events in the history of the Old West. A dozen major mines yielded $35 million worth of ore during the heyday. In one year alone, 1882, production was over $5 million in silver. Then trouble developed. Flooding of the mines became a major problem, and in time the price of silver dropped to half of what it had been immediately after the Civil War. These two factors combined to make it unprofitable to continue to work the mines.

Other celebrated matters are the great "lost" mines which supposedly once existed in Arizona. The most famous is the Lost Dutchman in the Superstition Mountains east of Phoenix. Did Jacob Waltz, who died in Phoenix in 1891, really know the whereabouts of a rich gold mine? Was there really an Escalante Mine in the Santa Catalina Mountains near Tucson or a true "Glory Hole" near Salome? No one knows for certain.

Over the years there have also been problems with the "salting" of mines, planting things of value in a worthless claim. Probably the most famous example of this was the great diamond mine hoax of the 1870s. A pair of enterprising swindlers claimed to know the location of a valuable diamond mine although they were vague as to its location. Diamond fever swept Arizona; the United States marshal for the territory abandoned his office to seek the precious stones. Finally the "salted" mine was located in Utah.

"Red metal," copper, was not important until a need for it developed, and then new ways of removing the pure metal from ore had to be found. Small quantities of copper had long been mined; from Span-

ish days the rock and earth were separated and the resulting mixture was heated until the relatively pure ore could be removed.

With the coming of the industrial revolution following the Civil War, many new uses for copper were found. Electrical and telephone wires were two very important ones. A Canadian mining engineer, Dr. James Douglas, was one of the men who developed modern methods of producing pure copper ore, and in 1880 he received the first copper bars sent from the great Copper Queen Mine in Arizona to Pennsylvania for refining. Douglas soon came to Arizona as the representative of the Phelps Dodge Corporation and ultimately he was the patriarch of an important Arizona family.

At first, copper mining, like the digging for gold and silver, was done on an individual basis with one or two men working with pick and shovel. In the 1880s and 1890s large-scale mining came to be done by corporations; local owners generally sold out and absentee ownership became an issue in the territory. By 1888 copper was the leading mineral produced.

Several areas of Arizona had productive copper mines. Jerome and Clarkdale were famous for the United Verde properties; Clifton and Morenci had several productive mines; Globe was the site of the Old Dominion Mine; and Bisbee had the Copper Queen. Ajo, Miami, and the Ray-Superior districts proved also to be rich in ore. Starting in 1894 Arizona began to produce at least 10 million tons of copper per year, a minimum of one-fifth of all copper produced in the United States.

In addition to the three leading minerals—gold, silver, and copper—other wealth has been taken from the earth in Arizona. There were, for example, mercury mines in operation in the Phoenix area until the early 1940s.

Also important to Arizona's economy was cattle, which were raised in the Southwest since the days of Father Kino. During gold rush days in California, the demand for animals was so great that they sold for $300 per head. William S. Oury is said to have been the first resident cattleman when he bought a herd of about 100 animals from a drover headed from Illinois to California. Oury settled his animals near Tucson and in 1862 he imported some blooded stock from Kentucky. For the most part, however, animals were of the Texas longhorn variety until the fall of 1883 when Colin Cameron, who with his brother Brewster Cameron operated the San Rafael Cattle Company, brought 57 Hereford bulls to Arizona. Although there was some doubt as to whether the animals could survive the weather and the open range, they flourished.

Henry Clay Hooker of Sulphur Springs Valley operated the Sierra Bonita Ranch, which covered 800 square miles and was in its day the largest of the cattle spreads. Some say Hooker got his start in the West by buying and then driving a flock of turkeys to Carson City, Nevada, where he sold them for as much as five dollars apiece. With this capital he moved south and one day was surrounded by a large number of Apaches. To show he was not afraid he drove into the camp of Cochise who told him that though they could have killed him they did not because they appreciated the fact that he had brought livestock into the area.

John H. Slaughter of Cochise County was the owner of another noted ranch, the San Bernardino, which he purchased in 1883 and which was located along the Mexican border. The early ranches were mostly located south of the Gila River, but later northern Arizona was also opened to livestock. Between Flagstaff and Holbrook the "Hashknife outfit," officially the Aztec Land and Cattle Company, grazed 60,000 head of cattle in the mid-1880s.

Although droughts were at times a problem, as in 1892 and 1893, the cattle industry continued to be important to Arizona. After the introduction of barbed wire as a fencing material the open range came to an end. In time cattlemen began to dig wells and provide winter food for the animals instead of letting them fend for themselves as had been the way in earlier times.

Sheep were also brought to the Southwest in Spanish times, and in the period following the Civil War herds increased in numbers. The Candelaria family, originally from New Mexico, had many head in Apache County. James M. Baker, Isadore Solomon, and the Daggs brothers were other prominent sheep ranchers. Since these animals would clip the grass much closer to the ground than did cattle, some cattlemen objected to sheep ranching.

Also vital to the economy were the dairy cattle, turkeys, and chickens which were raised in substantial numbers. In 1888 a few ostriches were brought from California, and soon the Salt River valley had over 6,000 birds on several farms. The feathers were used to trim women's hats, and the industry remained important until styles changed about the time of the First World War. People associated with ostrich farming long remembered that one nice thing about ostriches was that a single egg would make an omelet for an entire family. Ostrich racing was also a popular sport.

Farming became important in Arizona as soon as the population began to grow. In the southern desert all crops were dependent upon irrigation, but in some other portions of the territory there was almost enough rainfall to engage in dry farming. Corn and wheat were the principal foodstuffs, but alfalfa and hay were also grown to feed livestock

Jerome was once one of the great copper mining camps in Arizona until the Phelps Dodge Mine closed in 1952 when the ore gave out. Built on the steep slopes of the Black Hills, Jerome houses are supported by props and stilts as they cling precariously to the hillside. Beneath them, millions of tons of copper ore had been mined nearly to the surface, causing some buildings in the business section to collapse. Notice the steep wooden steps climbing the hillside in this modern view of Jerome. Courtesy, Arizona Historical Society Museum

and farm animals.

Mills to grind grain into flour were also found throughout the area. In Phoenix John Y.T. Smith and King S. Woolsey were partners in an early mill, and for many years Charles T. Hayden produced flour at Tempe.

Citrus farming on a commercial scale dates from the early 1890s, although some people had orange trees in their gardens earlier. Vegetables of all varieties were produced as were many kinds of fruits. For some time it was not possible to ship many food items from outside the territory, and therefore only things grown locally could be obtained fresh.

One of the wonderful qualities of the pioneers is that they would try anything. One day the clerk in the general store at Maricopa had a customer who said he had finally found the ideal crop to grow on his land. He asked to purchase 10 pounds of seed macaroni!

In territorial days there were few rich people in Arizona and correspondingly few really poor ones. The first $1-million estate was not probated until 1924, but there were some who had substantial fortunes before that. Unfortunately it was the general rule that if one really made money one moved away, most likely to California where the climate was considered better.

It was possible to get along in Arizona with a relatively small income, and perhaps it is best to say it the way Mark Twain did in describing his boyhood: "We were all poor but didn't know it." Miners worked for about $2.50 per day, a workday being 10 to 12

hours. Schoolteachers were lucky to be paid $60 a month, but then Congress most years only paid the governor $3,000.

All the usual professions were to be found in the territory, including physicians, lawyers, and clergymen. Banks opened for the first time in Arizona in the late 1870s. For years Tucson had a combination taxidermist and dentist. Several of the early dentists were Eastern residents who were in Arizona only during the winter months when they wanted to get away from the cold. Mechanics worked on the railroads and in the mines. Carpenters, photographers, and morticians all played roles in the Arizona story.

One of the striking characteristics of Arizona was that it was separated from other major Western settlements by great distances. To the west the California towns were largely along the coast. To the north Utah was sparsely settled until one got close to Salt Lake City. Santa Fe and Albuquerque were quite a way to the east, and the Republic of Mexico had few settlements in its northern states.

Arizona's cities and towns were settled usually for one of about a half-dozen reasons. The missionary activities of the Mormons resulted in the founding of a number of settlements all over Arizona. Jacob Hamblin was an explorer who had contact with the Hopi peoples in the late 1850s and 1860s. He often guided settlers into northern Arizona and lived for several years at Edgar. Bishop Anson Call founded a town called Callville in what is now southern Nevada but which was once a part of Arizona. It is now at the bottom of Lake Mead, but it is said that when the water is clear one can still see the stone corrals built by Bishop Call. John Doyle Lee operated a noted ferry at the settlement named for him on the Colorado River. Other substantial and lasting LDS towns and cities were Springerville, Snowflake, Joseph City, St. David, Mesa, and Thatcher.

The railroad also caused towns to grow. Although John C. Fremont is said to have camped years before on the site, the city of Flagstaff was not a permanent settlement until the coming of the Santa Fe. Other railroad towns in the north were Kingman, Ash Fork, and Williams, while in the south there were Benson, Bowie, and Maricopa.

Bisbee, Tombstone, Clifton, and Jerome are examples of mining towns. Jerome was named for a New York family who invested in the mines; a member of that family was the mother of Sir Winston Churchill.

Phoenix and Florence were trading centers. The year after the Civil War, John Y.T. Smith was the first non-Indian to live in Phoenix. Smith harvested

wild hay where Phoenix Sky Harbor International Airport is now located, and sold his produce to Fort McDowell. Florence was either named for Governor McCormick's sister or because it reminded the early settlers of Florence, Italy. Nogales was founded because of its strategic location on the international border, and Prescott was established to be the capital city.

Most Arizona towns in the late nineteenth century were small, and in the southern part of the territory they resembled dusty Mexican villages. The buildings were mostly made of adobe and had flat roofs. Trees of any kind were highly prized. The people of Tucson and Phoenix did not have paved streets until about the time Arizona became a state. Every-

John H. Slaughter, rancher of the historic San Bernardino Ranch on the Mexican border, was also the sheriff who brought peace to Tombstone and Cochise County. Depicted here in the early 1890s, wearing his duck-hunting garb, Slaughter had been a Civil War soldier, Texas Ranger, army scout, and trail driver. Courtesy, Arizona Historical Society Library, Tucson

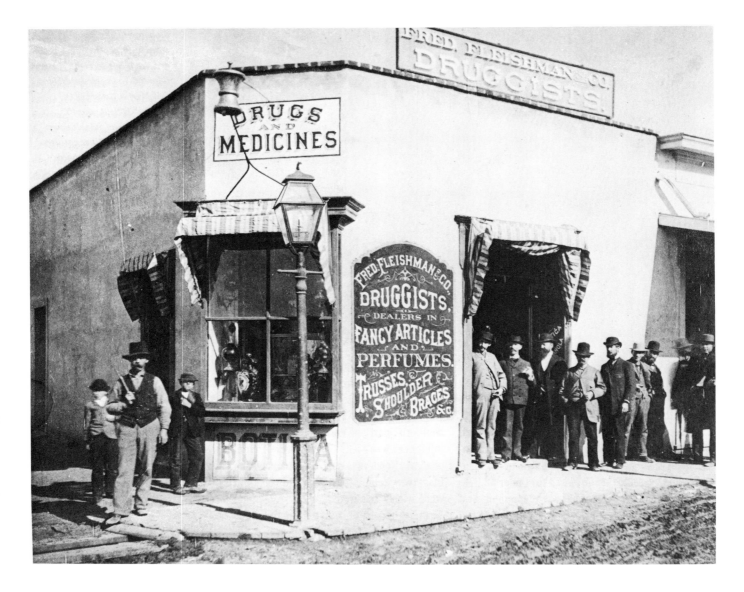

Among the settlers who brought their skills to Tucson was Frederick Fleishman, who came to Arizona in 1880 and opened a drugstore at the corner of Congress and Court. Fleishman sold "fancy articles and perfumes, trusses and shoulder braces" along with drugs and medicines. Note the board sidewalk and muddy street in front of the gas streetlight. Courtesy, Arizona Historical Society, Tucson

to gamble, meet one's friends, talk politics, and transact business.

The first woman's club was organized in Prescott in the 1880s, and soon almost every town had a ladies' social or cultural organization. Men, too, had their fraternal and benevolent groups, with the Masonic Order, the Odd Fellows, and the Knights of Pythias among the most prominent.

In the early days there was a shortage of women in the territory, but in time the ratio became more equal, even though the tradition of the mail-order bride continued for many years. Respectable ladies had families, and a few were teachers, typesetters, and telegraph operators. "Fancy ladies" and dance hall girls were present but frowned upon by some. The legislature in the 1890s banned houses of prostitution within 400 yards of any public school building.

Pearl Hart was the famous "girl bandit" at the

turn of the century. She and a friend, Joe Boot, robbed the stage that ran between Globe and Florence and tried to escape on foot. On trial in the territorial court Pearl was acquitted because of her story that she needed the money to visit her poor sick mother. In federal court, however, she was tried and convicted of tampering with the United States mail and sentenced to prison. Putting a pillow under her dress, she won the sympathy of chivalrous Governor Brodie who did not think it was proper for a child to be born in prison. Hart received a pardon.

In territorial days there were as many reasons for people coming west as there were people who came. The migrants' point of origin included all parts of the United States and many foreign nations. There were some who came to get a new start in life, and it was considered an insult to ask if a name was the individual's true one. Unless people told about their past one did not ask questions. There are some mysterious cases of people whose stories can never be known.

In the 1860s John T. Alsap, later to be the first mayor of Phoenix, and a companion were engaged in a skirmish with the Apaches and were winning. One of the men took aim at a figure in native dress and as she cried out just before the bullet killed her it became obvious that she was an Anglo woman. What was her story and what was she doing there? No one knows.

About the turn of the century a man appeared in Phoenix who said he was a Russian, despite the name he gave, which was DeRyland. The gentleman dressed in Russian costume and said he had come with his servants to supervise the exhibits of his country at the Chicago World's Fair of 1893. A victim of tuberculosis, he had ample funds, was friendly, and was welcome to pass his time in the better saloons of the town. One day the visitor died and immediately the servants disappeared. The undertaker was called and informed the sorrowing friends and acquaintances that the deceased was not male but female.

What became known as New Town, Flagstaff, arose about one-half mile west of Old Town after it was destroyed by an 1884 fire. These buildings at San Francisco and Santa Fe streets were the James Vail house on the left and Brannen's Pioneer General Store on the right. Both were rebuilt after an 1886 fire, and the Vail structure was rebuilt of brick after another fire in 1888. Courtesy, Phoenix Public Library

When the first workers building the Atlantic and Pacific Railroad selected this original Flagstaff settlement in 1880, it was probably for the fine spring water found at Antelope Spring. Located somewhat west of today's business district, this area known as Old Town was nearly destroyed by fire in 1884. Courtesy, Museum of Northern Arizona

ABOVE: This 1890s view of Winslow shows the churches on Front Street. The steeple of the Methodist Church is on the left, the next and larger building is St. Joseph's Catholic Church, and the next large building is St. Paul's Episcopal Church. Front Street, the heart of Winslow, runs along the railroad tracks. The coal cars were for the use of teamsters who daily hauled coal to the pumphouse south of town. Courtesy, Phoenix Public Library

The mysterious DeRyland was buried in Phoenix but to this day no one knows who she was.

People worked long hours and often had little time for recreation and entertainment. When they did, their amusements were simple. There were races and walking matches; cock fighting was legal and horse racing was also enjoyed. A good bit of gambling took place and betting was legal until 1907. Sports were popular and strictly amateur. There was a little prize fighting but more important were the

town baseball teams. On the Fourth of July 1888 Prescott is said to have held the world's first rodeo. Speakers and lecturers on all subjects were to be found in Arizona, and the Chautauqua, a group that combined education with entertainment, played an important role in the lives of many people.

Arizonans in those pioneer days had many wonderful stories to remember and to tell. A women remembered that in 1897, as a young girl, she and her father went for a ride out of town, she on a burro

RIGHT: The Babbitt and Riordan families were vital to Flagstaff's economic and civic development. Shown here are several members of the Riordan family on the porch of the Arizona Lumber and Timber Company Commissary in 1899. The Babbitts were in merchandising, and the Riordans were in lumbering, cattle, ranching, and financing. Both families produced many civic leaders for Flagstaff. Courtesy, Arizona Historical Society, Pioneer Museum

LEFT: This is a faro bank at Morenci in 1895. Until gambling was outlawed in 1907, faro was very popular in Arizona gambling houses. Courtesy, Arizona Historical Society, Tucson

BELOW: The Palace Saloon in Tucson, shown in 1903, was typical of saloons found in the Arizona Territory. Note the spittoons, the mirrored bar, and the gaming table. Courtesy, Arizona Historical Society Museum

instead of a horse. Out on the desert the burro decided to stop and there was no way to make the animal go except literally to light a fire under it. A small pile of leaves and twigs was ignited to which the animal strongly objected, throwing its rider into a thorny bush where the girl's new dress was torn and she was scratched. Another girl remembered a dance her parents gave in Prescott in honor of her older sister and friends who had come for a visit from an Eastern college. The guests were the young officers from Fort Whipple who danced with their swords and spurs on, except that they did take the rowels out of the spurs to keep them from catching on the young ladies' long gowns. A man remembered that as a boy he and his family arrived in their covered wagon from Texas and went north from Phoenix until they reached what is now the intersection of Central and McDowell. They stayed there until they moved way out of town to 13th Street

ABOVE: Life in the Arizona Territory around 1885 could be quite hard for women, as this Mexican woman washing clothes near Bisbee might testify. Courtesy, Bisbee Mining and Historical Museum, Sweet Collection

RIGHT: Pearl Hart, who committed the last stagecoach robbery in Arizona with her friend Joe Boot, is shown here, center, with two other inmates in a cell at Yuma Territorial Prison, probably in 1902. With Hart are Elena Estrada in the doorway and Rosa Duran with a guitar. After serving three years of her sentence, Pearl was pardoned, tried to become an actress, then married and lived in central Arizona. Courtesy, Arizona Historical Society, Tucson

and McDowell.

Most towns had auditoriums, with removable chairs, which also functioned as dance and banquet halls. There were a few local amateur theatrical groups, but most productions were done by traveling professionals. As early as the 1870s Yuma saw plays not only in English but in Spanish and Japanese as well. Gilbert and Sullivan productions were all the rage. An actor named J. Harry Carpenter and his young daughter, "Little Buttercup" Carpenter, decided to settle down in Arizona, and he later became

a member of the territorial legislature. Pauline Markham and her troupe were playing Prescott when the star disappeared and a search was launched. It was found that she had gone prospecting for a few days. In 1897 Phoenix was treated to a full production, with orchestra and scenery, of Verdi's *Othello*. Each town had a band which presented concerts and serenades.

Without doubt the best remembered theater in Arizona was the Bird Cage in Tombstone. Actually the more "respectable" citizens, especially ladies, did

Desert outings and picnics have always been an enjoyable part of Arizona social life. This 1907 picnic wagon seated 21 and was rented out by the Stevens and Wiggins Palo Alto Stables located at First Avenue and Adams Street in Phoenix. C.W. Stevens is standing in front of the wagon, waving a flag. Courtesy, Arizona Historical Society Museum

Teams of firemen pulling fire hoses raced each other for sport in many Arizona towns. Here is the Milton team, winner of the Fourth of July tournament in Flagstaff. They are on Birch Street, looking west. Milton, originally Milltown, was owned wholly by the Arizona Lumber Company. The small village just a mile from Flagstaff became part of the city in 1920. Courtesy, Arizona Historical Society, Pioneer Museum

RUSSELL & SHELDON.

Rambler and Ideal

BICYCLES.

RENTING. REPAIRING. PARTS AND SUNDRIES.

ELECTRIC WIRING.
BELLS
BATTERIES
FIXTURES
&
APPLIANCES

GAS STOVES
& RANGES
FOR COOKING
HEATING.
FIXTURES

The Russell & Sheldon bicycle shop stood on Church Street in downtown Tucson across from the Pima County Courthouse. Eddy Johnson stands in the doorway and the boy on the right is Frank Ganz. Courtesy, Arizona Historical Society Library, Tucson

not go there. They went to Schieffelin Hall instead.

By the 1880s Arizona had acquired a reputation as a good place to go to improve one's health, especially for respiratory problems. It was also considered a good place to winter, and by the 1890s Tucson had become a place where some wealthy Easterners spent a few months each year. It was not until later, however, that large numbers of people would begin to visit.

Arizona's population increased substantially with people seeking to improve their health. Often the results seemed to be nothing short of miraculous. In 1881 doctors told 19-year-old Elias S. Clark of Maine that he had no more than six months to live. When he died in Phoenix in 1955 he could look back upon a distinguished career as a lawyer, territorial attorney general, and one who came within a few hundred votes of being elected governor.

Hospitals and sanitariums did their best for people although often they operated under great difficulty. In those days one did not go to a hospital until one was nearly dead and that diminished a hospital's reputation for recovery.

The early physicians were often very colorful. Dr. John C. Handy of Tucson was considered the best of the lot until he was shot and killed by his wife's

attorney during a stormy divorce proceeding. Dr. George E. Goodfellow tried to save Handy but could not. Goodfellow was an expert on gunshot wounds, but then he had many chances to practice. He is also credited with performing the first successful prostate operation in the nation.

Newspapers were extremely important in the lives of people who had no other way of learning what was happening in the world. The first Arizona newspaper was called the *Weekly Arizonan* or *Arizonian*—depending upon how the editor felt—and was produced in Tubac before the Civil War. The second was the *Arizona Miner*, which was founded at Fort Whipple in 1864 by Richard C. McCormick. Later he sold it and established the *Citizen* of Tucson in 1870. Louis C. Hughes and his wife, E. Josephine Hughes, founded the *Star* in 1877. It was a Democratic paper, while McCormick's journals were Republican. Papers were violently opinionated politically and since one could be started with an investment of around $1,000 there were many of them. Phoenix had the *Gazette* and also the *Herald*, which was established in the late 1870s. In 1891 the *Republican*, which later became the *Arizona Republic*, was formed, and later absorbed the *Herald*. Yuma had the *Sentinel*, a good paper, and another prominent

St. Mary's Hospital in Tucson was founded in 1880 by the Sisters of St. Joseph and was Arizona's first hospital. The sisters also began an Indian school at San Xavier and St. John's Komatke, a hospital and orphanage in Prescott, and schools in Florence and Fort Yuma. This 1900 photo shows the sanitorium, de-signed to take continuous advantage of the sunshine. It had a shaded porch on each level onto which individual rooms opened. The isolation cottage is on the right, and one of the sisters is standing on the second-floor porch. Courtesy, St. Mary's Hospital and Health Center

journal was the *Silver Belt*, published in both Globe and Miami.

Editors were generally strong-minded individuals. One of the most famous was John H. Marion of Pres-cott who never recovered from the Civil War and was certain that somehow all Republicans were in league with the devil. He was such a loyal Democrat that he once supported the straight party ticket despite the fact that in the middle of a campaign the candi-date for county attorney ran away with Mrs. Marion.

His Republican counterpart was Charles W. Beach, who devoutly believed that Democrats were Lucifer's agents on earth. Beach was once indicted by the grand jury for attempting to bite off the ear of the young boy who swept the floors and ran er-rands for his office. When Beach was murdered the jury convicted his killer but asked for mercy because the crime must have been done under "extreme prov-ocation."

At the time of the founding of Arizona Territory the legislature appropriated some money for public schools, but for several years not much was done about the matter. Towns threatened by Indian attack could hardly be expected to operate schools.

In 1871 Governor Safford and Estevan Ochoa per-suaded the legislature to create the first comprehen-sive school system. Safford was so interested in the matter that he advanced money out of his own

pocket to pay the transportation costs to bring some of the first teachers to Arizona.

The school system was revised a few years later under the influence of Moses H. Sherman, the first territorial superintendent of schools, who took office in 1879. Soon most places in Arizona had a school system operating from the first through the eighth grade. Although Prescott earlier had something called a high school, it was 1895 before the legisla-ture authorized districts to provide this level of edu-cation. The Phoenix Union High School District was the first organized under the new law. A 1909 statute allowed schools to segregate their students of "African ancestry," and this was done in some situa-tions until the early 1950s.

It was believed necessary for a territory to have a university, and in the 1860s a board of regents was authorized for the proposed University of Ari-zona. Unfortunately two of the first three regents were killed in an Indian raid while on their way to a meeting, and the matter of a university was for-gotten for some years. In 1885 the legislature for-mally created the University of Arizona and placed it in Tucson. Although not opened until 1891, once it was in existence it functioned well as the leading institution of higher learning in the territory and state.

A few days before the university was created the

ABOVE: This group of young women in white muslin dresses and wide hairbows typical of 1910 is the Bisbee High School Girl's Glee Club. Their teacher, Clarence Kimball, is in the middle of the back row. Courtesy, Bisbee Mining and Historical Museum, Caretto Collection

RIGHT: The original building of the University of Arizona, Old Main, was completed in July 1891. It officially opened on October 1, 1891, with six faculty members and 32 students. The building was and is the focal point of the Tucson campus. Courtesy, Special Collections, University of Arizona Library

legislature also felt a need for a training school for teachers, and one was authorized at Tempe. It is properly regarded as Arizona's oldest institution of higher education. Much later, after several name changes, it became Arizona State University. In the 1890s a building owned by the territory in Flagstaff had been used for a time as a reform school. The governor urged that it be converted into another normal school and this was done in 1899. Long afterward it became Northern Arizona University.

The first public library in Arizona was the Territorial Library, which started with a few books which Richard C. McCormick brought with him across the plains in 1863. The collection was added to what became the first law library in the territory. By the 1870s there were private rental libraries in Tucson and elsewhere, and towns began to accumulate collections which were loaned for a small fee. In 1899 the legislature authorized free public libraries, and several were established and supplemented by grants from the Carnegie Foundation.

The great majority of Arizonans of the territorial period had some sort of formal religious affiliation.

The oldest Christian group in the area was the Catholic Church, dating from the period of Spanish rule. Next were the Mormons, who were also one of the larger groups in terms of membership. Protestants began to arrive in substantial numbers after the Civil War, and for a while towns had community Protestant worship services where several denominations participated. By the late 1870s the Presbyterians and Methodists began to create separate congregations and to establish churches. The oldest Protestant religious building still standing in Arizona is the Episcopal Church of Tombstone. Members of the Jewish faith lived in Arizona for some time before the first formal synagogue was organized. With the arrival of people of Asiatic ancestry, which occurred early in the territorial period, Buddhist temples came into existence.

The pioneers who came to Arizona in the territorial period brought with them not only their religions, but also their ideas, their attitudes, and, above all, their rugged individualism. They built the cities, the economy, the institutions, and the social structure on which the future would be constructed.

These young women are in a home economics class at Tempe Normal School in the 1910s. Tempe Normal was established in the territory in 1885, became Arizona State College in 1926, and became Arizona State University in 1958. Courtesy, Arizona Historical Foundation

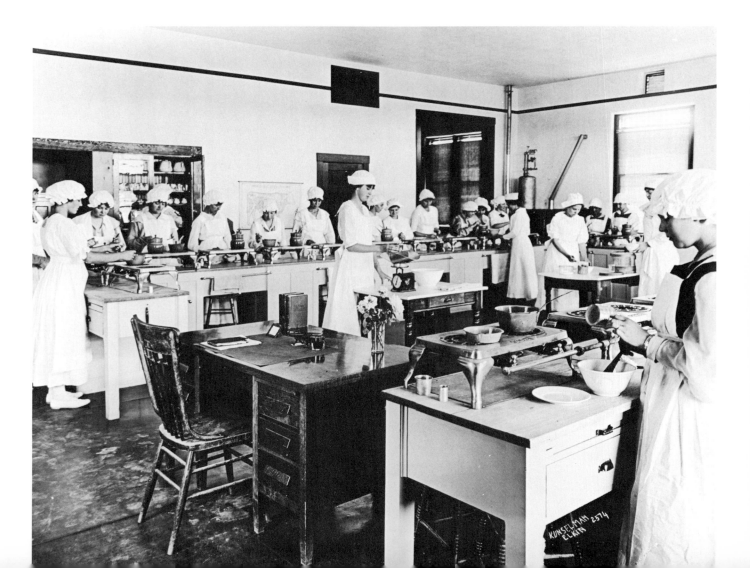

Statehood at Last

Road races were popular sport, and a race between Barney Oldfield, the famous race-car driver, and Harold Steinfeld gave Tucson's Speedway Boulevard its name. Oldfield is shown here in 1915 after winning a 103-mile race in his Maxwell special racing car. Courtesy, Arizona Historical Society, Tucson

If one had been a resident of Arizona Territory at the beginning of the twentieth century one would undoubtedly have been aware that for a long time Arizonans had wanted statehood. There was a big difference between a territory and a state, and by this time only Oklahoma, Arizona, and New Mexico of all the continental possessions had not become full-fledged members of the Union. People in Arizona felt they were in a lesser position and complained about "territorial vassalage," and their subservience to the federal government. They could not vote for the president and vice president in a period of intense political partisanship. There were no senators nor representatives from Arizona and therefore its citizens had no voice in the making of national laws. Officials of the territory were appointed, often from other states, and not elected.

There was some talk of Arizona being admitted in the 1870s, but the idea was not taken seriously. At that time the population was not large enough and the area had not yet been settled for a long enough time or made politically stable. Also, the Indian wars were still underway.

With the passage of time other factors would work against the goal. There was a view in the East that the land was wild and untamed, and cowboys shot up the towns each Saturday night. It was also thought that the population was not sophisticated enough to govern itself.

A more realistic factor was that the majority of the people of Arizona were Democrats, and a good bit of the time the Republicans controlled Congress. They had no burning desire to create two new Democratic senators and a representative.

In the late nineteenth century the country was embroiled in the great currency controversy. What should be the metal backing all United States money? Regardless of party, the gold standard supporters were in the lead in Congress, and Arizona was a strong free-silver territory.

The usual procedure for admission into the Union begins with Congress passing an enabling act which allows the territory to hold a constitutional convention. The convention then drafts a proposed fundamental charter which must be approved by the people of the area, a majority of both houses of Congress, and the president.

In 1889 and 1890 six new states were created, and that interested Arizonans very much. Since they had not been able to secure an enabling act, the people of the territory, acting through the legislature, decided to bypass step one in the admission process and proceed to the writing of a constitution.

This was done at a gathering held in Phoenix in September of 1891. A short, practical, and workable constitution was written and approved by the voters.

Mark Smith as delegate to Congress introduced a proposal to admit Arizona as a state on the first day of the year 1893. The United States House of Representatives approved it, but the United States Senate took no action.

In succeeding years many Arizonans, especially Mark Smith and Governor Nathan O. Murphy, worked very hard to achieve statehood but with no immediate success. Delegations of prominent people from the territory went to Washington to lobby for admission; the constitution written in 1891 was brought forth again and again.

When the Spanish American War began in 1898 there were those who thought that if men from Arizona made a particularly good showing this would call attention to the statehood issue. Accordingly, a number of them volunteered to serve in the Rough Riders, regiments of volunteer cavalry. One of the heroes of the conflict, "Bucky" O'Neill, made the famous remark, "Who would not die to place another star in the flag?" This remarkable man, who was killed by a sniper in battle in Cuba, was not talking of obtaining more possessions for the United States but of making Arizona a state. When a former Rough Rider, Theodore Roosevelt, became president, Arizonans felt they had a friend in the White House.

Unfortunately they also had an enemy in the United States Senate. For reasons never fully explained, Senator Albert J. Beveridge of Indiana was very skeptical about the Southwest, although probably his dislike was more directed toward New Mexico. Beveridge proposed combining the two territories and making one single state. Its name would be Arizona, but to the residents of the territory of Arizona that would mean the capital would return to Santa Fe, and New Mexico, with its larger population, would be dominant. Most Arizonans vigorously fought the idea of "joint statehood," but the man who saved the day was Senator Joseph B. Foraker of Ohio. He amended the jointure proposal so that it would not take effect until both areas, voting separately, had approved it. New Mexico voted in favor, but Arizona was much opposed to the referendum held in November 1906. The total vote in Arizona was just over 3,000 in favor and almost 13,000 opposed.

Both major political parties endorsed statehood for Arizona in their platforms for the presidential election of 1908, and Theodore Roosevelt called for it in his last message as president to Congress. When the new president, William Howard Taft, visited the Southwest in the fall of 1909 he, too, said that he was in favor, but cautioned that Arizona should not be "radical" in its approach to constitution writing.

At last in June of 1910 the long-sought enabling act passed. Governor Richard E. Sloan set September 12 as the date on which the voters would choose 52 delegates to sit at the constitutional convention. Delegates were elected from the counties, the number from each determined by population. There were vigorous contests, and when it was all over 41 Democrats and 11 Republicans had been chosen as the "founding fathers."

The convention, which first met in the chamber of the house of representatives in the capitol at noon October 9, 1910, contained some remarkable and interesting delegates. Only three of the delegates were natives of Arizona. One delegate had been born in Ireland and another in what is now Czechoslovakia.

Many different trades and professions were represented. There were lawyers, businessmen, and ranchers, as well as a pharmacist, a plumber, and a railroad switchman. One of the delegates died within five years after the convention, while the last probably lived until 1974. There is no certainty because three of the delegates simply disappeared. A later chief justice of the state supreme court became a hermit on the desert, another was last heard from while living in Australia, while the third simply moved away from Arizona.

Young Michael G. Cunniff was a graduate of Harvard and had been an English instructor there and an editor of a New York magazine before his tuberculosis caused him to seek a drier climate in Arizona. He would help to write its constitution, serve as chairman of the committee that put it in its final wording, and serve as a state senator all within a life span of less than 40 years. Three of the delegates, George W.P. Hunt, Benjamin B. Moeur, and Sidney P. Osborn, would serve as governors of the new state for over a quarter century. John Langdon, the only Republican to later sign the constitution, had worked his way up from machinist to the position of master mechanic for a mining company. The Reverend James E. Crutchfield, a Methodist, once announced to the convention that he was a "communist," and he was firmly committed to sharing the wealth of Arizona with all. Judge Edmund Wells, a delegate from Prescott, was called "Arizona's first millionaire." He was a self-made lawyer, banker, and mine owner.

When the group organized they selected George W.P. Hunt as president, and would later designate

Morris Goldwater and his brother Baron, sons of Michel, expanded the Goldwater stores to Phoenix, where their first store at First and Adams was a model of elegance and luxury. Goldwater, shown here in 1888, was also a member of the territorial legislature, vice-president of the constitutional convention, and mayor of Prescott. He was the uncle of Senator Barry Goldwater. Courtesy, Sharlot Hall Museum

Morris Goldwater as vice president. The latter, a Prescott businessman, was the uncle of future Senator Barry M. Goldwater. Delegates were asked to submit proposals, "propositions" they were called, of materials to be included in the constitution, and about 150 were introduced. The work was then done in large measure in the committees appointed by the president; the committees would report what they felt should be included in the charter.

The delegates had exactly two months in which to finish their task, and all was not peace and harmony. They quarreled, often about very insignificant things. Although some thought at the time that the "radical element" was in control, such was not the case. Special interest groups—business, labor, farmers, and others—were well in balance, and no one really got all that he or his group wanted.

At this time some devices of direct democracy were new, and had vigorous supporters and staunch opponents. The initiative allowed the voters to directly write laws, and the referendum allowed voters to insist upon a vote of the public before a law enacted by the legislature went into effect. Most controversial of all was the recall, which allowed the voters to end the term of a public official at any time. The major fight in the convention was over the recall of judges, which many insisted would lessen the independence of the judiciary. When the smoke cleared a majority of the delegates favored all three

The loquacious Henry Fountain Ashurst was a senator from 1912 until 1940. Courtesy, Phoenix Public Library

devices of direct democracy, and the constitution provided for the recall of all state officials.

When the delegates had finished their work 11 of them, 10 Republicans and one Democrat, refused to sign the proposed constitution. The minority considered it too radical a document. The voters on February 9, 1911, approved the constitution by a vote of 12,187 to 3,302; curiously the vote total was considerably less than the number of those who usually voted in an election.

Governor Sloan, a conservative Republican who did not approve of many of the features of the constitution, urged approval so that Arizona could get into the Union. Changes could later be made as they were felt necessary. After more delays and disappointments, Congress at last voted approval in August 1911; unfortunately there was trouble ahead.

President Taft disapproved of the recall in general and especially the recall of judges. He had been a federal judge and would later be chief justice of the United States and had strong feelings about the independence of the judiciary. The very colorful chaplain of the constitutional convention, the 73-year-old Reverend Seaborn Crutchfield, who had been a Confederate soldier and Union prisoner of war, which made him skeptical about Republicans in general, had asked God not to let "Billy Taft" be so "narrow-minded" as to keep Arizona out of the Union over a little thing like the recall. It was all to no avail, for Taft was firm on the issue and the offending provision had to go.

The recall of judges was taken out of the consti-

tution by another special election in December 1911. However, once the state was admitted the voters put it back in again, where it has remained ever since.

The Flood Resolution, named for the Virginia congressman who authored it, was signed by the chief executive on February 14, 1912. Arizona was at last the 48th state. Before admission took place, new state officials, almost all Democrats, were elected. That November President Taft ran for reelection, and people in the "Baby State" were so angry at him that in Arizona he ran fourth behind the Democratic, Progressive, and Socialist nominees.

The two new United States senators from Arizona were Mark Smith and Henry F. Ashurst. The former was the long-time delegate to Congress and the other was a delightful character known as the "Silver-Tongued Orator of the Colorado," or "Five-Syllable Henry" for his talents as a speech maker. Ashurst served in the Senate until 1941, and on more than one occasion was known to have switched sides on an issue. Once, when he had changed his mind, a colleague said to him, "Well, Henry, I see you have seen the light." His response was, "No, I have merely felt the heat."

At the same time the two new senators went east, the first representative from Arizona, Carl Hayden, also went to Washington and remained in office for 57 years, a record of service unparalleled in American history. Hayden, a native of Tempe, which was originally called "Hayden's Ferry," served in the House until 1927 when he moved to the United States Senate. Quiet, modest, and rarely known to make a speech, he was hardworking and dedicated, and had a considerable effect on not only state but national politics. His efforts brought massive federal grants to Arizona.

In Phoenix on the day the new state was admitted to the Union plans were made for great celebrations. The governor-elect, George W.P. Hunt, decided that since he had walked into Arizona, he would walk to his inauguration. Retiring Governor Sloan observed that it was the last time the portly chief executive was ever seen walking anywhere, as he dearly loved the state limousine. Hunt walked west on Washington Street to the capitol, and the crowd followed from the old Ford Hotel. At the capitol William Jennings Bryan was waiting to beam his approval over the launching of the State of Arizona. That evening there was a party in front of the Adams Hotel, speeches were made, and there was dancing in the streets until midnight when the band played "Home, Sweet Home."

Governor Hunt was a unique character in Arizona

history. Born in Missouri in 1859, he ran away from home at an early age and for three years wandered over the West until finally arriving in Globe in 1881. At first he worked at odd jobs such as miner, restaurant worker, and grocery clerk, but eventually became the well-to-do president of the Old Dominion Commercial Company, a general store and bank. He had served in the legislature and was well known for his support of labor unions and political reforms. His methods were those of the old-fashioned "machine" politician, and he kept careful records of those who contributed to his campaigns and those who did not. However, he rarely made permanent enemies. Someone might be with him in one election, opposed the next, and then back in the fold. Hunt was elected governor in 1911, 1914, 1916 (so the courts ruled after a dispute with Republican Thomas E. Campbell who served almost a year before being ousted), 1922, 1924, 1926, and 1930. He did not run in 1918, was defeated in 1928, and lost in the primaries of 1932 and 1934. Had he lived he might well have won again in 1936.

The man was about five feet, nine inches tall, weighed anywhere between 250 and 300 pounds, was totally bald, and had a handlebar mustache. Early in his career as governor his mustache was waxed so that it stuck out beyond his ears but later

was allowed to droop, causing his enemies to dub him "The Old Walrus." He was fond of wearing white linen suits, which he appears to have replaced at least once a month. Beneath it all he was an extremely astute politician who, although he became too fond of office and did not know when to quit, accomplished a great deal.

Hunt loved to have his picture taken, and that sometimes got him into difficulty. When police raided the offices of the radical Industrial Workers of the World, they found photographs of the governor taken with its leaders. Army intelligence considered him an IWW member, which he was not. Many an Arizona family of that era also had its photograph taken with Hunt when he came to have Sunday dinner with them. He would send aides out to buy cases of jams and jelly and then have the labels washed off. When he would go to dinner he would take a jar out of his pocket and say to the pleased lady of the house, "My wife was making jelly the other day and she wanted you folks to have a jar . . ."

Although the governor was controversial the First Lady was not. A much respected woman was Helen ("Duett") Ellison Hunt; she is supposed to have been the model for some Zane Grey heroines. Owing to her parents' need to have her at their ranch in Gila

From left to right are U.S. senators Carl Hayden, Ernest McFarland, and Lyndon Johnson, with Congressman Stewart Udall in 1951. Hayden was the first representative from Arizona and in 1927 became a senator, serving the state until 1969. McFarland was later governor of Arizona and chief justice of the Arizona Supreme Court, while Udall later served as Secretary of the Interior. Courtesy, McFarland Archives, McFarland Historical State Park

Helen Duett Ellison Hunt was the respected but seldom photographed wife of the very much photographed Governor George W.P. Hunt. She was first lady of Arizona for the seven terms her husband served as governor from 1911 to 1930. Courtesy, Arizona Department of Library, Archives, and Public Records

County, she and Hunt were engaged for almost 15 years before they finally married in 1904. Mrs. Hunt was devoted to her husband and their only child and did not take an active part in social events. She was an accomplished horsewoman and once shot a bear while on a hunting trip. When her husband was involved in politics she could and did operate the business in Globe.

In the new state government the Democrats set about the task of reworking the territorial system, and new codes of law were passed. Arizona was very much a supporter of the Progressive principles of Theodore Roosevelt and Woodrow Wilson. During the Hunt years only twice did the Republicans manage to capture the governorship. Thomas E. Campbell, declared the loser in the disputed election of 1916, served two terms, 1919 to 1921 and 1921 to 1923. A mining engineer and one who believed in efficiency in government, Campbell tried to put into effect a better state budget system.

A Phoenix attorney, John C. Phillips, served as chief executive from 1929 to 1931 after defeating Hunt. Ralph H. Cameron, former territorial delegate, served one term as a Republican United States senator from 1921 to 1927, but generally those were the days, as Barry Goldwater later remarked, when "a state Republican convention could have been held in a telephone booth."

The achievement of statehood for Arizona was a source of much pride to its citizens. They had come from all parts of the world to this new land and they

Governor Thomas Campbell went fishing in the Gulf of California on a visit to the international boundary at San Luis in 1921. He was there to look into plans for a 200,000-acre development on the border to be called the "Empire of the Gulf of California." Standing with Governor Campbell are Charles Johnston and A.L. Verdugo on the right. Courtesy, Arizona Historical Society, Yuma

were building a new way of life. The people had a strong identification with the state.

One of the great dreams of this time was that somehow the state would be able to build a giant dam on the Colorado River and generate electricity. The power would be sold all over the West, and the state would receive so much money it would never have any taxes. Toward that end a provision was put into the Arizona constitution which allowed the state to engage in industrial pursuits. Unfortunately there were two major problems. The needed capital to build the great dam was not available, and the other side of the dam had to be anchored to some other state.

As Arizona entered the twentieth century there was general prosperity across the land. The farmers were able to make some profits from the crops they shipped out of the territory, although freight rates were of much concern. The mines were booming, and copper was pouring forth and selling at about 10 cents per pound.

Those who worked in the mines, on the railroads, and at other similar occupations were paid around $2.50 to $3 per day for 10 hours' work. Those who had a skill were paid a little more. The companies which owned the mines were large and controlled from the East, where stockholders were concerned with profits. Disputes naturally arose between employers and workers over wages, and the result was the organization of labor unions.

The first unions were formed in Arizona in the 1880s for railroad workers. Before too many years most of those who worked in that field of transportation were members.

The miners at first created local organizations not affiliated with larger unions, but in 1896 the first local of the Western Federation of Miners was chartered at Globe in the midst of a strike at the Old Dominion Mine. There would be other strikes from time to time caused by controversies over wages, working conditions, and union representation.

There was a blacklist of names of known or suspected union members, and some employers would not hire these men. A later prominent Phoenix resident did not know her family's real last name until she was nearly grown because her father changed it with each new job.

In 1903 the legislature reduced the standard workday from 10 to 8 hours. Such skilled trades as printers, barbers, steamfitters, and machinists all had their own trade unions and were generally better off than the average general laborer.

After World War I, cotton became the king of crops in Arizona. This 1952 cotton crop was being harvested near the Mathieu Ranch in Yuma Valley, but farmers in the Salt River Valley, Graham and Greenlee counties, in the Casa Grande Valley, and along the Santa Cruz and San Pedro rivers made Arizona one of the leading producers of high quality premium cotton. Courtesy, Emil's Photography

RIGHT: With the advent of cars, people began talking about a road to San Diego across the sand dunes just west of Yuma. A one-way plank road consisting of planks nailed to cross ties made a track 25 inches wide for each wheel. Hazards were great, and the wise motorist loaded up with oil cans, water jugs, and extra tires. Portions of the plank road can still be seen along Interstate 8. Courtesy, Arizona Historical Society, Yuma

BELOW: Before the automobile, the streetcar was basic transportation. This first horse-drawn car is shown in December 1887 on Washington Street, looking east at Seventh Avenue. The first line was electrified in 1895, and streetcars ran in Phoenix until 1948. Courtesy, Arizona Historical Society Museum

New technology made itself felt in Arizona. It is not certain who owned the first automobile in Arizona but it was probably a Locomobile steamer which arrived just as the nineteenth century was giving way to the twentieth. In time this new form of transportation would change Arizonans' lives.

About the time of the First World War a type of cotton was needed for use in automobile tires. The result was the growth in Arizona of long-staple cotton and the founding of new towns such as Goodyear, which was established near Phoenix in 1916. The growth of the new crop was a significant factor in the economy of Arizona. In 1911 only two bales of cotton were produced, but by the year 1914 there were over 17,000 acres under cultivation. By 1917

that number had jumped to over 40,000 acres, and by 1920, 230,000 acres of land were planted.

The first paved street in Arizona, which made automobile travel much more pleasant, was in Phoenix in 1911. The following January that city also had its first automobile show. The "Good Roads" movement was important to the state. The area was large and the automobile was a good way to get from one place to another, not to mention the fact that it brought tourists to explore the Southwest. By 1920 Arizona was ninth in per capita auto ownership.

Some of those who first tried to learn to drive finally gave up. Governor Hunt, who never managed it, described a day as being like an automobile drive: "In the morning you start out with exhilaration and

by night you are towed home in humiliation." Judge Joseph H. Kibbey, the legal architect of the Salt River Project, discovered that he could control the machine in first and second gear, but not in third, so he used only those two gears. This slowed his progress, but he managed to reach his destinations.

The automobile led to new businesses: garages, auto dealers, and to something first called "tourist camps," and later called motels. In time businesses moved from the center of towns to the outskirts. Road races were popular in the early days of motoring, and manufacturers of autos brought large quantities of copper to use in their production.

Two and a half years after Arizona became a state the First World War broke out in Europe. At first it was feared that the conflict would cause hard times in Arizona, but quite the opposite proved to be true. When the fighting began, copper was selling at 13.5 cents per pound, and by the time the United States entered the war in 1917 the price had more than doubled. There were increased markets also for cattle, other livestock, and agricultural products as well. Unfortunately labor unrest became a major problem.

Workers wanted increases in salaries, and there were also rivalries between two labor unions.

The major trouble started in the Clifton-Morenci mines in September 1915. Eight thousand miners struck for higher wages and union recognition. Their pay then averaged about $2.50 per day. There was some violence, and troops of the national guard were used to keep order. In January there was a settlement, but no union recognition, and wages were raised to $3.40 per day.

Into the picture at this time came the Industrial Workers of the World, a radical union which came into conflict with the more established Western Federation of Miners, later the International Mine Mill and Smelter Union. In May of 1917, just after American entry into the war, there was a strike at Jerome which spread to nearby Clarkdale. About 65 alleged members of the IWW were put into cattle cars by non-strikers and taken toward California. A federal mediator had some success in calming the Jerome situation, but then there was trouble in Globe. United States troops had to be used there to maintain order and prevent violence in what developed

Miners struck in Clifton-Morenci in June 1903. The Mexican, Italian, and Slavonian miners walked out to demand $2.50 for the compulsory eight-hour day that had just become law. When the miners threatened violence, federal troops, the national guard, and the Arizona Rangers combined to set up this camp along the railroad and main street of Morenci. Courtesy, Arizona Historical Society Library, Tucson

into a long and bitter strike.

On the night of July 11, 1917, the most talked-of event in Arizona labor history took place, the Bisbee Deportation. A group calling itself the Citizens Protective League, a vigilante organization led by some important citizens, rounded up over 1,200 suspected members of the IWW. Mostly men, but with a few women included, the deportees were taken in cattle cars to the New Mexico desert and left there. President Wilson considered declaring martial law in the area. The army rescued those who had been deported, and although some people were later brought to trial for having led the event, no one was ever convicted. For many years the Bisbee Deportation was a bitter memory.

Despite these upheavals, Arizonans participated wholeheartedly in the great war effort of 1917 and 1918. Frank Luke, Jr., was one of its heroes. He volunteered for service and took pilot's training in Texas and California. Commissioned as a second lieutenant by July of 1918, he was on duty in France with the 27th Aero Squadron. Luke, born and raised in Phoenix, was not one to accept discipline well, but he is believed to have shot down nearly two dozen enemy aircraft. Called the "balloon buster" because of his destruction of German observation equipment, he was forced down after an air fight in September 1918. Refusing to surrender he defended himself with only an automatic pistol until he was killed. It was said of him that he was the "greatest fighter who ever went into the air." Later a statue of him was erected at the Arizona state capitol, and during World War II an air force base was named in his honor.

Other Arizonans served with the armed forces, bought liberty bonds to support the war effort, worked hard at their usual occupations, and, like Governor Hunt, even took up knitting to produce scarves for military personnel.

When the conflict ended in November 1918 there was great celebrating in Arizona as elsewhere. The troops came home and people tried to resume their lives. Senators Smith and Ashurst strongly supported President Wilson's hopes for the League of Nations. Both wanted the United States to join the new peace organization.

Arizonans' optimism following the war was matched by the state's growth rate. The census of 1920 confirmed the fact that Phoenix with a population of 29,053 had become the state's largest city, while Tucson, formerly the most populous, had 20,292.

The "Roaring Twenties" are famous for a number of things; one of them was Prohibition. Arizonans outlawed liquor in 1914, but the scheme did not work in the state any better than it did elsewhere. The *Arizona Daily Star* noted that while in 1914 Tucson had 30 saloons, in 1926 there were 150 bootleggers in operation. Federal agents used the sewer system of a Phoenix hotel for destroying confiscated booze, until it was discovered that employees had tunneled into the pipes below the basement floor and were reclaiming the liquor for resale. Prohibition lasted until 1933.

Two new forms of entertainment came upon the scene about this time that were important in the lives of Arizonans. The motion picture gradually evolved from the "nickelodeon." The first movie theaters were simply halls, but in the 1920s they became more elaborate. One which opened in Phoenix in 1931, the Fox, was the first refrigerated building in the state.

Some movies were filmed in Arizona. Governor Thomas E. Campbell served as an advisor for the making of Samuel Goldwyn's film, *The Winning of Barbara Worth*. The movie starred Ronald Coleman and Vilma Banky, and introduced a new actor, Gary Cooper.

Radio was at first a novelty but soon became very important in the lives of people in a large, thinly populated state. Arizonans later elected two radio announcers, Howard Pyle and Jack Williams, to the governorship. The first radio station on the air in Arizona was KFAD in Phoenix, later renamed KTAR. It began broadcasting in June of 1922.

During this era, Arizona also had its share of famous and colorful writers. At the inaugural ball of President Coolidge in March of 1925 Arizona's "poetess laureate," Sharlot Hall, wore a gown made of copper to promote the state's great industry. She was a writer of considerable talent who had a distinguished career writing for magazines and newspapers. Earlier she was territorial historian by the

On July 12, 1917, suspected members of the International Workers of the World were herded to the railroad station in Bisbee, loaded on cattle cars, and deported to the New Mexico desert. First in line, and holding a rifle, was George Cobb, chief clerk at the shaft and captain of the deporters. Courtesy, Arizona Historical Society, Tucson

Frank Luke, Jr., standing beside his Spad XIII biplane in 1918, was the first American flier to win the Congressional Medal of Honor in World War I, and the only one to be so honored during the course of the war. This Phoenix man was the epitome of the brave, brash, undisciplined Yank aviator. Known as the balloon buster, he downed no less than 15 enemy balloons and four German airplanes in 10 combat patrols. Courtesy, Arizona Historical Society Museum

Among the many Arizonans who volunteered during World War I were these women at the Tucson canteen. Courtesy, Arizona Historical Society, Tucson

appointment of Governor Sloan. In the late 1920s
she became a prime mover in the restoration of the
old log-cabin governor's mansion in Prescott, which
is now named in her memory.

Another prominent literary figure of this period
was the humorist De Forest Hall, who signed himself
at first as "Dick Wickenburg" Hall, and then became
"Dick Wick Hall." Through the pages of the *Saturday
Evening Post*, Hall made Arizona known for the
Laughing Gas Station and the Greasewood Golf
Course in Salome. One of his characters was the
Salome Frog which was seven years old and, being
a desert dweller, had not yet learned to swim. Hall
had a quiet, gentle humor, somewhat in the style
of Mark Twain.

Writings such as Hall's stimulated interest in visiting Arizona. Some people came on official tours.
After the First World War, King Albert and Queen
Elisabeth of Belgium came on a state visit to view
the Grand Canyon. Later Lord and Lady Mountbat-
ten, he being the last British viceroy of India, honeymooned there. Albert Einstein also arrived to take
a look at the great natural wonder.

Herbert Hoover was in Arizona several times
while he was secretary of commerce to discuss the
development of the Colorado River. Franklin D.
Roosevelt campaigned in the state during his first
race for the White House. In 1928, when a statue

called "the Madonna of the Trails" was dedicated in
Springerville, the principal speaker was a county
judge from Missouri, Harry S. Truman.

Some of the most welcome visitors were entertain-
ers. They ranged from dancers trained by Isadora
Duncan to the noted music hall entertainer Sir Harry

Among the many celebrities who visited the Grand Canyon was Albert Einstein. In the late 1930s, he posed in Indian headdress at Hopi House at the canyon with his wife on his left. Among the Hopis are Leo Andrews, Chester Dannis, and Porter Pimeche at the drum. The bald man is Herman Schweitzer, head of Fred Harvey Curios. Courtesy, Museum of Northern Arizona and Fred Harvey Corporation

Lauder, who always included Phoenix and Tucson on his American tours. John Philip Sousa and his band did likewise, and the well-known ballerina Pavlova danced in Phoenix. Prominent singers who appeared during this period were John McCormick, Amelita Gali Curci, Rosa Ponselle, and the much beloved Ernestine Schumann-Heink. The pianists Arthur Rubenstein and Ignace Paderewski performed, as did the Rumanian composer and violinist George Enesco. The world-traveler Lowell Thomas was in the state several times, General Billy Mitchell spoke on air power, and the poet Edwin Markham lectured on literary matters.

Cartoonist Bud Fisher, who drew "Mutt and Jeff," was several times a winter visitor. Once while being interviewed he remarked that the two funniest things he had ever seen were a Mexican army and an Arizona legislature.

President Coolidge, recently retired from the White House, came to Arizona to dedicate the dam bearing his name. Will Rogers, who was also present, looked at the as-yet waterless area behind the structure and commented, "If that was my dam I would plow it."

By the time of the First World War Arizona was making use of all available water within its boundaries except the resources of the Colorado River. That great stream remained to be developed not only for its water but also for the electrical power it could generate. In 1919 the legislature created a board to consider the development of the state's resources, and two years later the lawmakers brought into existence the office of state water com-

missioner.

The Colorado River touches seven states plus Mexico. Much discussion and negotiation would have to take place and the federal government would be involved in any river development. Governor Thomas E. Campbell was an advocate of cooperation in the planning for the river. California, among other states, was vitally interested because it needed both water and electricity for the rapidly growing Los Angeles area. Governor Campbell and some others recognized that California had more power politically and economically than did Arizona, and its desires had to be accommodated.

The federal government became involved when President Harding designated Secretary of Commerce Herbert Hoover to chair a conference on the future of the river, held in Santa Fe beginning in November 1922. Delegates from all seven states met, and although they discussed problems they seemed to be unable to agree on the apportionment of the water. Wyoming, Colorado, Utah, and New Mexico, which were called the upper basin states, feared that Nevada, California, and Arizona, designated the lower basin states, were developing more rapidly than they were and would use all of the water.

Herbert Hoover finally hit upon the solution when he proposed dividing the water between the two groups of states and then letting them decide among themselves how much each would get. In time the upper basin states divided the waters among themselves amicably. The lower basin states were not so fortunate.

In January of 1923 George W.P. Hunt again became governor of Arizona, and while at first he was uncertain about the Santa Fe Compact, as the results of the meeting were called, soon he was in full opposition to it. In order to proceed it was necessary for all seven states plus Congress to ratify the compact, and Hunt's firm opposition kept Arizona from agreement. At one point the legislature actually voted in favor but the governor used his veto. Hunt's basic position was that California was getting more than its share of water and that Mexico, too, should not receive as much as proposed.

As the battle raged Arizonans learned to discuss "acre-feet of water," the amount of liquid necessary to cover one square acre of land to a depth of one foot, and all the other technical matters pertaining to the river. There were many conferences involving representatives from the various states but no resolution of the basic dispute. Tempers flared. When asked what California should do Hunt

LEFT: The Biltmore Resort, opened in 1925, arranged tours of the Arizona desert for their winter visitors on this "wonderbus," complete with chef and catered meals. Note the small boy in Western garb, and the woman smoking a cigarette. At least the sleeping accommodations were air-cooled! Courtesy, Arizona Historical Foundation

stormed, "Let the barbarians drink sea water!" In retaliation a California congressman urged that Arizona be returned to territorial status since it obviously lacked the required political maturity to function as a state. Hunt also managed to upset the Nevadans by referring to that state as "one big ghost town." A regional joke was that while Jesus walking on water was a miracle it was not unique,

because Arizona had a governor who regularly ran on the Colorado. The issue was always prominent in Hunt's reelection campaign.

Meanwhile, Senator Hiram W. Johnson of California and others were pushing for the building of a giant dam on the river so that electrical production could start. In 1924 Congress began to hold hearings on the Swing-Johnson bill, as the dam

BELOW: This groundbreaking for Tucson's Temple of Music and Art in 1926 was hailed as the greatest day in Tucson's artistic history. The temple became the home for the Saturday Morning Musical Club. Founded by Madeline Dreyfuss Heineman in 1907, the club included most of Tucson's cultural leaders. Standing in black behind the shovel was Amelita Galli-Curci, the Metropolitan Opera's famed coloratura soprano. Courtesy, Arizona Historical Society Library, Tucson

construction proposal was called. A part of the bill required that only six of the states would have to approve the Santa Fe Compact before work could begin. The overwhelming majority of Arizonans opposed the idea, and the state's senators and representative fought it as hard as they could. Before the passage of Swing-Johnson, Senators Ashurst and Hayden even conducted a filibuster against it but were joined by only one other member of the upper chamber. (The senator from South Carolina did not especially care about the issue but liked to filibuster.) The bill passed in the latter part of 1928.

There had been some discussion as to where the dam should be located. Although it was eventually built in Black Canyon instead of Boulder Canyon, the structure was for years called Boulder Dam until it was renamed for Herbert Hoover by President Truman. Arizona would receive 18 percent of the electricity generated, and a sum of money annually from the federal government since the state could not tax the project. Arizona went to court to fight the matter but President Hoover declared the compact in force. On March 11, 1931, the first contract was made to begin construction.

Arizona continued to exhibit hostility toward the dam project. In 1934 Parker Dam, downstream on the river, was under construction to take water to Los Angeles. Governor Moeur, Hunt's successor, ordered the Arizona National Guard into action, but there was very little they could do to stop construction. A detachment of troops boarded the "Arizona Navy," a barge owned by the state highway department, and from the middle of the river fired a few rounds of ammunition into the sand dunes on the California side to show how they felt about matters.

Hoover Dam was at last finished in 1936 and in the final analysis had, among other things, provided employment for a number of Arizonans. The state continued to battle for its water rights in the federal courts.

In the early 1920s there was a severe, but fortunately brief, economic depression. Some local banks had operating troubles, and copper and cotton prices went down. The livestock industry had many misfortunes. Governor Campbell said they were caused by overgrazing, and to add to the trouble there was an epidemic of hoof-and-mouth disease. Timber production dropped by 70 percent. Nationally the reason for these events was the almost overnight disbanding of the armed forces and the fact that the economy could not absorb so many people in the labor market.

By 1923 things were starting to look brighter, and there followed six years of solid prosperity. "Truck farming" became increasingly important because growers now had an easy and dependable way to take their produce to shipping points. Citrus production boomed. Canteloupe and other melons, lettuce, and tomatoes became increasingly important, and about 1922 table grapes also became a valuable product. By the late 1920s the lumber industry was producing $5 million worth of timber annually. The tourist industry also thrived, with people arriving not only by train but by automobile. Copper production remained high although the ore from which the pure metal was produced became less and less pure as the richer areas were worked out. Cotton production also made its contributions. Those were the days in which it was said that the Arizona economy was made up of the three C's: copper, cotton, and cattle.

In the years following the First World War Arizonans began to realize that with the passage of time the early pioneers were rapidly disappearing from the scene. One of the things they did in several cities was to hold annual reunions. This gave people an opportunity to gather the "old-timers" together, and the newspapers would run feature stories on interesting characters. Sadly, people were mostly

ABOVE: Dr. Clyde Tombaugh, who discovered the planet Pluto at Lowell Observatory in 1930, is shown here in 1938 examining planet-search photographs under the blink microscope comparator. He spent 7,000 hours at Lowell peering through the eyepiece during the years 1929 to 1945. Courtesy, Lowell Observatory

LEFT: This 40-foot dome was built in 1896 by Stanley and Godfrey Sykes. Left to right are Harry Hussey, secretary W. Louise Leonard, astronomer Vesto M. Slipher, founder and director Percival Lowell, Carol Lampland, and John C. Duncan. Courtesy, Lowell Observatory

remembered when stories of their death appeared in the press. In 1919 the last member of the Powell expedition through the Grand Canyon, William W. Hawkins, died. In 1922 Isaac Polhamus, best-known of the Colorado River steamer captains, passed away from the scene, and in 1928 Edward D. Tuttle, the only survivor of the first legislature in 1864, was gone.

While figures from the past disappeared, new generations arrived on the scene. In 1928 a young carpenter named Del E. Webb arrived in Arizona. He started a construction business and would later found Sun City. The year before Webb's arrival, Phoenix Junior College hired a mathematics instructor, Robert J. Hannelly, who would later be called the father of junior and community college education

in Arizona. In 1929 Lowell Observatory in Flagstaff hired 23-year-old Clyde W. Tombaugh, who had not yet graduated from college. The next year he would discover the planet Pluto. This is not to say that only those who moved to Arizona from somewhere else would shape its future. In 1925 a young woman named Lorna E. Lockwood graduated from the college of law of the University of Arizona, and in the 1960s she would become the first woman chief justice of a state supreme court.

The achievement of statehood, after so many years of striving, was a significant occasion for all Arizonans. Citizens of the new state now had all the privileges and responsibilities of full-fledged members of the Union. Arizona had become master of its own destiny.

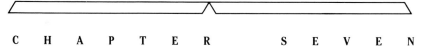

Depression, War, and New Prosperity

In November 1942 the first of the 32nd and 33rd Women's Army Auxiliary Corps (WAACS)
arrived at Fort Huachuca to serve beside the men of the 93rd division. Although
WAACS had been filling other positions in other areas, these were the first
to serve in the primary function of replacing soldiers so they might
serve in combat. Courtesy, Fort Huachuca Military Museum

During the 1920s many people believed there would be no more economic and business cycles, only great prosperity ahead. The world was wonderful and exciting, and when the stock market crashed in October of 1929 few could imagine the consequences.

It has often been said that the Great Depression was slow to make itself felt in Arizona, but once it fastened its grip upon the state it was very slow in releasing its gloomy hold. At first there were perhaps fewer tourists, prices dipped slightly, and there were no more wage increases. But by early 1931 it was obvious that things were going very wrong. The leading economic indicators demonstrated real trouble. Copper, which had been selling at 13 cents per pound in 1927 was at five and a half cents in 1932. Arizonans asked for a tariff to keep foreign metal out of the United States, and although a tariff was enacted it did not seem to help. Gold prices actually went up—to $25.56 in 1933 and to $34.95 an ounce a year later—as a result of the United States going off the gold standard, but by that time the metal was not terribly important to the state. In general, mining declined until 1936 when the bottom was finally reached.

Cattlemen endured hardships as the price of live animals went as low as $5 per 100 pounds. By 1938 it went up a little to $9 per 100. In 1931 cotton reached a low of five and a half cents per pound until, with government price supports, it came up to 12 cents

per pound a few years later. The best Arizona oranges sold at retail for about two cents per pound.

It has been estimated that Arizona actually lost population during the worst of the Depression, although by 1940 the census revealed an increase since 1930. People were often on the move during these troubled times.

In 1932 there was a march across the nation organized by veterans of the First World War. Its purpose was to ask Congress to pay a promised veterans' bonus early. The Bonus Expeditionary Force, so called because the army in the war had been the American Expeditionary Force, left Los Angeles on June 10. By the time the marchers reached Arizona there were somewhat over 2,000 men and women, including families with their children. They were allowed to stop briefly at the fairgrounds in Phoenix and the state prison at Florence, and then with their ranks swollen to nearly 3,000 they continued on their way to Washington.

The marchers undoubtedly passed many people heading west, seeking new homes. As if the economy were not in enough trouble, the weather combined with years of neglect of the land on the Great Plains to create the Dust Bowl. Thousands of people left drought-stricken areas and headed for California. Highway 66 across northern Arizona, as well as the southern highways, carried thousands of people in search of new lives. Governor R.C. Stanford, who was chief executive of Arizona from 1937 to 1939, recalled that never once during his term in office did he wake up in the morning not to find at least one stranded family parked in front of his home. They had come to ask the governor for help.

A substantial number of migrants remained in Arizona and became useful and substantial citizens. In communities such as Peoria, near Phoenix, later well-to-do residents would joke that they had a higher social position when they arrived because they had four or five mattresses tied to the top of their cars while others only had one or two.

Old Governor Hunt was in his last term as governor when the Depression fastened itself upon the land, and he like others felt the sorrow of it. In his diary he wrote, "So many wanting work. No work. So many people hungry." His political career came to an end in the primary election of 1932 when he was defeated by Benjamin B. Moeur.

"Doc" Moeur, as he was called, was the son and grandson of physicians, and although born in Tennessee he was raised in Texas. After graduating from medical school he came to Arizona and soon settled in Tempe where he was a "country doctor" for

During the Great Depression migrants and the unemployed lived in makeshift camps like this one. Called "Hoovervilles" after President Herbert Hoover, this camp was situated under the Central Avenue Bridge. The bridges and other areas along the Salt River still shelter their share of the homeless in the 1980s. Courtesy, Arizona Historical Foundation

over 30 years. Old-timers in the state still insist he could swear for up to 15 minutes without ever repeating himself—somewhat of an exaggeration. Actually, he was a kindly, well-intentioned, gruff humanitarian who even operated a free medical clinic in the capitol during his spare time as governor. Moeur was sworn into office in January 1933 and his most immediate and pressing problem was the banking crisis.

At this time Arizona had dozens of small local banks which were not particularly secure in the best of times. Several had failed in the 1920s, but that was nothing compared to the troubles of the Depression. Governor Moeur closed Arizona's banks on March 2, 1933, two days before Franklin D. Roosevelt became president. The new president also temporarily closed financial institutions, but in a few days those that were sound were allowed to reopen.

On the Arizona scene a major new figure in the banking field appeared. On the first day of 1933 Walter R. Bimson, newly arrived from Illinois, became president of the Valley Bank and Trust Company of Phoenix, then a rather small bank. After helping Doc Moeur draft his bank holiday proclamation he turned his attention to trying to salvage his own institution. Several smaller banks were merged to form the new Valley National Bank, a statewide financial institution. Similar mergers took place across Arizona, and within a few months the banks were secure once more and public confidence in them was renewed.

A major problem faced by the state was that the value of property was so depressed that tax revenues did not meet the needs of financing the government. Federal grants were to some extent helpful, particularly in welfare matters, but new ways to finance state expenditures had to be found. The legislature enacted the first Arizona sales tax and the first state income tax as well as levies on such items as beer, liquor, and cigarettes. A part of this new financial program was the reduction of state spending whenever possible. It was proposed that the colleges in Tempe and Flagstaff be closed to save money, but in the end this was not done. Salaries of government workers from the governor on down were cut, and somehow the state managed to pull through the economic crisis.

Jobs were among the great needs of the time. Respectable middle-class people simply could not find work. The federal government stepped in as an employer of last resort. Through the Reconstruction Finance Corporation, founded in 1932, several millions of dollars in federal funds were loaned to Arizona businesses to keep them operating.

Probably the most famous of the 1930s government agencies was the WPA. The letters stood for Works Projects Administration, but popularly it was said that WPA meant "We Poke Along." Sixteen thou-

sand Arizonans worked for the agency at one time or another at rates of between $15 and $25 a week. Employees did a variety of tasks: 1,714 miles of highway were built, as were 200 public buildings. In addition there was a Federal Music Project which sponsored over 1,000 free concerts and a Federal Theatre Project which performed plays for the public. A group of writers, headed by Ross Santee, a talented cowboy artist and short-story craftsman, produced the Arizona State Guide, one of the WPA Writer's Project volumes. Less well known was the PWA, the Public Works Administration of the Interior Department, which was responsible for the improvements at Tumacacori Mission and the national monuments at Montezuma Castle and Wupatki. The original buildings of Phoenix Junior College were constructed by the PWA in 1939.

The CCC was the Civilian Conservation Corps, a federal agency designed to provide outdoor work for young men. It was organized along military lines and operated a total of 27 camps in Arizona; between 1933 and 1942 more than 50,000 men at one time or another worked in camps in the state. They built nearly 6,000 miles of forest roads and erected 3,559

miles of telephone lines, designed to bring service to small communities. The corps built earthen dams, erected fences, planted seven and a half million trees, and constructed hundreds of picnic facilities, restrooms, and rock fireplaces. The program is estimated to have pumped more than $50 million into the economy of Arizona in the nine years it existed. In 1935 the Resettlement Administration, headed nationally by Rexford G. Tugwell, tried to establish a farm and dairy cooperative at Casa Grande, but after 60 adobe homes were built the project was abandoned.

For those who did not live during the 1930s, and for those who may have forgotten, prices then seem strange now. A family of four could easily live on $100 a month. Many managed with a good bit less. In 1934, in the sizable cities and towns of Arizona, a two-bedroom furnished apartment rented for $30 to $40 a month and a modest five-room house and lot sold for about $2,500. Physicians charged $2 for office calls, and a new automobile could be purchased for well under $1,000. A new overstuffed chair and footstool were advertised for $22.95.

For those preparing holiday dinners that year

there were some real "bargains" in the grocery store. Turkeys were 25 cents a pound and ham was 18 cents. Butter was at a rather high rate of 33 cents a pound but oleomargarine was two pounds for 25 cents. Lettuce was advertised at three heads for five cents and coffee was 19 cents per pound. If one decided to dine out, a full-course Christmas dinner including soup, salad, main course, dessert, and beverage was $1 in the better restaurants. If one wanted entertainment the movie theaters charged 20 cents admission. If one had some Christmas shopping to do chocolates were $1 for a two-and-a-half-pound box, brand-name men's shirts sold anywhere between $1.95 and $3.50, and men's or ladies' wristwatches were $14.95.

Except for a brief downturn in 1937, economic indicators showed gradual recovery by the late 1930s. Many mines were closed altogether for a while, but in 1937 and 1938 they began to reopen. In 1938 there were again 11,000 miners employed in Arizona, in 1939 there were 12,500, and 1940 saw approximately 14,000 on the payrolls. By 1940 the value of farmland in the state had reached a total of over $50 million, and so-called truck farming was once more on the road to recovery, as was livestock raising. For the most part manufacturing was not yet a part of the picture; the industrial revolution did not come to Arizona until the start of World War II.

Governor Moeur was reelected in 1934 but lost his bid for a third term in the Democratic primary of 1936. He was succeeded by two one-term chief executives: R.C. Stanford, who refused to run for reelection, preferring to be a supreme court judge instead; and Robert T. ("Bob") Jones, who was retired by the voters in the primary of 1940. Neither was especially important as governor although both were honorable and dedicated men. Stanford, born in Texas, was three years old when his family arrived in a covered wagon which they parked at the corner of Central and McDowell in Phoenix. A tall, impressive-looking man, Stanford was one of those individuals who always tried to please everyone, with the result that he now and then found himself on both sides of a question. Jones, who came originally from Tennessee, had worked as an engineer on the construction of the Panama Canal before arriving in Arizona. Later he was the owner of a drugstore, had ranching interests, and after leaving the governorship he owned and operated a Western-wear store in Phoenix.

The victor in the Democratic primary of 1940, who went on to easily defeat his Republican opponent in the general election, was Sidney P. Osborn.

He took office in January 1941 and was destined to be a major figure in Arizona history. The grandson of pioneers who came to the territory in the 1860s, Osborn was born in Phoenix in 1884. He was educated in the local public schools and was only 26 years old when he served in the constitutional convention. He was the new state's first secretary of state in 1912, but after leaving that post ran for several offices over the years and was always defeated.

Once he was elected governor he was very popular and was easily reelected in 1942, 1944, and 1946. Osborn was a modest, quiet man, not a character as George W.P. Hunt had been, but extremely able. He had the respect of all. When he decided that it was necessary to ratify the Santa Fe Compact in order to proceed legally in the courts to determine the apportionment of the Colorado River waters, and the legislature was reluctant, he told lawmakers he would

The Civilian Conservation Corps built dams, roads, and forest recreational facilities throughout Arizona during the 1930s. Courtesy, Arizona Historical Society, Tucson

call them into special session until they either ratified the compact or impeached him. They approved the compact.

Osborn was considered a strong governor. He solved the problem of the inability of the chief executive to remove individuals from office in the administration once they had been appointed by requiring each nominee to submit in advance a signed, undated letter of resignation. If at any time the appointment did not work out the governor simply reached into his "little black box," as the press called it, dated the letter, and made it public.

Sadly, Osborn developed the muscular disorder known as "Lou Gehrig's disease." "I have set many precedents as governor," he said one day, "and now I am going to establish another. I will be the first governor to die in office." Until the end of May of 1948 this brave man was carried daily to his office, and having lost the power of speech he communicated by holding a pencil in his mouth and pointing to an alphabet chart.

As the decade of the 1930s ended Arizonans became increasingly concerned over the disintegration of international peace. There was no agreement, however, whether the United States should end its "isolationist" stance in world affairs. The debate ended the morning of December 7, 1941, when the Japanese bombed Hawaii. The attack had a particular meaning for the people of the Southwest because their battleship, the *Arizona,* was one of those vessels lost.

The ship had been in the planning stages at the time of statehood. It was launched with not only the traditional bottle of champagne but also a bottle of water from Roosevelt Lake. A ship of 32,600 tons, the *Arizona* was placed in commission in October 1916. The great battleship was 608 feet in length and saw regular service until modernized in 1929. At that time it was equipped with tripod masts, new guns, new boilers, and its engines were given a complete overhaul.

The *Arizona* joined the Pacific Fleet in 1931 and was rated as a first-line fighting ship. However in December 1941 it was a sitting duck in the harbor when the attack came. Nearly 1,200 seamen lost their lives on the *Arizona,* and it settled into the waters of Pearl Harbor, flag still flying from the stern, never to be raised again. In 1950 with a simple ceremony a 50-foot flagpole was erected on its superstructure and the commander-in-chief of the Pacific Fleet declared: "From today on, the *Arizona* will fly our country's flag as proudly as it did on the morning of December 7, 1941." A memorial and museum have been erected at the ship, which also serves as a tomb for those who lost their lives. The anchor of the *Arizona* now rests near the state capitol and its ceremonial silver is on display within the building.

World War II brought many changes to Arizona. There were increases in population, although not all were voluntary. After the bombing of Pearl Harbor it was the policy of the United States government to remove Japanese Americans from the Pacific Coast areas and place them inland in "relocation centers." Although it would later be recognized that this was a gross violation of the rights of these Americans, at the time it was considered a military necessity.

The town of Poston on the Colorado River had a relocation center housing approximately 18,000 individuals and was for a time the third-largest settlement in the state. Altogether 20,000 people were located on the Colorado River Indian Reservation starting in April of 1942. There was another sizable camp of 15,000 Japanese near Sacaton on the Gila River Indian Reservation southeast of Phoenix. During the summer of 1942 the Navajo Tribal Council authorized the relocation of 2,000 Japanese to facilities near Winslow. In addition there were a number of prisoner-of-war camps within Arizona. A substantial German group was housed in Papago Park, near Phoenix, and some Italian prisoners were also in the area.

Sidney P. Osborn, shown here in 1948, was a popular and strong Arizona governor from 1942 to 1948. He also served in the constitutional convention and was Arizona's first secretary of state in 1912. During his years as governor he faced World War II, the postwar industrial and population boom, the building of huge military installations, and the acute water shortage. Courtesy, Arizona Department of Library, Archives, and Public Records

LEFT: The USS Arizona *was modernized in 1929 and joined the Pacific Fleet stationed at Pearl Harbor in 1931. The great battleship was commissioned in 1916 and has never been decommissioned. Courtesy, McFarland Historical State Park, McFarland Archives*

Because of nearly ideal weather conditions Arizona became the site of several military airbases. Principal among them were Luke Field, Thunderbird fields numbers one and two, Davis-Monthan Field, Williams Field, and Falcon Field, as well as training facilities in the Yuma area. Not only Americans but men from Allied nations were trained there, especially Great Britain and China. Apart from flying fields there were other types of training facilities to be found in the Southwest. A major gunnery range was located near Kingman, while Camp Horn near Wickenburg and Camp Hyder near Yuma taught soldiers the tactics of desert warfare. The military was still racially segregated at this time and Fort Huachuca was an important base for black soldiers.

One of the most interesting stories from World War II is that of the Navajo code talkers. The Navajo language is so complicated and unusual that Navajo men were used in the Pacific theater of war operations in communications. The enemy could not "break the code" and understand what the Navajo men were saying to one another. The greatest numbers of the code talkers served in the Marine Corps although the other services also utilized these communications specialists.

Probably the best-known Arizona hero of the war was Ira Hayes. Of Pima ancestry, he was born on the Gila River Reservation and joined the United States Marines. A corporal, he was with the paratroopers and spent nearly two years in the war zone of the Pacific. In early 1945, after a very bloody fight, the United States flag was raised on Mt. Suribachi after the Battle of Iwo Jima. Hayes was one of the flag raisers. The years after the war were not good ones for Hayes, and he died in 1955 at the early age of 32. He was buried in Arlington National Cemetery.

In all, over 30,000 men and women of the state served in the armed forces during World War II. Nearly 8 percent of those were native Americans.

While some figures would indicate that the industrial revolution in Arizona began in the 1930s, the weight of the evidence shows that it did not begin un-

ABOVE: On December 7, 1941, the Japanese bombed Pearl Harbor and sank the USS Arizona, *killing 1,177 men on board. This is the wreckage of the great battleship just before it sank. A memorial and museum have been erected at the site to honor the ship and those who died. Courtesy, McFarland Historical State Park, McFarland Archives*

til World War II. In 1940 manufacturing in the state produced gross sales of about $17 million, but by the end of the war that annual figure had increased to $85 million. Most of the new plants were related to the war effort. There were new steel and aluminum fabricating plants and factories for the making of aircraft and aircraft parts. Some tank parts were also produced, as were steel pontoon bridges.

When the war ended many of these operations came to a halt. During the first full year of peace, manufacturing dropped to gross sales of $53 million. Fifteen thousand skilled and semiskilled workers also lost their jobs at that time. However, the idea that Arizona could share permanently in the industrial development of the nation was firmly planted, and the state in the postwar years would actively seek new industry and businesses.

To create an industrial society is not an easy task. One needs capital, which was not readily available in Arizona, but investments from other states and foreign nations, plus government grants, provided needed funds. Raw materials, another necessary ingredient, were not indigenous to the state and so had to be shipped, which added transportation costs to expenses. Skilled workers are also a necessity, and these were drawn from other states or trained locally once the population began to increase. Finally, markets are needed, and for the most part these were located a distance from Arizona, so more transportation costs entered into the picture. Despite the handicaps, private groups and state agencies such as the Arizona Development Board went in search of new industries and businesses which might wish to relocate in the Southwest.

For corporations to move, several factors are im-

portant. A favorable tax climate is very significant, and that was to be found in Arizona. Also companies wanted to know what facilities were available for their personnel. The climate was well known but schools, highways, and recreational areas also make an area attractive. Trying to provide these facilities for a growing population would tax the abilities of the state.

For a variety of reasons the years following World War II saw the greatest westward movement the United States has ever experienced. Arizona had a population of about a half-million in 1940 which grew to three-quarters of a million in 1950, and a decade after that it was well over a million and a quarter. Most of the time about half of that population was centered in Maricopa County in the Phoenix urban area, and a second good-sized population center was in Pima County around Tucson. People came from all over. The desert areas grew the most, but other parts of Arizona experienced increases in population as well.

The development of air conditioning made much of Arizona a more pleasant place. Although the identity of the inventor is uncertain, "evaporative coolers" were being manufactured in substantial numbers by the 1930s. Refrigeration, which is much more expensive to operate, was known earlier but was rather rarely used in Arizona until after the close of World War II. Then it became very popular, and by the early 1950s automobiles came so equipped.

Amazingly, jobs seemed to be available for most of the new arrivals. AiResearch, which had closed its Phoenix plant in 1946, reopened in 1951. That same year Hughes Aircraft began a facility in Tucson. Reynolds Aluminum took over the Alcoa plant in Phoe-

nix. Motorola, General Electric, and Sperry-Phoenix became important employers. By 1960 nearly 40,000 individuals were employed in manufacturing. Land which had once been used for farming was converted into miles of urban tract housing. Pioneer homebuilders, such as John F. Long, provided good single-family dwellings at reasonable prices. New homes were on the market for under $10,000.

Long and his wife Mary built a new home for themselves in 1947 and received an offer to sell it for $8,400. Work was started on another and there was another sale. Soon Long was building homes as a career, and in 1950 he started his first tract development at 26th Avenue and Glendale in the northwest part of Phoenix. Soon many others joined Long, and by 1962 the area had 80 homebuilders. Three years later that number was reduced to 20.

As the population grew so did school enrollments. In the middle 1940s there were approximately 100,000 elementary school pupils and not quite 25,000 in high schools. By 1960 those respective figures were nearly 275,000 and almost 100,000. For years school districts were hard-pressed to build enough buildings, obtain needed teachers, and find the financial resources to operate their systems.

ABOVE: During World War II, Navajo code talkers effectively prevented the Japanese from breaking their communications code. It is said that the language of the Navajo Indians cannot be mastered except by those who have grown up with it. Depicted here are a few of the code talkers, Navajo Marines in formation at Camp Pendleton, circa 1943-1944. Courtesy, Special Collections Library, Northern Arizona University, Flagstaff

Higher education in the state showed similar trends. In the late 1930s the University of Arizona enrolled about 4,000 students; what is now Arizona State University had 1,500; and what is now Northern Arizona University had 700. During the Second World War those figures dropped to 2,000, 700, and 500, as young men joined the armed forces. When the veterans returned after the war, many of them were educated under the G.I. Bill of Rights, which was the creation of Senator Ernest W. McFarland of Arizona. The figures went up to nearly 6,000, nearly 5,000, and almost 1,000 respectively in the three schools. With the influx of population by 1960 totals were nearly 20,000, over 12,000, and nearly 3,000.

This postwar era also saw an increase in road building. Whereas in 1930 Arizona had only 281 miles of paved highways, 20 years later the area contained 4,000 miles of paved state highways plus 16,000 miles of county roads. The automobile had truly arrived, and it did so at the expense of the railroads. The latter began to decline, especially passenger travel, in the 1950s. In 1950 Arizonans owned almost 300,000 motor vehicles, and in the next decade that number more than doubled. Trucks and buses also played important roles in the Arizona economy.

To handle the traffic the Interstate Highway System was authorized by the United States Congress. Some of Interstate 15 crossed the northern part of Arizona. Old and famous Highway 66 became Interstate 40 while Interstate 10 linked New Mexico to California. Interstate 8 connected Casa Grande and Yuma while other interstates, 19 and 17, ran from Flagstaff to the Mexican border.

Airlines became more and more important. During the 1920s several cities and towns built airports, although in many instances they were little more than open fields. In 1927 regular air service was inaugurated among Arizona cities such as Tucson and Phoenix, connecting them to the West Coast. By 1948 Phoenix Sky Harbor airport ranked fourth in the nation in numbers of passengers passing through the terminal.

In addition to transportation improvements, Arizonans also took increased interest in politics during this period. In national politics, from statehood until the presidential election of 1952, Arizona had the distinction of always being on the side of the winning presidential candidate; in state politics it was overwhelmingly Democratic. When Governor Osborn died he was succeeded in office by Secretary of State Dan E. Garvey, who was elected to a term of his own as chief executive in 1948. Two years later the Republicans captured the governorship when J. Howard Pyle narrowly won over Ana Frohmiller. This was merely a prelude of things to come. The Eisenhower landslide of 1952—a triumph for the Republican party—had an important impact upon Arizona. Ernest W. McFarland, a United States senator since 1941 and Senate majority leader, lost his bid for reelection to a newcomer in politics, Republican Barry M. Goldwater of Phoenix. Grandson of a pioneer merchant, the new senator would become a major figure not only in state but national matters. At the same time John J. Rhodes, who would later become Republican leader of the United States House of Representatives, was elected to that body. Also in 1952 Governor Pyle was reelected.

The Republicans concentrated on winning the top offices in the state and gradually built up their strength for battles at all levels. Several things worked to the advantage of the party. There was a long tradition of Democrats feuding among themselves, and the party reflected Will Rogers' famous comment, "I am a member of no organized political party. I am a Democrat." In contrast, the Republicans adopted what was called the "California Eleventh Commandment," which is "Thou shalt not speak ill of any other Republican."

The greatest number of new Arizonans who came to the state following World War II came from two geographical areas. Foremost were the large number of voters who came from the Midwestern states—Illinois, Indiana, Ohio, Kansas, and Nebras-

U.S. Senator Ernest W. McFarland, the 1952 Democratic Senate majority leader, later became the only man in U.S. history to hold the three top political positions in a state. From 1954-1958 he served as governor and in 1968 became chief justice of the Arizona Supreme Court. McFarland co-authored the GI Bill to aid veterans, and he sponsored water and reclamation legislation, including the vital Central Arizona Project and the Wellton-Mohawk Irrigation Project. Courtesy, McFarland Historical State Park, McFarland Archives

ka—where Republican voters were in the majority. Substantial numbers of people also came from the Southern states, where people were largely Democrat in name only. Once they reached Arizona, these Southerners openly declared their allegiance to the Republican cause. The Republican party also benefited from strong newspaper support and the tendency of the Democrats to nominate weak candidates. In this they were often helped in the primaries by "pinto Democrats"—Republicans who registered as Democrats so they could influence that party's selection process.

In 1954 Ernest W. McFarland ran for the governorship and won. He was then on his way to holding the "triple crown of Arizona politics," being senator, governor, and chief justice of the state supreme court. After two terms as governor McFarland made another race for the senate against Goldwater but again lost. The Republicans won the governorship with Phoenix businessman Paul J. Fannin, a popular man who was twice reelected as chief executive and then served two terms in the United States Senate.

Politicians weren't the only ones interested in Arizona at this time. Archaeologists and anthropologists had long been familiar with its unique story. The Arizona State Museum in Tucson, the Heard Museum in Phoenix, and the Museum of Northern Arizona in Flagstaff all provided showplaces of Arizona's past. During the Depression there were few funds to finance archaeological research, but after the Second World War when grants and other funds became more available there was increased activity.

Owing to the work of writers and the film industry the "Old West" became a unique American export to the world. Films were frequently made in the state as movie sets utilized Arizona's "Western" scenery. "Old Tucson," originally created for the film *Arizona,* is a replica of what Tucson was supposed to be like in the 1860s. Today "Old Tucson" attracts visitors from all over the nation and the world.

Several prominent writers had some contact with Arizona and they wrote about it. Zane Grey is perhaps the best known of this group and for some time he spent at least a part of each year in the mountains of the state. Harold Bell Wright, another prominent novelist, lived for a time in Tucson, and Owen Wister visited and knew Arizona people. Although some may argue that the picture of the Old West which was presented was not always accurate, the work of these people generated great interest in the frontier. One great writer had an imagined connection with the state. Samuel L. Clemens at times signed himself: "Mark Twain, M.A., Professor of Belles Letters

in the Veterinary College of Arizona."

In the late 1920s a unique publication developed in Arizona which served to make the state of interest to people outside its boundaries. This was *Arizona Highways,* sponsored by the State Highway Department, which originally began as simply a mimeographed publication, but by the middle 1930s was a monthly publication featuring both excellent black-and-white photography and stories about Arizona's past. In 1948 the magazine added color photography and then moved away from its literary efforts. The latter was resumed in more recent times.

Arizona has been an important center for astronomy since Percival Lowell founded his observatory on Mars Hill in Flagstaff in the 1890s. In 1958 land was leased from the Papago people for the establishment of Kitt Peak National Observatory, which was named for a southern Arizona pioneer. In succeeding years it became an internationally known center for research. Its solar telescope has accomplished significant work as has its 150-inch telescope and other smaller instruments.

On February 14, 1962, Arizonans celebrated a half century of statehood. Much had happened in the last 50 years in the "Baby State," and the land which had seen so many changes was about to experience many more.

Dr. Emil Haury was head of the Department of Anthropology at the University of Arizona and director of the State Museum until 1964. He was noted for his archaeological activities at Ventana Cave, Mogollon Village, Snaketown, and many other sites. He is shown here in 1964 at the Gila Pueblo site in Snaketown. Courtesy, Arizona State Museum, University of Arizona, Helga Teiwes, photographer

The Recent Past

To celebrate the Fourth of July, a World Champion Inner Tube Race was held on the Colorado River, starting just north of Yuma. A group of intrepid racers is shown here just starting out in 1969 or 1970, most of them well-protected from the Arizona sun. The race was held from the 1960s until 1983, when flooding made the course unsafe. Courtesy, Mr. and Mrs. Alan Martel, Don Cordery, photographer

In the years following World War II there seemed to be an accelerated decline in state government in the United States. Many predicted that by the end of the twentieth century the states would be mere administrative units in a unitary national government. Then from the United States Supreme Court came rulings that would ultimately revitalize the states and give them a new lease on life.

The problem presented by the "one person, one vote" issue was nowhere more evident than in Arizona. The state senate had two senators elected from each county. Thus Maricopa with approximately half the state population elected one-fourteenth of the members of the upper house. When Arizona was ordered to redraw its legislative district boundaries, and make them approximately equal in population, the legislature was unable to take any action, and so the federal courts created 30 new districts. In each, one senator and two representatives were to be chosen.

The application of "one person, one vote" had two immediate effects upon the state. It transferred political power from the rural areas to the cities, and, unlike the situation in most other states, in 1966 it gave the Republicans a majority in both branches of the legislature for the first time. Clearly changes were in the immediate future.

Paul Fannin was three times elected governor—in 1958, 1960, and 1962. He was succeeded as chief executive in January 1965 by Samuel P. Goddard, a Missouri-born Tucson attorney. Goddard was one of those new Arizonans who arrived following World War II (while he was stationed in the state on active military duty, his wife found the climate beneficial to her health). A Democrat elected in a Republican era, Goddard was a capable governor whose many constructive ideas were never accepted. He felt, for example, that the state ought to modify its restrictions on state debt so that needed facilities could be constructed. However, "pay as you go" was a deeply imbedded Arizona belief, and eventually a costly one in light of later inflation.

The victor in the 1966 governor's race was John R. ("Jack") Williams, a Phoenix radio personality and newspaper columnist who had been mayor of Phoenix. Governor Williams, a very popular Republican, was reelected in 1968 and 1970, the latter time for the first four-year term given an Arizona governor.

In the 1960s Arizona underwent a major constitutional revision. Unlike some states which, when faced with the need for modernization, adopted entirely new fundamental charters, Arizona instead remodeled its constitution of 1910. Credit for these accomplishments goes largely to Republican legislators and the voters of Arizona who were able to make state government more effective than it had been. Instead of electing executive officials every two years, terms were increased to four years, and this principle was applied to county officials as well. The court system was entirely modernized with a new court of appeals, and in the 1970s methods of selecting judges were improved. Budget procedures that had lagged far behind other states were made more efficient, and a new state civil service system was created. The power of the governor generally increased, and while some thought other changes, such as a four-year term for members of the legislature, might still be accomplished, there was a statewide feeling that by the 1970s Arizona had a much improved and more effective state government.

In national political affairs Arizona has in modern times become more prominent. Once the state exerted influence because of a tendency to reelect its United States senators and representatives; due to the seniority system in Congress those officials rose to positions of prominence. In the 75 years after statehood, only nine different individuals have held the office of senator. In the House of Representatives Arizona was allotted a third member in 1963, a fourth in 1973, and a fifth in 1983. The state's influence grew not only in terms of numbers but also in terms of the prestige of its elected officials. Representative John J. Rhodes, a Republican, served as his party's leader in the House, and Representative Morris Udall has been a prominent Democratic leader.

The first Arizonan to serve in the president's cabinet was Stewart L. Udall, secretary of the Interior from 1961 to 1969, and the second was Richard G. Kleindienst, who was attorney general of the United States from 1972 to 1973. Although the great majority of the justices of the United States Supreme Court have been appointed from states east of the Mississippi River, and very few from the Far West, two former residents of Arizona serve on the high tribunal. In 1971 President Nixon appointed William H. Rehnquist, a former Phoenix attorney, to be an associate justice, and in 1986 President Reagan advanced him to the office of chief justice of the United States. Sandra Day O'Connor, formerly judge of the Arizona Court of Appeals, was in 1981 appointed as the first woman to serve on the United States Supreme Court.

Probably the best-known Arizonan of modern times is Barry Goldwater. Born in Phoenix in 1909, he is the son and grandson of pioneer merchants, and the nephew of Morris Goldwater, a mayor of Prescott and delegate to the constitutional convention of 1910. He grew up in his native city, attended its schools, and left the University of Arizona following the death of his father in 1929. Goldwater's Department Store, the family business, occupied his attention for many years. In addition, he learned to fly and would later rise to the rank of brigadier general in the United States Air Force. Facts not so well known include his lifetime interest in Arizona's history, geography, and people, especially the native Indian population. He first entered politics as a member of the Phoenix City Council, and when he first ran for the United States Senate he had no idea that he could defeat Ernest W. McFarland. But he did.

The new senator from Arizona soon became very well known. Regarded as the father of the modern American conservative movement, he was concerned about the growth of the power of the federal government and its intrusion into the lives of people. He also championed building the nation's military power to a strength greater than that of any other nation. Reelected to the Senate in 1958, Goldwater was spoken of as a leading contender for the Republican nomination for president of the United States. That distinction came to him in 1964, and he mounted a vigorous campaign against the incumbent Democratic chief executive, Lyndon B. Johnson. Although Goldwater was not elected, he carried his native state, Arizona, where his popularity grew.

When Senator Carl Hayden announced his retirement from the Senate it was a foregone conclusion that Goldwater would be his successor. Now a leading elder statesman, the Arizonan continues to speak out on any and all issues. Although often labeled conservative, he is too independent and individualistic to be tied to any particular doctrine. At a retirement banquet a friend said Goldwater's approach to rhetoric was "Ready, shoot, aim!" In 1974 and 1980 the senator was reelected, but in 1986 he decided to retire and left office in January 1987.

Governor Williams left office in January of 1975 and was succeeded by a Democrat, Raul H. Castro of Tucson. A native of Mexico and a naturalized citizen, he had taught at the University of Arizona while attending law school. A judge and United States ambassador first to El Salvador and then Bolivia, Governor Castro resigned as chief executive of Arizona, the first governor to do so, on October 20, 1977, to accept an appointment as ambassador to Argentina. He was succeeded in office by longtime Secretary of State Wesley Bolin, also a Democrat. Governor

Bolin died suddenly on March 4, 1978, and was succeeded by another Democrat, Attorney General Bruce Babbitt.

The 16th state governor was the grandson of one of five brothers who in the 1880s founded Babbitt Brothers Trading Company, a major firm in the economic development of northern Arizona. Babbitt was a geology major in college before attending law school. He practiced in Phoenix and was elected attorney general of the state. Not quite 40 years old when he became governor, he was elected in his own right in 1978 and 1982. In January of 1987 he voluntarily retired from office. He was generally recognized as the most important and effective governor since Sidney P. Osborn. A believer in strong executive leadership, Babbitt had the distinction of vetoing more bills than all other Arizona state governors combined. Despite this fact he got along fairly well with the Republican-controlled legislatures.

Closely related to Arizona politics, especially in recent decades, is the continued problem of bringing an adequate water supply to the state. No other single issue will bring members of Congress and state leaders of both parties closer to working in harmony. As early as the 1920s there was talk of bringing Colorado River water to metropolitan Phoenix and Tucson, but for a long time the idea was considered impractical. In 1947 a proposal called the Central Arizona Project was introduced in Congress to do just that. Senator Carl Hayden probably worked

At the 1964 Republican Convention, Barry Goldwater was chosen to be that party's candidate for president. He lost to Lyndon Johnson, but continued to serve Arizona as a U.S. senator until he retired in 1986. Courtesy, Arizona Historical Foundation

The military continues to be a vital part of Yuma's economy. In March 1987 the arrival of the AV-8b Harrier II at the Marine Corps Air Station in Yuma marked one of the first steps in the transition to a fully tactical Marine Aircraft Group. The Harrier II is a short takeoff, vertical landing light attack aircraft, here being readied for the welcoming ceremony at its new home base. Courtesy, Marine Corps Air Station, Yuma

longer and harder than anyone else for passage, but the entire Arizona delegation to Congress strongly supported it. In 1952 a suit was filed before the United States Supreme Court to determine Arizona's water rights in the Colorado. A decade later, after much litigation, a favorable decision was forthcoming. Arizona was to receive its fair share of the water, but passage of the CAP was required to bring the water to the desert. The Senate was generally in favor but the House, where the California delegation was especially numerous, was not. More compromises had to be made.

At last in the fall of 1968, as Senator Hayden's long tenure in the Senate was coming to an end, Congress approved and President Johnson signed legislation to authorize the Central Arizona Project. Unfortunately no construction funds were included; that took several more years. By the middle 1980s much work had been done but the project was not yet finished and water was not yet flowing.

Concern over water may continue as the state's population increases. Population figures are very important in explaining much of the state's recent history. According to the census of 1960 there were 1,301,161 Arizonans; in 1970 there were 1,775,399; and in 1980 the total was 2,718,425. It was estimated that on the 75th anniversary of statehood, February

14, 1987, the number was well over three million.

Approximately 125,000 Arizonans are native Americans or Indians. About 100,000 are blacks, and about half a million people living in the state have Hispanic family names.

Arizona is said to have a young population. Although between 1970 and 1985 the number of children under 14 years of age actually declined, during the same period the group between 25 and 34 increased by one quarter. The state is also known as a good place to retire. Senior citizens, those over 65, constitute more than 12 percent of the population.

More than one third of modern Arizonans have some college education, while at least another third graduated from high school. While in recent years the numbers of people engaged in mining and farming have declined, manufacturing provided jobs in the middle 1980s for nearly 200,000, and service industries provided jobs for nearly 300,000. In 1985 government at various levels employed over 200,000.

The impact of the new arrivals in the state has been major in many ways. Air quality, once one of the great features of Arizona, and so important for the tourist industry, has degenerated in many places, causing great concern. The growth of industry has brought the pollution of groundwater, disturbing the delicate balance within nature. An important author and conservationist, Joseph Wood Krutch, spent the later years of his life in Tucson and wrote eloquently on those problems.

The institutions of society have also been put under stress by the great growth in population. Many building programs have been started or expanded. A state park system is under development.

It has been necessary for the state to provide new correctional institutions: prisons, jails, and halfway houses. The state hospital and other facilities for the treatment of the mentally ill have also necessarily been expanded. Once in a rare while some medical advance allows the closing of a facility. In the 1930s the federal government built a tuberculosis sanitorium near Tempe, but because of modern medicine the facility was recently closed.

Educational institutions are ever-present, and in Arizona the need has been to expand them as fast as possible. In the late 1950s there was discussion whether more colleges ought to be founded, and the result was the state Junior College Act of 1960. It allowed counties to establish junior colleges. By the middle 1980s a majority of Arizona counties had established "community colleges," as it became the fashion to call these schools. Maricopa County's system, which is the largest, enrolls more than 40,000 students. Pima has about half that number, and the statewide total approaches 70,000. At the same time university enrollments continue to increase. Arizona State University has more than 40,000 students, the University of Arizona over 30,000, and Northern Arizona University enrolls nearly 12,000. Another indication of the population growth is the fact that even with declines in the birthrate the average daily at-

tendance in all of the elementary and high school districts is in excess of half a million.

In the last quarter century one of the major trends in Arizona's economy has been the acquisition of local businesses by larger and sometimes national firms. This practice existed in the past: the great mining companies and the railroads were always controlled by absentee owners. Still, most other businesses were locally owned.

The new trend started during the Depression

ABOVE: The historic Rosson House at Sixth and Monroe in Phoenix has been preserved as part of Arizona's heritage. This classic Victorian mansion was built in 1895 by Phoenix physician Roland Rosson at a cost of $7,500. It is now restored and listed on the National Register of Historic Places, and is the center of Heritage Square, site of many cultural activities. Courtesy, Arizona Historical Society Museum

LEFT: Irrigation has made the Yuma Valley one of the leading agricultural areas in the state. Alfalfa, citrus, dates melons, cotton, bermuda grass seed, and garden vegetables are shipped to markets in all parts of the country. Here romaine and endive are being harvested and boxed in 1952 on the Mathieu Ranch in the Yuma Valley, against a backdrop of date palms. Courtesy, Emil's Photography

when locally owned banks were reorganized and became much larger; in the 1980s most then became units of even larger banking corporations. In the 1960s and 1970s the major department stores of Arizona—Korricks', Jacome's, Goldwater's, Steinfeld's, and Diamond's—either went out of business or became parts of large chains. In the 1970s many of the larger apartment complexes in Arizona metropolitan areas were acquired by out-of-state interests.

Not only is there substantial investment in the state by investors from other states, but increasingly capital from outside the United States finds its way into Arizona. Canadian and also Japanese money is more and more important. The Southwest has long realized that Mexico is an important trading partner, and the relationships, economic and social, between citizens of Arizona and Mexico are very significant to all.

Investment created a building boom, and Arizona became a focus of well-known architects. The group at Taliesin West, founded by Frank Lloyd Wright, continues the work started by him. Benny Gonzalez is a well-known contemporary architect, while Paolo Soleri and his Arcosanti in central Arizona have also received attention. In recent years a number of important public buildings have been constructed in the state. The major cities have several relatively new art museums, concert halls, and other facilities for the performance of cultural events.

Tucson, Phoenix, Flagstaff, Scottsdale, and Sun City all have symphony orchestras, and a number of communities have "little theater" groups. The Heard Museum of Phoenix and the Museum of Northern Arizona near Flagstaff are important anthropological centers. In the 1880s a group in Tucson founded the Arizona Pioneers' Historical Society. For many decades it was one of the few groups in Arizona devoted to the preservation of the history of the territory and state. This group evolved into the Arizona Historical Society, a state institution with several chapters.

Arizona has long been an "artist's colony" with much emphasis on painting and sculpture. Although not considered by many critics to have been the most talented of the group, Ted DeGrazia was the best known of the state's painters in recent years. *Arizona Highways* magazine made him nationally and even internationally known. The state is a center for Western art, and there are many practitioners of traditional art as well as more modern artists. Professional and amateur photographers have also long found Arizona a source of inspiration.

In literary matters one of the questions which must be asked is what constitutes an "Arizona writer"? For example, the playwright Clare Boothe Luce lived in Phoenix for a number of years. The humorist Erma Bombeck has for several years made her home in the state. Neither has written on distinctly Arizona themes. Then there's Glendon Swarthout, a transplanted Midwesterner, who does write historical novels with Western settings.

By looking backward 100 years from now historians will be able to make a better judgment as to those individuals who were important in the cultural life of Arizona, and to acknowledge the contributions they made in the latter part of the twentieth century.

◆　◆　◆　◆　◆

It has been said that all the world is a stage, and we are the players upon it. If so, the story of Arizona has had many acts of high drama, comedy, mystery, and romance. As the play has unfolded, there has been spectacular scenery—the diverse and colorful geography of Arizona—and spectacular lighting, as any desert sunset or moon-lit night on the high plateau can attest. The "props," Arizona's natural resources, have played important roles as well.

Several acts in the play called "Arizona" were staged before there were written records. But though signs of the ancient peoples—the Hohokam, Mogollon, and Anasazi—have largely vanished, native Americans continue to play an important part in Arizona's story. The arrival of Spanish conquistadors and priests brought changes and new stories to Arizona, as did settlers from Mexico. Although Latin control of Arizona ended long ago, Hispanics still have pivotal roles in the state today. The pioneers of the territorial period, who came from all parts of the nation and the world, added greatly to the drama. Statehood, granted in 1912, began yet another act which has been unfolding for 75 years.

In history, as in the theater, there are the "stars:" Father Kino, Geronimo, Charles D. Poston, George W.P. Hunt, and Barry M. Goldwater are prominent examples. Yet perhaps most important to the story of Arizona are the forgotten individuals who played "bit parts." The now-unknown priests, the early Apache immigrants from the plains, the Mexican residents of long-ago Tubac, and those who lost their lives along pioneer trails—they all contributed to the success of the play.

The drama continues to unfold. What will be the Arizona story when the state celebrates its bicentennial in 2112? Whatever the answer, the story of Arizona will never be dull, and will continue to explore the sum of human experience.

In 1911, when she was 40 years old, Sharlot Hall, Arizona's beloved poet and territorial historian, spent 75 days traversing Arizona's strip, then an unknown region, with a team and wagon and a guide. Courtesy, Jo Proferes

In October 1863 Henry Wickenburg discovered the gold-bearing quartz ledge that would become the Vulture Mine, around which grew Vulture City, with its share of greed and violence. Nineteen men were hanged from the lower limb of the ironwood tree at the right in this painting. *Courtesy, Jo Proferes*

The Hubbell Trading Post is one of the state's commemorated historic sites. Photo by Mark E. Gibson

Arizona offers everything from mountains and deserts to lakes; rimmed with pine trees and cactus. Photos by Mark E. Gibson

LEFT: *Engraved into the desert varnish of the weathered sandstone block known as Newspaper Rock located in the Petrified Forest National Park are these ancient petroglyphs. Their entire meaning is now obscure, but some are identical to clan symbols used by today's Indians. Others may be religious and some may simply be the doodling of a long-gone artist. Photo by Matt Bradley*

OPPOSITE: *Arizona's Petrified Forest is a wonderful, unique national park. Photo by Matt Bradley*

The forces of erosion have created many awe-inspiring natural formations, like this one, known as Window Rock. Photo by Mark E. Gibson

An unrivaled collection of national monuments can be found in Arizona, featuring a variety of natural and manmade phenomena. Shown above is the Walnut Canyon National Monument, photo by Mark E. Gibson, and at left, the edge of the Painted Desert, photo by Phyllis Fockler Gray.

ABOVE: As light slants from the west, day recedes and the towers, temples, and horizontal striations of color stand out in startling relief. Carl Sandburg described sunset in the Grand Canyon by saying, "There goes God with an army of banners." Photo by Harry Fockler

ABOVE RIGHT: Protected by needle-sharp spines, the exotic blossoms of the barrel cactus await pollination by desert insects. The barrel cactus is widely distributed throughout the desert Southwest. Photo by Robert D. Stout

RIGHT: Sunsets behind San-guaro cacti are breathtaking in Arizona. Photo by Mark E. Gibson

RIGHT: An older community than Phoenix, Tucson is known as the "Old Pueblo," and the Spanish influence is much more apparent there than in other Arizona cities. Photo by Mark E. Gibson

OPPOSITE TOP: The Arizona Vietnam War Memorial sculpture, Fallen Warrior *by Jasper d'Ambrosi, is located in a quiet park across from the state capitol building in Phoenix. The sculpture is surrounded by vertical plinths engraved with the names of Arizona's Vietnam War dead. Arizona was one of the first states in the nation to erect a memorial to those who paid the ultimate price for participation in the Vietnam war. Photo by Harry Fockler*

OPPOSITE BOTTOM: A five hour drive from the Grand Canyon, Phoenix, the capital and largest city of Arizona and the seat of Maricopa County, is a popular resort and retirement spot. Photo by Mark E. Gibson

ABOVE AND OPPOSITE: Monument Valley is a well-known Arizona attraction where the forces of nature have sculpted some imposing geologic formations. Photo by Mark E. Gibson

RIGHT: An amazing array of cacti abound in Arizona. Photo by Robert D. Stout

Partners in Progress

The Modoc stagecoach, which could carry up to 25 passengers, ran between Tombstone and Bisbee from 1880 to 1890. "Sandy Bob" Crouch, part owner of the Arizona Mail and Stage Company, brought the Modoc from California where it had been in service for 30 years. Courtesy, Arizona Historical Society, Tucson

In the 76 years since Arizona attached its star to the flag of the United States, the state has undergone a vast transformation. The days when this was the last frontier, inaccessible except by slow train or by horse and wagon over primitive trails or roads, are now only distant memories. Gone also is the gold and silver mining that drew so many thousands of hardy souls to this often inhospitable frontier.

While some of Arizona's once-traditional industries have vanished with the years, others have not. Cotton farming, which began before the turn of the century, continues to be an important part of the state's economy, as do tourism and the cattle industry. Copper mining, severely hurt by low prices and high operating costs in the early 1980s, seems poised once again for a comeback.

As part of the Sun Belt, Arizona has grown in population tremendously in the four decades since the end of World War II. The state has become primarily urban. Maricopa County itself is home to more than half the state's population; in excess of two million Arizonans live in Phoenix and the surrounding Salt River Valley communities. This urban complex is now the 10th-largest in the United States. Another 600,000 people live in metropolitan Tucson. Sierra Vista, Flagstaff, and Yuma are growing also.

New economic activities have emerged, most notably the high-technology electronic industries. Clean and nonpolluting, these businesses are welcome corporate citizens of a state trying to preserve the livable environment for which it is famous and at the same time provide employment for its citizens.

Education in Arizona now is stronger than ever, with three public universities, community college systems in several of the state's counties, and private institutions from preschool through college. Also top ranked in the nation are some of the state's hospitals and health-care research facilities. And Arizona remains a leader in astronomy as it has for decades, a tribute to its clear, clean air and dark skies.

The state faces problems, of course, perhaps greatest among them a shortage of water in the urban areas. Water brought to the interior by the Central Arizona Project already is beginning to alleviate the shortfall in Maricopa County. Other problems associated with rapid population growth and economic change remain challenges as well. Yet Arizona has powerful resources to muster in the search for solutions to these problems. In this state ethnic diversity has produced cohesion rather than division. And Arizona has been blessed since the end of World War II with some extraordinary political leadership, on both the state and national levels. Above all, Arizonans of all ages are vigorous, independent, and civic in their attitudes.

With its economic, educational, and human resources, Arizona looks forward with confidence to its next 76 years of statehood and beyond. Leading that progress are the state's businesses, institutions of learning, and local government. The organizations whose histories are related on the following pages have chosen to support this important literary and civic project. They illustrate the variety of ways in which individuals and their businesses have contributed to Arizona's development, making the state an excellent place to live and work.

The Quechan Indian band, shown here in 1925, performed throughout Arizona and marched in presidential inaugural parades. The band is composed entirely of native Indians from the Fort Yuma Indian (Quechan) Reservation, which was established in 1884 at the site of Fort Yuma, across the Colorado River from Yuma. Courtesy, Arizona Historical Society, Yuma

ARIZONA HISTORICAL SOCIETY

The Arizona Historical Society's current headquarters at 949 East Second Street, Tucson. George Chambers, longtime supporter of the society, salvaged the stone facade from the San Agustín Church when it was demolished in 1936. He donated it to the society, and it was installed on the front of the building in the mid-1970s.

Founded in Tucson in 1884 as the Society of Arizona Pioneers, the Arizona Historical Society is the state's oldest cultural organization.

A year before the passage of legislation that created the University of Arizona and present-day Arizona State University, the territory's Anglo and Hispanic frontiersmen banded together to preserve the memory of their accomplishments. To this end they urged other pioneers to write down their recollections, which would then be preserved in a permanent archive. They also set about collecting territorial records, public documents, and, later, some works of history. And, from the beginning, they assembled the artifacts of the early years—from furniture and clothing, wagons and tack, to the armor of the Spanish conquistadores. These early acquisitions formed the core of what is today one of the finest research collections in the Southwest.

The primary focus of the society in its first 105 years has been the collection of the artifacts and documents of state history, and their preservation for future generations of Arizonans. This mission involves the Arizona Historical Society in a variety of efforts, including publication of books, a bimonthly magazine, and a quarterly scholarly journal; statewide education programs; and the maintenance of libraries and museums in all regions of the state.

In Tucson, where the society's headquarters is located, the library and archives contain more than 2,000 collections of private papers, diaries, journals, letters, and business and government records; 90,000 bound volumes, pamphlets, and newspapers; and more than 500,000 photographs dating from the 1870s to the 1950s. The museum collections include hundreds of thousands of artifacts reflecting every phase of life and endeavor. The society also owns or maintains a number of historic buildings that are in use as museums or operated as commercial properties.

The Arizona Pioneers' Historical Society rented this space in the Consolidated Bank Building for $15 in 1903. This was the society's home until 1922.

The society's collections are supplemented by regional division repositories in Phoenix, Flagstaff, and Yuma—each of which has archives related to the geographic area in which it is located. The Phoenix division preserves the family and business papers of longtime Salt River Valley residents, together with more than 100,000 photographs. The Yuma library and archives contain about 120 shelf feet of regional records and 5,000 photographs. The Flagstaff museum houses materials on early land, timber, and cattle companies, as well as the papers of Michael J. Riordan, George Hochderffer, and other pioneers.

Expansion of the society's facilities is under way at the Hubbel Trading Post in Winslow and the Douglas/Williams House in Douglas.

With a large staff of professionals and volunteers, and public and private funding, the Arizona Historical Society today is a far cry from the organization founded by Arizona pioneers more than a century ago. But its mission—the preservation of the state's historic past—is as timely and important as ever.

KCEE RADIO

This photo taken in the early days of KCEE Radio featured (second from left) Dan Russel, who prepared bits of programming dealing with proper pronunciation; David Drubeck, the guiding hand in the establishment of KCEE; Cliff Gill, who held an interest in the station and was an engineering adviser; and Ray Owen, manager of KCEE from its inception to 1967 and now with WAPA in San Juan, Puerto Rico. The man on the left is unidentified.

KCEE Radio was founded in 1958 by Associated Broadcasters of Tucson, whose principals were Cliff Gill, Dave Drubeck, and Barney Sorkin. Gill was general manager of Metro Media's flagship station in Los Angeles and chairman of the Radio Code Review Board for the National Association of Broadcasters, the board responsible for writing the code of ethics for the radio industry. Drubeck, a radio station music director, also was a jazz musician with the Benny Goodman orchestra. Sorkin was a society band leader in Los Angeles.

KCEE went on the air with 1,000 watts of daytime power, at 790 on the AM dial, with a beautiful-music format. It was the first beautiful-music station in Tucson. Its principals constructed the original studio building and two towers at 2100 North Silverbell Road. A third tower was added in 1962 in order to boost daytime power to 5,000 watts and add nighttime service of 750 watts.

In 1965 Associated Broadcasters sold the station to Strauss Broadcasting. The purchase price of $395,000 included a construction permit to build an FM station. Robert A. Strauss, president of the company, was very active in the community both in politics and in civic activities. His father, Robert S. Strauss, vice-president of the company, was chairman of the National Democratic Party and served the Carter Administration as an adviser and as federal trade representative.

In 1966 Strauss Broadcasting built the KCEE-FM towers and studio on South Alvernon

Way. The FM station later was sold to Lotus Broadcasting and was renamed KLPX.

A partnership named 790 Inc. acquired KCEE from Strauss Broadcasting in 1980 for $1.3 million. The principal owners were Dennis Behan, Marvin Strait, Sam Young, and Steve Jacobs. Jacobs, the general manager of an AM/FM radio station in San Diego, moved to Tucson to become KCEE general manager. The new owners changed KCEE's programming to an all-oldies format. Later they added current music to become an adult-contemporary radio station.

In 1984, four years after purchasing KCEE, 790 Inc. acquired Tucson radio station KWFM from Sandusky Newspapers for $4.5 million. At the same time the partnership merged its holdings with those of other Behan stations under the corporate name of Behan Broadcasting.

Behan Broadcasting sold both KCEE and KWFM to American Media in 1987 for $10 million. American Media, a Long Island-based corporation, has radio stations in six cities. Alan Beck and Art Kern are the principals. Laury Browning, who became general manager for Behan Broadcasting in 1985, retained his position for American Media.

KCEE is a full-service adult-contemporary radio station that has been a part of the Tucson entertainment scene for nearly three decades. The station has served the best interests of a generation of Tucsonans, and counts on continuing its service for years to come.

RALPH'S TRANSFER, INC.

A few years ago Ralph's Transfer, Inc., got an unusual job: The firm was hired to move a 1925 Boeing fighter plane from the Pima Air Museum outside Tucson to the Smithsonian Institution in Washington, D.C.

The fragile aircraft, virtually the only one of its type still in existence, had to be disassembled—wings unbolted from the fuselage, engine taken out, tail assembly removed—before it could be packed onto the transcontinental moving van. On the other end, more than 2,000 miles away, the process was reversed and the plane was put back together again, not a bit the worse for wear.

The skill involved in the move of this rare airplane is typical of Ralph's Transfer, Arizona's oldest agent for northAmerican Van Lines. The firm is equipped to handle the transport of all kinds of goods, from the smallest and most fragile to the largest and heaviest.

Ralph's Transfer was founded in 1926 by Ralph Montiel, a native of the Mexican city of Alamos in the state of Sonora. Originally named Ralph's Transfer & Storage Co.—Montiel gave the firm his first name because, he said, every-

Ralph's Transfer & Storage Co. shortly after it became affiliated with northAmerican Van Lines, with the old adobe warehouse in the background.

one in town knew him that way—the enterprise was located on Fifth Street west of Stone Avenue. Montiel started with a Model T Ford truck and a Republic truck, and began hauling both locally and statewide. Ralph's became an affiliate of northAmerican Van Lines in 1947.

The period of the company's most dynamic growth began in 1973, when Fred Stang and Marie Wicks purchased Ralph's Transfer from Fermin Montiel, son of the founder, and moved its offices and main warehouse to its present location at 747 South Freeway. Both Mr. Stang and Mrs. Wicks had come to Tucson in the 1950s and had backgrounds in the moving business before the purchase. Ralph's currently employs between 80 and 100 people and operates more than 100 vehicles, and the firm continues to grow.

With the advent of deregulated transportation in Arizona in the 1970s, Ralph's expanded into all facets of transportation—the company even had a helicopter at one time—and into various nontransport activities. In addition to moving statewide in its own equipment and nationally through its affiliation with northAmerican, Ralph's operates up to 650,000 square feet of warehouse space in Tucson. The firm owns more than 250,000 square feet of this total in three Tucson locations; the rest is leased.

As Tucson's electronics industry has expanded since the late 1970s, Ralph's has been increasingly involved in moving computers and other equipment for those companies. Special air-ride trailers are used in the moves, and this aspect of the business amounts to several million dollars annually. For other customers, Ralph's has been a local pioneer in the "customer load/company haul" program, in association with northAmerican. This cost-saving innovation has been very well received.

Every year since 1983 Ralph's Transfer, Inc., has been honored by northAmerican with its Commitment to Excellence Award. In 1985 this honor went only to the top 26 of northAmerican's agencies nationwide—and there are more than 900 northAmerican agencies. The award is appropriate recognition for a business that always puts its best foot forward.

Ralph's Transfer, Inc., bears the name of its owner, Ralph Montiel, who founded the firm in 1926. Shown are the offices in 1973.

EVERGREEN AIR CENTER

Not long ago a Boeing 747 flew into Marana Air Park, headquarters for Evergreen Air Center. The plane, recalls one senior Evergreen employee, was "an empty tube" behind the pilots' area. Eight weeks and 40,000 man-hours later, the same 747 emerged completely refitted, transformed from a shell to one of the most luxurious aircraft in the sky, ready to inaugurate a new route from Dallas, Texas, to Tokyo, Japan.

Modification of a large commercial aircraft is one of the things Evergreen Air Center does best. Aircraft maintenance on all levels is another. With a force of about 400 mechanics—80 percent of the firm's total number of employees—Evergreen is one of the top-ranked businesses in the United States in both maintenance and modification. Its employees are recruited nationwide, and its technical people are licensed by federal agencies. Because of Evergreen's total aircraft capability and the quality of its work, some people say it's the best company in the business.

Evergreen moved to Pinal Air Park in 1975, after its parent firm, Evergreen International, bought out Intermountain Air, a regional freight carrier also engaged in aircraft maintenance and modification. The air park, which is leased from Pinal County, dates from World War II, when military aviators were trained there. It is 2,080 acres in size, large enough not only for Evergreen's service functions but also for aircraft storage and for the cutting up, for parts and scrap, of airplanes and helicopters that are no longer serviceable.

At any single time there are apt to be four or five aircraft receiving more or less major modifications at Evergreen. Many more are there for scheduled inspections and maintenance, whether "C" checks, which require seven to 10 days to complete, or "D" checks, which take six weeks. Some helicopters are in for rotor work. Some fixed-wing aircraft are there simply for painting and refinishing.

However, Evergreen's aircraft-related work occupies only part of the Pinal Air Park area. Much of the rest of it is leased by Evergreen to various federal agencies for training purposes. One tenant is the National Advance Resource Technology Center, where U.S. Forest Service supervisors are trained. The Western Zone Fire Cache, a depot for Forest Service fire-fighting equipment, is located there. At the Federal Law Enforcement Training Center, also an Evergreen tenant, U.S. Customs Service agents and

employees of other federal law-enforcement agencies receive training. The Bureau of Indian Affairs also maintains its national police academy there.

Pinal Air Park is an attractive location for these agencies because of its remoteness and the space that is available for such things as driver's training for law enforcement officers. An average of 150 people receive training through these agencies at any single time. To accommodate them, Evergreen provides a motel and restaurant that can serve as many as 300 people at a meal.

A leader in its field, Evergreen Air Center is growing fast to keep up with the industry it serves.

Evergreen Air Center in Marana serves as a training school for hundreds of law enforcement trainees each year.

Evergreen's hangar area will accommodate the largest airplanes flying today.

W.L. GORE & ASSOCIATES, INC.

The physical distance separating Arizona and the earth's moon is vast, yet the creative human mind is able to leap this void in an instant. Such inspiration and insight have always propelled a stream of innovative products from W.L. Gore & Associates, a privately owned high-technology company with divisions in Phoenix and Flagstaff.

GORE-TEX® wire and cable assemblies manufactured in Arizona accompanied the U.S. Apollo Moon Lander on its historic journey into the cold of space for mankind's first step onto another world. From the immense reaches of space to the warm worlds within us requires another leap of the imagination, but Gore Associates in Arizona have pioneered these regions as well. GORE-TEX® Vascular Grafts (synthetic blood vessels) replace diseased arteries carrying blood to save limbs—and lives. Where the human body is pushed to its physical limits at the outer rim of the world is likewise familiar

Microwave coaxial cable assemblies, manufactured by W.L. Gore & Associates, Inc., in Phoenix and Flagstaff, are space qualified and have operated in a wide variety of spacecraft without failure.

Signals transmitted through GORE-TEX® insulated flat cables operate the cargo bay arm on the Space Shuttle Columbia's manned space flights.

terrain to the Gore organization. Mountaineering expeditions worldwide overwhelmingly rely on GORE-TEX® fabric outerwear to cope with extremes of weather at high elevations.

The time is 1967; Bill Gore and his wife, companion, and business partner, Vieve, have set out, map in hand, from Newark, Delaware, the base of operations for their wire and cable business. They are on their way west to establish a manufacturing plant to serve West Coast customers. The trip is a successful one. All the places circled on their map have been carefully evaluated in rational business terms—market size, suppliers, distance to markets. And yet there is that one place on the road that draws them back—a place of towering peaks, cool pines, and haunting beauty; a place where a millennium of human culture left its mark on the ageless bare stone; a place where raw frontier grit raised a modern civilization among tall trees sighing in the wind.

Bill and Vieve Gore returned to this place, Flagstaff, and purchased the 37 forested acres that four of the seven Arizona plants of W.L. Gore & Associates occupy today. There Gore Associates started producing insulated wire, and round and ribbon cables—a modest beginning for an Arizona division that would, by 1987, grow to 800 associates and be the largest commercial enterprise in the city. However, that was still far in the future. Events and inventions unleashed by the Gore philosophy of enterprise—self-motivation, commitment, open communication—would first intervene to catapult the firm toward the twenty-first century.

The Gore business had always been based on fabricating unique products from polytetrafluoroethylene (PTFE), more widely known as Teflon®. Bill and Vieve's son, Bob, revolutionized the business in 1969 with a method for expanding PTFE. This unforeseen event soon had Gore Associates fabricating unheard-of products from the new material—fibers so tough and resistant to temperature extremes they were woven into the space suits of NASA astronauts, filters and seals immune to chemical attack, and membrane filters to clean up the emissions of industrial America, to name a few.

The restless innovation that had become the hallmark of the company took another unanticipated turn in the early spring of 1971 at a ski resort in Vail, Colorado. It was there that Bill Gore showed a piece of GORE-TEX® expanded PTFE to Ben Eiseman, M.D., of the University

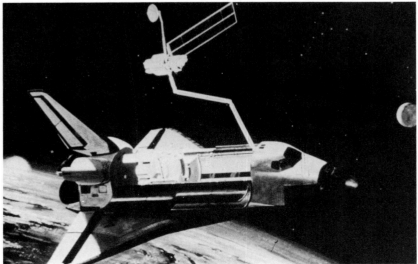

of Colorado. Working with Gore Associates in Flagstaff, Eiseman had great success with GORE-TEX® tubes used as blood vessel substitutes in pigs.

Late that year a woman came to Denver General Hospital with a cancerous tumor invading a major blood vessel of the abdomen. The previously inoperable tumor was removed and a GORE-TEX® tube substituted for the vessel. Two weeks later she walked out of the hospital, the first patient of what would be millions worldwide to receive a GORE-TEX® medical implant.

Gore Associates soon tested and perfected other devices made of expanded PTFE to sustain diseased or injured body structures— patches to reinforce the body wall, artificial knee ligaments, sutures, and dental materials to overcome the effects of periodontal disease.

By 1973 Gore engineers had designed machines to stretch GORE-TEX® membrane wide enough to be incorporated into many fabrics. Boots, gloves, hats, and coats of windproof, waterproof, and breathable GORE-TEX® fabric appeared and were everywhere adopted by outdoor enthusiasts. They have sailed with Jeff MacInnis through Canada's Northwest Passage in a 20-foot boat, ascended Mt. Everest with

John Roskelley on his climb, accompanied Steve Newman on a four-year walk around the world, and raced across America in less than nine days with bicycle marathoners.

The fabrication of soft, flexible, expanded PTFE led to a quiet revolution in the Electronics Products Division as well. Insulated wire and cable to carry digital signals at 93 percent of the speed of light were designed for supercomputers. GORE-TEX® cables were built to transmit the signals that operated the arm on the cargo bay of the space shuttle and to participate in the fly-by of Jupiter on the Voyager spacecraft. GORE-TEX® wire and cable was designed for neighborhoods as well. Miles of it in the electronic switches at the local telephone company ensure that calls go through as dialed.

Unharnessing the creative mind; being fair to customers, suppliers, and fellow associates; having the freedom to dream—and the ability to make those dreams come true—are elements of the culture of W.L. Gore & Associates, Inc. A sense of adventure pervades all aspects of the company's operations uniting its past, present, and future.

GORE-TEX® is a trademark of W.L. Gore and Associates, Inc. Teflon® is a trademark of E.I. du Pont de Nemours Company, Inc.

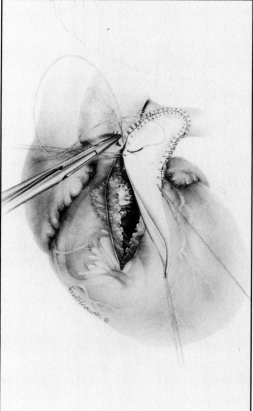

GORE-TEX® Cardiovascular Patch makes repair of congenital heart defects possible, allowing a baby's life to unfold and blossom while transforming a parent's despair into joy.

Even under extremes of exertion, fabrics made of waterproof, breathable GORE-TEX® keep the wearer dry on the rocks.

SHAMROCK FOODS COMPANY

Winifred and William T. McClelland, founders. Photo circa 1918

Shamrock Foods Company, the nation's ninth-largest institutional food distribution firm, is a hardy Tucson native. In its 65 years of life, the company has left an important mark on the city, the state, and the West.

The firm began in 1922 as Shamrock Dairy. Its founder, W. T. McClelland, was a native of County Down, Ireland, who spent his early years on his family's small farm, raising potatoes and keeping a small herd of cows, sheep, and hogs. Orphaned at the age of 17, McClelland came to the United States four years later and settled near the town of Oracle, Arizona, a few miles north of Tucson. The year was 1912. Arizona was a brand-new state, and optimism was in the air everywhere.

McClelland worked briefly on a ranch, then took a job in Tucson with a man who ran a holstein dairy. There he worked—with time out for service in the U.S. Army in France during World War I and in Germany after the war—until 1920, when he bought the Modern Dairy. That same year he married Winifred Parker. In 1921 he sold the dairy and moved with his wife to California, but returned the following year and founded Shamrock Dairy on Ruthrauff Road, northwest of Tucson. The love McClelland and his wife bore for their homeland accounted for the dairy's name, but their hard work and sensible management were responsible for its astonishing growth and diversification.

"Mr. Mac," as he was known, began Shamrock Dairy with a herd of 20 cows and a Model T truck. He milked the cows twice daily, at 3 a.m. and at noon, and Earl Bates, the first route driver, would start deliveries immediately after the milking was done. There were between 40 and 50 customers, and milk—bottled only in pint and quart glass bottles—sold for 12 cents a quart. Mrs. McClelland kept the books and sometimes helped out in the little plant.

Business prospered. Mr. Mac added his second route in 1925, before the dairy was three years old. The third came three years later. By 1933, when W.J. Parker, Mrs. McClelland's brother, came from California to join the organization, there were four routes—three retail and one wholesale. Mr. Mac had already begun his guernsey herd, in which he took a special pride and interest; the herd grew to become, at its peak, one of the largest in the country. Shamrock also had begun improving its technology, adding first a pasteurizer, then a rotary bottle-filler and bottle-washer. These were only the first of a series of technological improvements and innovations that have continued, in ever-increasing numbers, until the present day.

By 1933 the dairy had 10 employees. Mr. and Mrs. McClelland also had become parents. Their son, Norman P. McClelland, is now president of Shamrock Foods, and their daughter, Frances, is secretary/treasurer.

Good management kept Shamrock Dairy growing during the Great Depression, and the growth of Tucson and southern Arizona during World War II led the business to expand. Between 1949 and 1953 Shamrock established service in Benson, Bisbee, Douglas, Nogales, Gila Bend, Ajo, Yuma, and San Manuel. In 1954 three delivery routes were established in the Phoenix area, selling milk packaged in Tucson. Two years later Shamrock opened a processing plant in Phoenix from which the entire metropolitan area was served. Meanwhile, growth continued in central, southern, and western Arizona, fueled in part by the acquisition of land and additional dairy properties. By 1965 Shamrock was supplying more than 30 percent of the total volume of dairy products in Arizona.

The 1960s saw expansion into many new communities, from San Luis on the Mexican border to Flagstaff. At the same time the company began diversifying its products. Ice cream had been added in 1959. Six years later the acquisition of a distribution and foods operation made Shamrock a distributor of retail frozen-food products and led to the development of Shamrock's foods division, which delivered institutional foods to northwestern Arizona, Phoe-

The Dairy Division in Phoenix and Tucson, Arizona.

nix and its surrounding area, and Tucson and southern Arizona.

The twin patterns of geographical expansion and product diversification have continued, matched every step of the way with the use of the most advanced, state-of-the-art technology in food production, packaging, and transportation. Under the banner of Shamrock Foods Company, a new corporate structure created in 1967 to embrace all the varied activities of the firm, the corporation today markets food products and supplies in 10 states: Arizona, Colorado, California, Wyoming, Kansas, Nebraska, Utah, Texas, Nevada, and New Mexico. Its goods range from the fine dairy products that first established the good name of Shamrock through fresh and frozen meats and fish, orange juice, bottled water, canned and dry groceries, delicatessen items, produce, and a complete line of more than 4,000 restaurant supplies and equipment. Shamrock Foods does more than $300 million in business per year.

As Arizona has been good to Shamrock, so Shamrock has been an excellent corporate citizen in return. In 1968 scholarships in the name of W.T. and Winifred McClelland were established for worthy upperclassmen or graduate students in the University of Arizona's College of Agriculture. In 1976 the company endowed McClelland Educational Park in the Flowing Wells School District in Tucson. In 1983 the McClelland family pledged the sum of $300,000 to endow the McClelland Centennial Professorship in the Karl Eller Center at the University of Arizona's College of Business and Public Administration. The endowment is intended to fund a preeminent national scholar in the university's business college.

Mr. Mac died in 1968, four years before his company marked the beginning of its second half-century. His wife followed him in death nine years later. Yet their spirit lingers still in a firm that is never too large to care for the quality of its goods and the services it provides, nor too impersonal to take an interest in each of its

Norman P. McClelland, president of Shamrock Foods Company, and son W. Kent McClelland, president of the Colorado Division.

employees. As company president Norman P. McClelland recently wrote, "It is the intent of the owners and management of Shamrock Foods Company to conduct our business so as to warrant and merit the respect, understanding, and esteem of all our customers, employees, and of the people in communities that we are privileged to serve."

The Foods Division in Phoenix, Arizona, and Commerce City, Colorado.

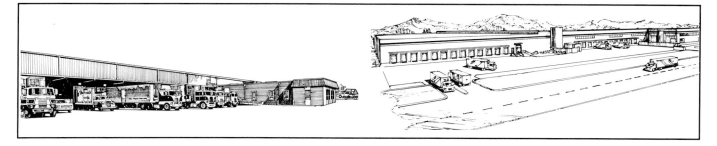

GOLDEN EAGLE DISTRIBUTORS INC.

In August 1985 Golden Eagle Distributors broke ground for its new headquarters at 705 East Ajo Way on Tucson's south side. On hand were all of the company's executives and over 100 employees from around the state. Also in attendance were various photographers, who later documented every step in the 20-month construction project. However, one presence nearly always available at such ceremonial occasions was missing; there were no alcoholic beverages.

For William M. Clements, president and chief executive officer of Golden Eagle Distributors Inc., Tucson's largest beer distributor, the decision was entirely in character. Clements, who is very proud of the quality Anheuser-Busch beers that he sells, is also keenly aware that there are some people who abuse them. It is for this reason that he has implemented many comprehensive programs to encourage the responsible use of his products.

Clements and his father, the late Dudley Clements, founded Golden Eagle Distributors in 1974, as an adjunct to All American Distributing

Co., a Phoenix-based wholesaler of liquor, beer, and wine that once operated statewide. Golden Eagle's focus was more specific. The new business was directed exclusively toward the sale of beer; specifically the products of Anheuser-Busch, brewers of Budweiser, Bud Light, Michelob, and other malt beverages.

Golden Eagle was originally located at Golf Links Road and the Aviation Highway, on Tucson's southeast side. However, before long the size and logistical needs of the operation made moving a necessity. Clements and his father already had bought the land on Ajo Way, convenient to rail service and only a few blocks off Interstate 10. It was there that they built a new headquarters in 1975, designed—as Clements says—"to provide adequate space for a long time to come." This original structure contained 29,000 square feet. The company outgrew it in only seven years. In the spring of 1982, 80,000 square feet of warehouse space was added, and in the winter of 1987 a 45,000-square-foot addition brought Golden Eagle's expansion to completion. The new building

Ground was broken for Golden Eagle Distributors' new headquarters building at 705 East Ajo Way, Tucson, in 1985.

stands on the site of the old, and incorporates the earlier structure.

Growth and change have gone hand in hand. Clements is now out of the liquor distributing business (All American was sold in 1982). However, Golden Eagle has grown from a Tucson business to a statewide concern that has branch operations in Casa Grande, Buckeye, Flagstaff, Holbrook, and Globe. Several of those branches also are expanding. The Tucson operation is headquarters for the state, and serves southeastern Arizona and the entire metropolitan Tucson area.

As a distributorship, Golden Eagle supplies its retail customers while serving their needs. Its warehouse, designed by Clements to conserve maximum refrigeration, is capable of stocking one million cases of beer. Inventory is computerized, and the Tucson operation takes care of ordering for its branches statewide. However, there are less obvious aspects of service that the company provides. Although Anheuser-Busch produces its own national ad-

vertising, Golden Eagle often localizes for the different communities it serves. It also provides training in beer handling, along with personal touches such as repair and rehabilitation of customers' old glass bar signs that are no longer functional.

Tucson and Arizona have been good to Golden Eagle, and Golden Eagle, in turn, has been good to them. The firm now employs over 185 people statewide and does $70 million in business per year. Golden Eagle Distributors Inc., under the direction of its energetic chief executive, William M. Clements, can be counted on to roll up its sleeves and pitch in on virtually any worthy civic cause. These organizations and groups encompass the areas of education, health care, leadership development, medical research, and cultural enrichment.

Golden Eagle continually meets the new challenges of today, while striving for higher levels of excellence. Golden Eagle has made a commitment to selling quality products and being a good corporate citizen.

Today, after additional expansions, Golden Eagle Distributors' headquarters (shown here) and branches in Casa Grande, Buckeye, Flagstaff, Holbrook, and Globe service metropolitan Tucson and southeastern Arizona. Courtesy, Chris Mooney, Balfour Walker Photography

EAGLE MILLING COMPANY

The Eagle Milling Company, Arizona's largest supplier of feed grains for livestock of all kinds, is one of Tucson's oldest businesses. The firm traces its origins back to the time just after the Gadsden Purchase added Tucson to the map of the United States and before Arizona was created as a federal territory in 1863.

In 1857 Alfred M. and William M. Rowlett built a dam on the Santa Cruz River and began milling flour. In the course of the next half-century, at least four prominent southern Arizona pioneers owned the property and enlarged the mills, interweaving the story of the business and their own stories with the history of the region.

One of these men was William S. Grant, a major contractor for the U.S. Army in Arizona before the Civil War, who lost everything when the soldiers withdrew eastward to fight, burning their posts—and Grant's mills—so they would not fall into Confederate hands. After the war Charles Trumbull Hayden, the founder of Tempe and father of the later Senator Carl Hayden, owned the property. His successors built a steam mill, one of the early marvels of industrial Tucson. They, in turn, sold the business and mill to Edward Nye Fish, one of Tucson's most notable early entrepreneurs. Fish sold it to Leo Goldschmidt, who first gave the firm the Eagle Milling Company name. In 1899 Goldschmidt built a new mill on Toole Avenue, on the northernmost edge of the city by the railroad tracks. His family owned the business until after Arizona became a state. Ownership then passed to the Viault family, owners of flour mills in Phoenix and Mesa, and subsequently to a group of associates headed by T.J. Melczer.

Until the 1930s the principal output of the mills was flour from Arizona wheat. It was a perfect family baking flour; Chinese grocers retailed it, big ranches bought it by the ton, Indian

villages subsisted on it, and the flour tortilla, an innovation of northern Sonoran and Arizona cooking, was made from it. But since Arizona wheat is only semihard, it was less than perfect for commercial baking, and, as bakeries turned to wheat from the Midwest, the company, by now called the Arizona Flour Mills, began moving toward production of feed grains.

This departure necessitated research, which led to the establishment of the first feed company experimental farm in the West, as well as to the improvement of storage facilities necessary for several types of grains. By the early 1940s the firm was producing a salt-limited range feed that enabled ranchers to increase the size of their herds on the same land. Good weight gains and improved calf production also resulted. Soon this grain and others were being marketed throughout the Southwest and northern Mexico.

Research and improvements continued. In 1955 Arizona Flour Mills became one of the first organizations in the United States licensed to use diethylstilbestrol, a growth-stimulating hormone, in beef feed rations. By that time a separate but affiliated company already had been created to produce and market a particularly successful feed supplement first made by Arizona Flour Mills. This firm eventually merged with its parent under the name Arizona Feeds. Rapid expansion and diversification followed, and the company passed into out-of-state ownership. An Arizona-based firm purchased Arizona Feeds in 1985, returning ownership and control to local people. In recognition of this new beginning, the corporation took the name it had borne 90 years ago—Eagle Milling Company.

Under the Arizona Feeds label, Eagle Milling today provides a full range of feed products for animals of all types, including cattle, horses, poultry, swine, pet food, fish food, and bird seed. Its products include feed-lot supplements, poultry feed, rolled grain for dairy cattle, seed for wild birds, and a wide variety of specialty products. Eagle has mills in Tucson and Casa Grande, several warehouses throughout the state, and five retail outlets covering the state from Flagstaff to Yuma. In addition, some 80 dealers throughout Arizona carry its products.

Eagle Milling Company, a firm born on the frontier in the nineteenth century, looks forward to continuing to serve the needs of ranchers, feed-lot operators, and owners of backyard livestock in the twenty-first century.

The new Eagle Flour Mills were completed in May 1899, establishing the Eagle Milling Company as one of Tucson's oldest business enterprises.

ARIZONA STATE SAVINGS AND CREDIT UNION

It all started in October 1951, with 10 charter members and an office in a desk drawer at the Industrial Commission of Arizona. Today the Arizona State Savings and Credit Union has more than 50,000 members—a figure that places it among the 200 largest of America's 17,000 credit unions. It employs a staff of 100 in eight offices throughout Arizona, and its resources now exceed $150 million. Without doubt, this is one of Arizona's most exciting success stories.

The slow early progress of the organization gave little indication of such future growth, however. Three months after its charter was granted, the credit union had coaxed only 74 state employees into joining. Almost five years passed before the membership reached 1,000. The first full-time manager, Martha Hayes, was appointed in April 1957 and resigned 18 months later. The next two managers had even shorter tenures.

What turned around the fortunes of the Arizona State Savings and Credit Union was the appointment of R.C. "Dick" Robertson as manager on November 1, 1959. Robertson, who had organized a credit union at the Reynolds Metals Co. plant at Troutdale, Oregon, used an intriguing mix of enthusiasm, philosophy, sound professional methods, and outstanding leadership abilities to put the organization on the road to success.

Within three years he had persuaded the membership to erect its own building near the state capitol at 1812 West Monroe Street in Phoenix—expandable to accommodate rapid growth—and put together a management team that brought new members in by the thousands.

New offices of the credit union were opened in Prescott, Flagstaff, at Metro Tech in Phoenix, Arizona State University in Tempe, and two in Tucson. A new East Valley office officially opened in Mesa on February 22, 1988.

State and university employees and their families have found the Arizona State Savings and Credit Union meets their needs for many kinds of loans: automobile, education, personal, and real estate, to name a few. The loss rate on these loans over the years has been less than three-quarters of one percent—an amazingly good record.

Little wonder that Dick Robertson has been the only person ever elected president of every major state, national, and international credit union association, and that he was named national Credit Union Executive of the Year for 1986-1987.

This unique financial cooperative organization is building upon its success and is committed to serving the savings, credit, and financial needs of its members throughout Arizona in the future.

R.C. "Dick" Robertson, president, has headed the organization since 1959.

Headquarters offices of the Arizona State Savings and Credit Union are housed in this building at 1812 West Monroe Street in Phoenix.

THOMAS-DAVIS MEDICAL CENTERS, P.C.

Founded in 1920 as the Thomas-Davis Clinic, the health care organization is now known as the Thomas-Davis Medical Centers with its main facility, shown here, and six other branches in the Tucson area plus one in Tempe and one in Green Valley.

The Thomas-Davis Clinic, as it was previously known, for decades one of Tucson's primary providers of health care, was founded in 1920 by Charles Anselm Thomas, M.D., a surgeon, and Stirley C. Davis, an internist. Neither man was a native Arizonan. Thomas, born in Mississippi, practiced medicine in Oklahoma before moving to Arizona in 1912 for his wife's health. He set up his practice in Tucson on February 12 of that year, the same day Arizona became the nation's 48th state. Davis, a native of Kentucky, practiced in that state and in Oklahoma before moving to Arizona in 1920.

The clinic first was located in the building, on Pennington Street near Stone Avenue, where Thomas had his offices. Later that year the two physicians moved to the new Roskruge Hotel (since demolished), at the corner of Broadway and Scott Street. At that time they still constituted the entire medical staff of the clinic. However, the organization grew in the 1920s—and outgrew its quarters. In 1928 Thomas and Davis built a new facility at 130 South Scott Avenue. When the clinic moved early the following year, there were six physicians.

In the 1930s Tucson was a small city, both in its population and its physical size. Activity centered downtown, and nearly all the doctors had their offices there. Interestingly, more than half of those practicing at that time began their professional lives in the Thomas-Davis Clinic or the Tucson Clinic.

In the early years of this century many people with tuberculosis came to Arizona seeking a cure in the mild, dry climate. But medical facilities to serve them were too few and often too expensive. In 1931 Drs. Thomas and Davis converted an old railroad warehouse into a tuber-

culosis sanitorium. This facility eventually became the Southern Pacific Hospital and finally Carl Hayden Hospital, and was staffed by clinic doctors for a number of years.

World War II brought change and growth to Tucson, and Thomas-Davis Clinic grew and changed as well. New doctors joined the staff. Even before the war most clinic physicians became partners rather than employees. Soon the clinic began to outgrow its quarters. The eye and pediatric departments moved across the street into the old Santa Rita Hotel, but that helped only for a while. In 1960 planning began for a new facility at East Fifth Street and North Alvernon Way. With the help of Fred Emery, a former Tucson mayor who was then the clinic's executive director, the proper zoning was obtained and the building erected. March 9, 1962, a Friday, was the last day in the old clinic; Monday, March 12th, was the first day in the new one. The staff then included 17 doctors.

And Thomas-Davis Medical Centers has kept right on growing. In 1979 an office was opened in Green Valley; five years later another was started in Tempe. Meanwhile, the main facility in Tucson has been enlarged three times, and a total of six branches around the city have been opened. The medical staff now amounts to more than 80 people. Moreover, Thomas-Davis owns and operates Intergroup, a health maintenance organization that today accounts for 45 percent of all the practice of Thomas-Davis physicians.

Thomas-Davis Medical Centers today is still what it has been for nearly 70 years—a mainstay of Tucson's health care community and a good citizen wherever it operates.

MESSINGER MORTUARY & CHAPEL, INC.

In the days before Scottsdale developed into a world-renowned resort city, former Arizona State Representative Paul R. Messinger went about his daily tasks of milking the cows at the family's Grade A dairy located on 20 acres of land at the southeast corner of Miller and Indian School roads, where the city's first mortuary, Messinger Mortuary & Chapel, now stands.

When the mortuary opened its doors on May 10, 1959, Indian School Road was still a two-lane paved country road bounded on the south by a major irrigation ditch and on the north by a wastewater ditch lined with pomegranate trees. Miller Road had just been paved, and the new mortuary was still surrounded by a dairy farm, an alfalfa field, and new building projects of Our Lady of Perpetual Help Church. The Messinger family had sold the 10-acre parcel in 1955 to the Catholic diocese.

The summer before the mortuary was built, when Scottsdale was less than one square mile in size, the Messinger family asked the city to annex their 10 acres at Miller and Indian School roads so that the proposed mortuary could be inspected by the town's only building inspector, Walter Donn, because Maricopa County did no inspections. The city fathers agreed to rezone the property only if the family agreed to provide Scottsdale with 24-hour-a-day, seven-day-a-week ambulance service, which they did until 1968. At one time the Messingers operated five ambulances, with the service being the first commercially operated service in the city.

Messinger Mortuary & Chapel, Inc., 7601 East Indian School Road, is a family business founded by the Messinger family: Paul R. Messinger, funeral director and embalmer; his wife, Cora R., corporate secretary in charge of general office operation; William H. Messinger, treasurer, with wife, Vera F. Messinger, who died in 1987 and 1980, respectively; and Paul's brother, Philip W. Messinger, vice-president. However, it is Paul and Cora Messinger, and their son Kendrick, a licensed funeral director, embalmer, and vice-president, who are actively involved in the business today.

During the first year of operation the Messingers had only two employees, Ray Morehead and Jerry Bullock. They served 75 families that first year; today, more than a quarter-century later, there are 20 employees and more than 14,000 families have been served.

The Messingers joined with four other funeral directors and two individuals to start Paradise Memorial Gardens, 9300 East Shea Boulevard, in 1968. The city granted zoning, but the state denied a state license. Court action followed with the Arizona Supreme Court ruling in favor of the applicants, thus paving the way for the cemetery and the first interment in February 1974. Nine years later the Messingers became the sole owners of Paradise Memorial Gardens, a 40-acre cemetery.

Paul Messinger served on the Scottsdale City Council from 1971 to 1976 and as vice-mayor from 1974 to 1975. He was chairman of the citizens committee that brought Scottsdale Community College to Scottsdale, served on Scottsdale's first airport advisory commission, served three terms in the Arizona House of Representatives (1979 to 1985), and both Paul and son Ken have served as directors of national professional associations.

Scottsdale's first mortuary, Messinger Mortuary and Chapel, on Indian School Road, opened its doors in May 1959.

The 40-acre Paradise Memorial Gardens, on East Shea Boulevard, is another Messinger family enterprise.

TUCSON MEDICAL CENTER

Tucson Medical Center, the largest hospital in southern Arizona, has grown up with the city whose name it bears. Its history is intertwined with Tucson's, even as it is with the story of 60 years of medical progress. For much of that time TMC has been what it preeminently is today—an institution at the forefront of medical development, especially in the area of patient care.

The Desert Sanatorium, the institution from which TMC grew, was founded in 1925 by Dr. Bernard L. Wyatt as a tuberculosis sanatorium and research center. It originally consisted of four separate units, each built around an open court and containing eight to 12 rooms with individual screened porches, used for heliotherapy or prescribed sunbathing, which was believed then to cure tuberculosis. Two years later Alfred W. Erickson, a New York advertising executive, provided funds for four additional patient units and two other buildings, one used for outpatients and research, the other as a residence for nurses. In 1927 Erickson and his wife took over the project, built themselves a home on the property, and became frequent

The main entrance to the Desert Sanatorium, Tucson Medical Center's predecessor. Today this spot is one of Tucson's busiest intersections, Beverly and Grant, and the hospital's outpatient entrance.

Mrs. Alfred W. Erickson, whose gift of the Desert Sanatorium's land and buildings to the community made possible the establishment of Tucson Medical Center.

visitors to Tucson. That same year, under new medical leadership, the "Desert San" shifted its focus to become a respiratory and arthritis center, using only one building to house tuberculosis patients.

In the 1930s the Desert San had some famous patients, including General John J. Pershing, whose hospitalization there brought national attention to Tucson. But gradually the institution became better known as a luxury private health resort, to which prominent and affluent people came for rest and relaxation. All this ended with the coming of World War II. A growing population, in part due to the defense industry that sprang up in Tucson, and a shortage of hospital beds made it necessary to devote some of the Desert San's beds to local patient care. In 1943 wartime shortages of medical supplies and trained personnel made Mrs. Erickson, by now a widow, decide to close the sanatorium.

Concerned with the possible loss of 91 hospital beds, the Reverend George Ferguson, founding rector of St. Philip's in the Hills Episcopal parish, went to New York to see about the possible purchase of the Desert San property for a community hospital. Instead, Mrs. Erickson offered to donate the 133 acres, 15 buildings, and all the equipment to the citizens of Tucson, provided the community raise the money to convert the sanatorium into a general hospital and run it for five years.

Tucson rose to the challenge. A nonprofit corporation—Tucson Medical Center, Inc.—was formed with an unpaid board of directors responsible for its operation. The first board began operating in November 1943, and successfully conducted a fund drive that made possible the conversion of the Desert San into a 142-bed community hospital.

Tucson Medical Center admitted its first patient on November 9, 1944. From that day on, the hospital's record has been one of unbroken progress. After the hospital opened, plans for an additional 108 beds immediately became a priority. Maintenance and renovation preceded other plans in the years between 1946 and 1951, when gradual and cautious building began. In 1963, with the renovation of two court buildings, the number of beds increased to 441. Another 90 beds were added in 1968, and a major four-year renovation and expansion project, completed in 1981, brought the hospital's licensed bed total to 650.

A distinguishing feature of Tucson Medical

Center over the years has been its buildings and grounds. Though the hospital could not build upward in its first five years according to the terms of the original gift, its board has always chosen not to. This unique one-story design provides 28 private patios that aid in patient morale and recovery. Every TMC patient has a room with a view.

TMC consistently has been a center of medical innovation. In the late 1940s, spurred by advances resulting from the war, medical specialization developed nationally, and TMC became the Tucson hospital where specialists practiced. Thus, it was the first facility offering gastroenterological and cardiac care, and the first hospital to establish an intensive care unit. Many other significant "firsts" for southern Arizona followed: first intensive care nursery (1968); first pacemaker clinic (1971); first pediatric intensive care unit (1972), first clinical use of a CAT scanner (1975); first coronary angioplasty, a noninvasive opening of blocked arteries (1979); and the first clinical use of magnetic resonance imaging (1985). TMC was the first hospital in Arizona to open a cardiac care unit (1968), to reattach a severed hand successfully (1977), and to use a heart-assist device following heart bypass surgery (1984).

As of 1985, with the implementation of a joint trauma program with University Medical Center, TMC and UMC are the two southern Arizona hospitals where patients with life-threatening injuries are taken. When necessary, trauma patients in outlying areas are transported to TMC or UMC by the air rescue helicopter of the Arizona Department of Public Safety.

TMC has set the pace not only for medical advancements, but also in finding ways to deliver care in a cost-efficient manner. In 1973 TMC was a pioneer nationally in opening a one-day surgery center. Through the late 1970s and the 1980s TMC has been a leader in offering an increasing number of tests and treatments on an outpatient basis and in developing "step-down units," areas that provide a bridge between levels of nursing care at a reduced cost.

TMC's efforts at holding down the cost of health care have also included the establishment of alternatives to traditional insurance. These alternatives include a preferred provider organization, TMCare Health Network (1985), and a health maintenance organization, Partners (1986). Both organizations manage the

delivery of care and hold costs to set fees or premiums.

Today Tucson Medical Center is the birthplace of more than half of Tucson's babies, and the hospital of choice for most high-risk mothers. Independent surveys over the past decade have indicated a consumer preference for TMC for most serious illness or injuries. TMC's most enduring reputation, however, is that of a true community hospital. As such, millions of dollars of indigent care, community service, and education are provided each year.

To keep pace with a rapidly changing, more competitive environment, and to ensure a continuance of its mission of community service, education, and quality care, TMC in 1984 created a holding company, TMCare, with three subsidiaries: TMC, the community hospital; TMC Health Enterprises, a profit-making company that is aimed at offsetting losses of TMC; and the TMC Foundation, which focuses its fund-raising efforts on supporting the hospital's equipment needs, trauma program, and children's unit.

The history of Tucson Medical Center is a history of growth and medical progress, but mostly it is a history of people—people who have dedicated their lives to providing special care, people who have donated their time and money to guide and support hospital operations, and people who have trusted their lives to their community hospital.

Tucson Medical Center has a totally horizontal configuration, which is unusual for a 650-bed medical center. One reason for retaining the one-level approach was the ability to continue using patios as an aid to patient morale and recovery. There are some 28 patios now, with the newer ones featuring more desert planting, and every patient at TMC has a room with a view.

One of many entrances to the hospital over the years. This photo was taken in 1962.

PALO VERDE HOSPITAL

Alan I. Levenson, M.D., president of Palo Verde Hospital and professor and head of the Department of Psychiatry at the University of Arizona College of Medicine (right).

Jack A. Marks, M.D., Palo Verde Hospital's senior psychiatric consultant and a private-practice psychiatrist who has been associated with Palo Verde since 1960, and Edward B. Berger, executive vice-president/general counsel of the hospital and president of the Palo Verde Hospital Foundation (below).

Tucson's need for inpatient psychiatric care was met when Palo Verde Hospital, Tucson's only nonprofit psychiatric hospital, opened November 21, 1960. At that time the private, 34-bed facility was situated on 16 desert acres along Pantano Road south of Broadway, well beyond city limits. Today Palo Verde Hospital, operated since 1978 under the corporate name of Palo Verde Mental Health Services, is an innovative 62-bed nonprofit community-based psychiatric facility centrally located on eight acres adjacent to Tucson Medical Center.

Palo Verde provides inpatient and partial hospitalization programs for people of all ages. A walk-in and call-in urgent care service is provided free to the community 24 hours a day, seven days a week. Palo Verde offers separate services for young people, active individualized services for adults, and expanded psychgerontology services. Specialized treatment is also offered for eating disorders and substance abuse problems. Palo Verde has the first hospital-based school in southern Arizona approved by the state and accredited by the North Central Association for students from preschool through 12th grade.

Palo Verde Hospital was founded by Boris Zemsky, M.D., Warren S. Williams, M.D., and Earloyde Edmonson, a psychiatric social worker. Dr. Zemsky died in 1965, the year before Palo Verde Hospital was incorporated as the Palo Verde Foundation for Mental Health, a nonprofit community organization.

Original incorporators were Zora Zemsky, Warren S. Williams, M.D., Roy Hewitt, M.D., William C. Voris, Edwin K. Erickson, Marvin D. Johnson, Ann Simmons, Jane Loew Shelton, Fred H. Landeen, M.D., Vernon L. Newell, George Rosenberg, William L. Raby, B.G. Thompson, Jr., Lowell E. Rothschild, and Edward B. Berger.

Edward Berger continues to serve on the board of trustees and is the executive vice-president and general counsel for Palo Verde Hospital and president of the Palo Verde Hospital Foundation Board of Directors, formed in 1984.

Zora Zemsky also continues to serve on the Palo Verde Mental Health Services Board of Trustees. She says her late husband, Boris, would be happy to see how well the hospital serves the community. "It was his dream for Palo Verde Hospital to become a nonprofit community facility," she says.

Palo Verde's history shows its ever-expanding commitment and capacity to serve the mental health needs of a growing Tucson. By 1970 Palo Verde had assumed operation of the Suicide Prevention Crisis Center, providing 24-hour, seven-day-a-week telephone crisis intervention for individuals experiencing any kind of social, family, or personal emergency.

In 1971 the Tucson Child Guidance Center, in existence since the 1950s, began operating as part of the Palo Verde Foundation for Mental Health. The center was the first psychiatric outpatient program for children in the Tucson area.

It was the first such program in Tucson to become accredited by the Joint Commission on Accreditation of Hospitals, the national accrediting body for all health care programs.

Beginning in 1972 and using a $3.3-million declining grant from the National Institute for Mental Health, Palo Verde expanded its services to include outpatient consultation, education, and outreach services coordinated through the Tucson East Community Mental Health Center. The Drug Help Line, a 24-hour telephone hotline for counseling individuals with drug-related problems, was established in 1974.

In 1978, responding to the reality that federal and state funds were decreasing and a recognition that Palo Verde needed to work toward self-sufficiency, a decision was reached to operate Palo Verde without funding from the National Institute for Mental Health. In 1982 the facility made additional strides toward becoming self-sufficient and chose to operate without funding from the Arizona Department of Behavioral Health Services.

"During that time period Palo Verde recognized that quality outpatient psychiatric care was well established in Tucson," says Alan I. Levenson, M.D., president of Palo Verde Hospital since 1971. "In order to use our resources more efficiently, avoid duplication of service in Tucson, and be responsive to the community's mental health needs, Palo Verde altered its focus to concentrate on inpatient, partial hospitalization, and urgent care services. Palo Verde also continued its education and advocacy efforts.

"Throughout the 1970s we nurtured a dream to build a new, accessible, state-of-the-art hospital," says Dr. Levenson. In 1981 the Arizona Department of Health awarded Palo Verde a certificate of need to build and operate a freestanding, 62-bed psychiatric hospital. The dream came to fruition when construction began in 1983, and the new Palo Verde Hospital, at 2695 North Craycroft Road, opened its doors November 19, 1984.

To help the hospital fulfill its mission, the Palo Verde Hospital Foundation was founded in 1984 to expand the funding base of the new or enhanced programs, capital improvements, research, community education/outreach, and the treatment of patients unable to afford care.

Support is continually sought from a broad base of private and corporate sources in partnership with the board and staff of Palo Verde

Hospital and the Palo Verde Ambassadors, a nonprofit social organization that provides financial assistance to Palo Verde Hospital.

"Palo Verde's mission has always been to provide the highest quality of care for the maximum number of patients possible who are suffering from mental illness and related disorders, to provide support to their families, and to promote mental health in the community through advocacy, professional leadership, and prevention programs," says Dr. Levenson. "There has been tremendous growth and progress in psychiatric treatment, and Palo Verde Hospital is committed to furthering this progress and reducing the stigma associated with seeking treatment."

Palo Verde Hospital's first facility, which opened in 1960 (above).

The new Palo Verde Hospital opened in 1984 (below).

FAIRFIELD HOMES

Fairfield Homes became a vital part of residential and community development in Arizona in 1972, when the firm acquired the 4,500 acres that make up the community of Green Valley, 25 miles south of Tucson. Development there had begun under another corporation, but had languished; Fairfield Homes was responsible for the growth of Green Valley from a village to the town of 16,000 to 18,000 residents that it is in the late 1980s.

Fairfield Homes is one of several divisions of Fairfield Communities Inc., a firm begun in 1966 and based in Little Rock, Arkansas. The parent company, through its homes and resorts division, has projects from St. Croix in the Caribbean to the Pacific, spanning the Sun Belt. Fairfield Homes is one of the 20 largest residential builders in the United States.

Residents of Tucson's Fairfield in the Foothills enjoy a new concept of cluster housing, which concentrates housing in certain areas to preserve the natural terrain.

Expanding north into the Tucson metropolitan area from Green Valley, Fairfield Homes has built or is building three major developments, each little communities separately master planned based on topography and a desire to maximize land use while maintaining the ambience of the area. Fairfield's planning and innovative land use has received commendations from the Pima County Board of Supervisors.

The nucleus of the first of these developments, Fairfield in the Foothills, is 1,600 acres on Tucson's northeast side, acquired in 1976-1977. In this community, Fairfield Homes created the prototype of cluster housing, a concept that concentrates residences in one area of the development in order to leave another in its natural state. The community, which when completed is projected to have 1,700 housing units, also has 22 acres dedicated to commercial use.

In 1984 Fairfield Homes acquired 133 acres opposite the prestigious Tucson National Golf Club on the city's northwest side and began development of La Cholla Hills, Tucson's first in-town retirement community. Plans call for about 500 residences, both single-family homes and town houses, when development is complete. These properties, designed for active people who are retired or approaching retirement, are deed restricted; owners must be at least 45 years old.

Late in 1985 Fairfield Homes purchased the land for its third Tucson development, Fairfield's Pusch Ridge at La Reserve. This community, located northwest of the city, will be situated on 275 acres and, when complete, will have about 300 homes. The land is spectacular, situated on the westernmost slopes of the Santa Catalina Mountains, facing into the granite cliffs of the Pusch Ridge wilderness area. There a special effort is being made to preserve the natural environment and accommodate the development to it; the community's next-door neighbor is a reserve for the desert bighorn sheep.

Fairfield plans to remain in Tucson, using the area and the Southwest Division of Fairfield Homes (created in 1981) as a base for further expansion in Arizona, as well as in New Mexico and Texas. With $55 million in sales annually and a reputation as one of Tucson's most reliable quality developers and builders, Fairfield Homes has carved out an enviable niche in southern Arizona's business community.

THE ARIZONA BILTMORE

Ronald and Nancy Reagan honeymooned at The Arizona Biltmore. Harpo Marx and his new bride startled dining room guests by skipping between the tables hand in hand. Clark Gable lost his wedding ring on the hotel golf course, and was eternally grateful to the maintenance employee who found it.

The list of famous guests would fill many pages—movie idols, giants of industry, American presidents, and many more. Little wonder that this storied resort hotel, located at 24th Street and Missouri in Phoenix, is a treasured Arizona resource.

Today The Arizona Biltmore holds the enviable distinction of winning the coveted Mobil Travel Guide Five-Star Award since its inception 30 years ago—a record unmatched in America. Basking in an exquisite setting in the foothills of Squaw Peak, the famed "Jewel in the Desert" has 500 guest rooms on its 39 acres of landscaped greenery; 2 championship golf courses, 17 tennis courts, 3 inviting swimming pools, and myriad other recreational resources; a 39,000-square-foot conference center; exquisite dining rooms and lounges; and the ultimate in service. All this—and a rich heritage and ambience that bring faithful patrons back year after year.

The idea of building such a hotel in the barren desert, eight miles northeast of Phoenix, was considered the wildest kind of folly in 1928, when it was being rushed to completion by a group of optimistic investors. A bejeweled throng of 600 celebrants attended the opening-night dinner February 23, 1929. They toasted the hotel's architect, Albert Chase McArthur, and his mentor, Frank Lloyd Wright, who had assisted in some phases of the planning. And they marveled at the cost of the project—a staggering $2.5 million.

The Arizona Biltmore's first season lasted only six weeks, and the reopening in the autumn of 1929 was seriously threatened by the tragedy of the stock market crash. Before 1929 was history, major stockholder William Wrigley of chewing gum fame took over the financially troubled property. The Wrigley family was to own the resort until June 6, 1973, when it was sold to Talley Industries. Two weeks after the sale was completed, much of the grand old hostelry burned to the ground, but its new owners rebuilt it in time to welcome guests for the 1973 fall season. Several major expansion projects have added considerably to the capacity and re-

Movie idol Clark Gable (second from right) was one of many celebrities who enjoyed playing golf at The Arizona Biltmore in the 1940s.

The Arizona Biltmore, 24th Street and Missouri Avenue, Phoenix, is one of the nation's great resort and conference hotels.

sources of the resort in recent years.

Today, thanks to the advances of air conditioning and the amazing growth of the Phoenix area, The Arizona Biltmore remains open year round. It is now owned by Lepercq/DBL Biltmore Associates Limited Partnership and is managed by Westin Hotels & Resorts of Seattle. Cecil Ravenswood, a charming and urbane native of Australia, is general manager.

A reporter who covered The Arizona Biltmore's opening in 1929 rhapsodized that "here one can find the solace of the desert, yet live in luxury unsurpassed."

Some things never change.

THE ESTES CO.

Three generations of the Estes family have been active in the company's operations (from left): William Estes III, William Estes, Jr., and William Estes, Sr.

The Estes Co., one of Arizona's largest real estate developers, creates modern dwellings such as this one in a Tucson subdivision.

Ventana Canyon Golf & Racquet Club, home to one of the most scenic golf courses in the nation, is part of the master-planned Ventana Canyon Resort, custom lots, single-family homes, apartment communities, and office buildings.

The Estes Co. was founded in Tucson in 1946 by William A. Estes. Sr.; his father, J.W. Estes; and his brother-in-law, Pete Church. The trio began the home-building business with only a little knowledge of construction. William Estes had spent the last year of World War II working in aircraft modification at Consolidated Vultee Aircraft Company. He had, however, remodeled a backyard shed into a home when he was living in Washington state, and this gave him the confidence to build this first house in Tucson.

The first decade was difficult for the young construction business. The company built homes on both contract and speculation. Estes bought a few lots at a time, improved and sold them, then invested in more lots. The firm's first office was the back of his truck. Ed Stratman, an early partner, supervised most of the organization's construction in its first two years.

As the business grew, Estes found it necessary to devote himself to administrative matters, while others performed the carpentry work he had previously done. In 1954 Max Estes, an attorney, became a partner in his brother's company. That same year the firm built two large subdivisions of 50 homes each in Tucson, one near St. Mary's Hospital, the other on North First Avenue. By the end of the decade The Estes Co. was building in several subdivisions simultaneously.

By that time the days of the truck-office were past. The next step had been to make headquarters in a model home built on speculation; when the home sold, the office was moved. In the early 1960s The Estes Co. opened its first permanent office at Broadway and Sarnoff, a move that reflected the city's rapid eastward expansion. The firm erected 160 homes on 90 acres in that area, in a subdivision called Centennial Park.

William A. Estes, Jr., now company president, joined his father's business in 1963. Nine years later the senior Estes sold the firm to the real estate arm of the Singer Co., then retired the following year. William A. Estes. Jr., and James N. Shedd, his partner and executive vice-president, reacquired the firm from Singer in 1978.

Since then The Estes Co. has grown rapidly, becoming one of America's largest and most diversified builder-developers, and gaining national recognition for long-range planning, strong management, and success across a broad spectrum of real estate development projects. The company now has five operating divisions, under the general direction of chief operating officer Jon Grove, with offices located in Tucson, Phoenix, Salt Lake City, and Minneapolis-St. Paul.

The guiding philosophy of Estes Homes, an Arizona limited partnership, headed by Chris Sheafe, makes people and the quality of their living environments a top priority. As a result, The Estes Co. experiences a large percentage of new home purchases from customer referrals.

More than 30,000 families currently live in Estes homes in Tucson, Phoenix, and Sierra Vista. This success has been built on innovative designs, quality construction, affordability, and customer satisfaction. It assures that new home construction will remain a primary, strong, and viable part of the company's business. The firm also maintains the same high standards with each new apartment community it builds, resulting in above-average market performance for every completed multifamily project.

The Estes Co. has become one of the nation's leading community development organizations. Estes Communities, an Arizona limited partnership, headed by Ron Haarer, has award-winning projects ranging from multiuse residential developments with commercial and retail facilities, to retail lot development and retirement/adult communities. Estes has become one of the few companies in the nation with the resources, personnel, and experience necessary to successfully develop large, master-planned communities.

Estes Properties, an Arizona limited partnership, headed by Kim Richards, received widespread acclaim and garnered numerous awards for its development of the environmentally sensitive Loews Ventana Canyon Resort in Tucson. In addition to world-class resorts and country clubs, this division also develops commercial hotels, such as the Days Inn in Flagstaff, and is involved in recreational and luxury housing land development, as well as recreation and asset management.

The Estes Co. has also devoted substantial resources in recent years to a far-reaching program of commercial and industrial development in Arizona, California, Utah, and Minnesota. Each project developed by Estes Development Co., an Arizona limited partnership, headed by Lee Hanley, is stamped with a unique identity and is designed to harmonize with its surroundings, creating a favorable and compatible environment for living, recreation, shopping, and working. Completed and ongoing projects include major industrial parks, shopping centers, office complexes, and urban redevelopment projects.

The company has developed a variety of other capabilities. It pioneered the concept of mortgage-secured bonds in 1982 by co-founding American Southwest Financial Corporation, one of the nation's largest issuers of mortgage-related securities. Estes Financial Services, an Arizona limited partnership, headed by Frank Parise, also founded a full-service mortgage banking subsidiary, Builder Mortgage Services Company, which originates and services both residential and commercial mortgage loans,

and founded and manages American Southwest Mortgage Investments Corporation, a publicly owned mortgage banking company trading on the American Stock Exchange under the symbol "ASR".

Estes Property Management Co. has gained extensive experience with commercial, industrial, and residential properties, and is recognized throughout the industry for competence, dependability, and a commitment to excellence. Through innovative marketing, relocation, and financing services, Estes Realtors has become a major force in the real estate brokerage field.

With the addition of these affiliates, The Estes Co. has become a full-service real estate organization. The firm is still growing, committing its experienced management team, multifaceted staff, research skills, and financial strength to new projects nationwide. This unusual blend of talent and 40 years of tradition indicate that the company will continue to be a responsive and dependable leader in the development community wherever it operates.

Court International, in St. Paul, Minnesota, was originally built in 1915 as an automobile assembly plant then acquired in 1928 for use as a factory by International Harvester. The Estes Co. renovated the formidable Twin Cities landmark in 1986, converting it into a four-story office building with 315,000 rentable square feet, two four-story atrium lobbies, six glass-enclosed elevators, a complete health club, and restaurant facilities.

The goal in the development of Estes shopping centers is a perfect fit. Each center, such as this one in Phoenix, must complement its surrounding neighborhood thus ensuring a pleasurable experience for both consumers and retailers.

DESERT SCHOOLS FEDERAL CREDIT UNION

The Desert Schools Federal Credit Union has its headquarters in this office building at 6633 North Black Canyon Highway, Phoenix.

Desert Schools Federal Credit Union has had only three chief executives: two, Betty Gregg (left) and Annis King (right), are shown with treasurer Jerry Winn in this 1964 photo.

It is Arizona's largest credit union today, but prospects for the new organization looked bleak after its founding meeting at Phoenix Junior College on May 17, 1939. Despite its worthy goal of providing low-cost loans for teachers, the credit union faced stiff opposition from some educational supervisors. "Teachers have no business borrowing money," declared one Depression-scarred school superintendent. "They should make do with what they have, and not go into debt."

But teachers in Maricopa County, Arizona's most populous county, did borrow money, and

their credit union thrived. Growth was surprisingly slow, however. The organization was managed by volunteers during its first decade; it did not acquire its first typewriter until 1947; and it was 1950 before it was able to move into its own office.

Before that the credit union used facilities in the Phoenix offices of the Arizona Education Association, and its name during the early years was AEA No. 1 Federal Credit Union. Growth brought in many teachers and schools not affiliated with the AEA, however, so the present name was adopted.

Desert Schools Federal Credit Union is notable for at least two reasons. One, it has had only three chief executives in its history, Annis King (1949-1968), Betty Gregg (1969-1988), and Kenneth Laubenstein (1988-). And two, it has served as a forerunner in innovation and expansion within the credit union movement.

A convincing example of this innovative character was the decision of Gregg to establish a marketing department—first in the credit union industry. Since 1969 marketing directors have conducted aggressive advertising and sales campaigns that have boosted current membership of Desert Schools to more than 79,000.

Growth in field of membership and services has radically changed Desert Schools Federal Credit Union since its birth in 1939. Today school personnel still make up 35 percent of the membership. In keeping with the educational nature of the credit union, students at local colleges, universities, and trade schools make up a large portion of the membership, as do family members of these same school employees and students. A relatively new program allows workers in Select Employee Groups (SEGs), businesses that meet required criteria, to enjoy membership eligibility in the organization as well.

Today Desert Schools Federal Credit Union has its headquarters in a strikingly modern building at 6633 North Black Canyon Highway, Phoenix, and operates branch offices at four other Maricopa County locations. The staff has grown to 125 people, and assets have skyrocketed to $235 million—by far the largest of any Arizona credit union.

This is financial democracy at its best—people working with each other in a not-for-profit enterprise to encourage thrift and provide low-cost borrowing ability.

LOEWS VENTANA CANYON RESORT

The Sonoran desert, unrivaled in its beauty, color, and dramatic scenery, is the backdrop for Loews Ventana Canyon Resort, vividly set in full view of an 80-foot natural waterfall. Nestled into the side of the Catalina Mountains, Loews Ventana Canyon Resort offers 400 expansive guest rooms and suites, whose private patios suggest the romance of cliff dwellings, the habitations for Arizona's earliest residents.

In this desert garden, the visitor can appreciate the history, archaeology, and geology of the saguaro-studded canyon. Named for the outcropping of rock that forms a window-shape opening high in the Catalina Mountains, Ventana (Spanish for "window") Canyon has existed as a designated area for ages. The trail leading up to the rock outcropping can be approached just behind the resort or begun from nearby Sabino Canyon.

Strolling around the 1,050-acre development, it is inspiring to recall that the 94-acre resort location was actually shifted from its original site to ensure the safety of a 300-year-old saguaro. Subsequently, architectural and construction guidelines emphasized the importance of preserving the natural environment. From the outset of its development, the resort was conceived as an integration of the building into the desert landscape.

Within the preserve of Loews Ventana Canyon Resort water gushes from the canyon waterfall to follow its natural stream course along the resort's signed nature trail. It empties into a shallow lake that graces the terrace side of the Flying V Bar and Grill, before being recirculated for continuous passage, traversing a habitat of more than 70 species of birds, small mammals, lizards, and frogs.

World class in service and amenities, Loews Ventana Canyon Resort is a proud addition to the emerging destination of Tucson, preserving the heritage of its natural environment while showcasing the beauty of its vegetation to visitors who acknowledge the wonder of the desert.

Harmony and tranquility—these are sentiments of guests who visit the canyon today. Human habitation of southern Arizona extends back at least 12,000 years. Although the evidence of paleo-Indian hunters has been reported in southeastern Arizona, little is known of what is commonly referred to as the Tucson Basin. On the site of the Ventana Canyon project, evidence was found of habitation during the archaic period, an era spanning from approximately 8,000 B.C. to one A.D.

Leaving the outside environment to explore the resort's interior, the visitor discovers further displays of Arizona's beauty in the custom-made, split-faced masonry block that forms a vertical ribbing along the resort's walls; native sandstone lobby floors topped with genuine fossil tables and bases of verde copper; and accents of polished copper in the Cascade Lounge contrasted with textural brick glass. Throughout the resort's interior, original juried pieces of art by Arizona artists are displayed. Lithographs published in Arizona enhance guest rooms, which are not only spacious and decorated in neutral tones, but also feature double-wide tubs as standard. Fine dining is enjoyed in the second-level Ventana Room. Overlooking the city skyline, the Ventana Room is acknowledged as the most romantic restaurant in Tucson. High tea in the Cascade Lounge alternates with the penetrating rhythms of the disco nightly at the Flying V. Mesquite-broiled hamburgers at Bill's Grill contrast with the daily buffet of the Canyon Cafe.

Casual elegance is the theme here; rugged exteriors merge with the mountain. At Loews Ventana Canyon Resort, nature is the entertainer. A joint ownership by The Estes Co. and Catalina Properties Inc., Loews Ventana Canyon Resort is managed by Loews Hotels, whose chairman is Robert J. Hausman and whose president is Jonathan Tisch.

World class in service and amenities, Loews Ventana Canyon Resort blends into its desert landscape and the Catalina Mountains in the background.

A canyon waterfall flows down its natural stream course forming a lake on the terrace side of the Flying V Bar and Grill.

TRAILSIDE GALLERIES

President Christine Mollring and her husband, vice-president Ted Mollring, have developed Trailside Galleries into an important Arizona art resource.

Beautiful Scottsdale Mall is the site of Trailside Galleries' Arizona gallery.

Around the world, Scottsdale is known as a community devoted to the finest in art, fashion, luxury resorts, and gracious living. One of Scottsdale's brightest jewels is Trailside Galleries, at 7330 Scottsdale Mall.

There, and in Trailside's other gallery in Jackson Hole, Wyoming, discerning patrons enjoy a never-ending feast of American contemporary art, and collectors find paintings and sculpture by many of America's finest artists.

The creators and moving spirits of Trailside

Galleries are president Christine Mollring and her husband, vice-president Ted Mollring. They purchased a small art gallery in Jackson Hole in 1972—a business that was grossing $187,000 per year—and moved it across the town square into a converted grocery store building. By 1976, when they established Trailside's Scottsdale gallery, their booming enterprise had annual sales of more than $6 million.

Such success does not come by magic. Years of hard work and faithful service to both patrons and artists have made the difference.

The Scottsdale gallery occupied only one-fourth of the present building in 1976, but it grew so spectacularly that it now has taken over the entire 6,000-square-foot structure. Its striking exterior is admirably complemented by interior viewing rooms that are a joy to visit.

"We took some chances, expanding in the mid-1970s when most other galleries were playing it safe," explains Christine. "We developed close relationships with some wonderful artists such as John Clymer, Harry Jackson, R. Brownell McGrew, Rod Goebel, and others. And we offered our clientele good service after the sale—annual appraisals, collecting advice, tax tips, and much more. We have four art shows each year in the Scottsdale gallery and two at Jackson Hole. It has all added up to a faithful clientele and a wonderfully exciting and successful operation."

Trailside Galleries has built an enviable reputation as the home of fine western art, but the Mollrings now enjoy an equally brisk sales volume in the works of American impressionists. The inventory ranges from relatively inexpensive art pieces and Indian jewelry to million-dollar masterpieces by Frederic Remington and Charles Russell.

The Mollrings are a fascinating pair. Christine was born in Brazil of British parents, visited Great Britain's great art galleries as a child, and studied art in Sao Paulo. Ted is an energetic Wyoming cowboy who studied at the Los Angeles Art School and has become a master at promoting Trailside Galleries. He can hang a collection with the best of them.

Maryvonne Leshe, who joined the Trailside staff in 1978, has been manager of the Scottsdale gallery since 1985.

Arizona owes much to Trailside Galleries, which has done much to cultivate art appreciation and develop the fine arts community during an eventful decade.

PCS, INC.

PCS, Inc., of Scottsdale, Arizona, entered the third-party prescription-drug claim-processing business in 1969. Today PCS is clearly the industry leader, approximately twice as large as its nearest competitor.

PCS derives its name from Pharmaceutical Card System, its primary business. Under the PCS card system, a cardholder presents his prescription along with the PCS card to any one of more than 60,000 member pharmacies. The prescription is filled, and the cardholder pays the deductible, typically three dollars. No further paperwork on claims filing is required of the cardholder—the rest is between PCS, the pharmacy, and the third party covering the individual. PCS provides claims processing and related services for more than 200 insurance companies, 50 HMOs and PPOs, 40 Blue Cross organizations, 500 labor unions—in all, more than 100,000 groups. By far the largest and best-known company in its industry, PCS is still enjoying phenomenal growth, and currently serves more than 16 million people.

This means that each business day more than 250,000 prescriptions are processed for holders of blue-and-white plastic PCS cards throughout the United States, Canada, and Puerto Rico. Every claim is checked with 56 edits, verified, and processed in the PCS operations center at 9060 East Via Linda in Scottsdale. More than 18 field offices worldwide complete the marketing and service network necessary to serve PCS clients. Altogether, 860 people work for PCS.

PCS, Inc., became a wholly owned subsidiary of the McKesson Corporation in 1972. On November 25, 1986, McKesson sold 2 million shares of PCS common stock in a public offering, but retained 86 percent of company ownership. Since 1981 the president and chief executive officer of PCS has been Donald B. Dahlin, a former senior executive of Massachusetts Mutual Life Insurance Company.

A PCS subsidiary, Pharmaceutical Data Services, Inc., collects and analyzes data on prescribing patterns, sale, and use of prescription drugs, primarily for the pharmaceutical industry. Virtually every major U.S. drug company is its client. Offices in Europe have been established to expand this service worldwide.

One of the latest innovations in PCS technology is electronic claims processing. The PCS on-line card has been given a magnetic stripe that contains the cardholder's eligibility date, thus permitting a pharmacist to obtain verification from the computer center on line within 30 seconds, much like point-of-sale credit card approvals. Because of its state-of-the-art computer system and the efficiencies made possible by specialization, it is little wonder that PCS claims-processing volume and revenues are increasing about 40 percent per year.

To help keep drug costs down, PCS has also designed incentive programs to promote the use of generic drugs where possible, and routinely provides cost-containment information to its clients. Such innovations are keeping PCS, Inc., in the forefront of its industry, and among Arizona's business leaders.

Donald B. Dahlin, president and chief executive officer of PCS, Inc., has led the corporation to rapid growth.

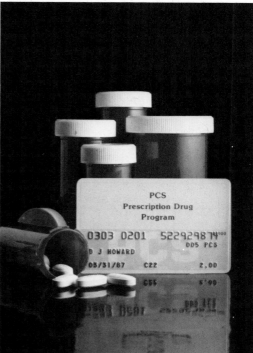

The PCS prescription card is honored in pharmacies throughout the United States, Canada, and Puerto Rico.

ANCHOR NATIONAL COMPANIES

Anchor Centre, 22nd Street and East Camelback Road, Phoenix, is headquarters for the Anchor National Companies.

Edward B. "Ben" Burr, founding chairman of the Anchor National Companies.

One of the most impressive of the new financial complexes in Arizona is Anchor Centre at 22nd Street and East Camelback Road in Phoenix. This beautiful six-story structure houses the home offices of the Anchor National Companies, respected nationally in the fields of life insurance and financial services.

Anchor National Life Insurance Company, which serves 49 states and the District of Columbia, is the only national life insurance firm with headquarters in Phoenix. It has long been known as a pioneer and innovator in the insurance and annuity business. Anchor National Financial Services, the other component of the Anchor National Companies, also is national in scope. A member of the Pacific Stock Exchange, its representatives sell mutual funds, direct participation programs, and securities.

The seeds of the Anchor National Companies were planted in 1924, when a New York City law firm and two New York Stock Exchange-member broker/dealers formed Investment Management Corporation to enter the mutual funds business. Hugh W. Long, a man who once aspired to a career as a concert violinist, became associated with Investment Management Corporation in the early 1930s, and eventually molded the firm and its offshoots into one of the nation's foremost mutual fund managers and distributors—Anchor Corporation. It was

Long who gave the present companies their name: "Anchor."

In 1962 Anchor purchased a small Arizona life insurance company called First Western Life, which eventually merged with a California-chartered life insurance company to become Anchor National Life. In 1971 Edward B. "Ben" Burr, chairman of Anchor National Life, moved from the East Coast to the firm's Phoenix headquarters, and Anchor continued its progress to national prominence in both life insurance and financial services. In 1968 Anchor National Life employed 30 people; today it employs 270. It currently has more than $4 billion of life insurance in force. Anchor's fixed annuities now total $1.8 billion, and its variable annuity more than a half-billion dollars.

Anchor's impact on the Arizona economy has been significant during the past quarter-century. On the occasion of the ground breaking for Anchor Centre in April 1982, Burr observed, "I am very proud of the fact that we have invested our assets in the Arizona economy at a rate four times greater than the returns we have realized in policy premiums from Arizona businesses and residents."

Burr retired in late 1985 as chairman and chief executive officer. In May 1986 the Anchor National Companies were purchased by Kaufman and Broad, Inc., of Los Angeles.

COLOSSAL CAVE

Colossal Cave, about 20 miles east of Tucson, is one of the city's most interesting natural attractions and a perennial lure for visitors and residents alike. The cave was first discovered in 1879 by Solomon Lick, who ran the Mountain Springs Hotel near the stage stop at Vail. A big cavern in an isolated area, it was a natural hiding place for outlaws in the still-untamed West, and legend has it that both Geronimo and Virgil Earp, brother of Tombstone's famous marshal, eluded their captors by concealing themselves there.

Colossal Cave was first mentioned in print in Frank Leslie's *Illustrated Weekly,* one of America's most popular magazines in the 1880s. A female reporter who signed herself "Miss Rose" described the cave for her readers, calling it the "Arizona Catacombs."

In the early 1930s about 500 workers for the Civilian Conservation Corps labored at Colossal Cave, erecting the buildings that still stand there more than 50 years later, and putting in the walkway in the cave itself. About the same time these same CCC workers and others built the General Hitchcock Highway up Mount Lemmon in the Catalina Mountains.

The cave was turned over to the Tucson Chamber of Commerce in 1944 and subsequently became a county park. But maintenance was poor, and, because county officials were reluctant to spend the sums to keep it up, the cave and the surrounding site deteriorated.

Then, in 1956, Joe Maierhauser, a native of South Dakota and a World War II Navy veteran, took a lease on the cave and the section of land on which it is located, and prepared to make it a prime tourist attraction. Of all the cave operators in the United States, he was the first to lease an entire park rather than simply operating the cave as a concession. Thirty-two years later he is still hard at work on what he calls "an extraordinary experiment."

There are several secrets to the success of Colossal Cave, now in the top 10 among commercial caves in the United States. For one thing, Maierhauser feels responsible for the natural phenomenon that he operates, so he sees that it is maintained every hour of every day of the year. Maintaining and operating the cave takes a staff of 15 to 18 people year round.

Visitors are not crowded through Colossal Cave, but are guided in small groups so they can best appreciate nature's impressive spectacle. Maierhauser has also fought long and hard to prevent encroachment on the site by developers, and this environmental battle continues.

Compared with other tourist attractions in Tucson, Colossal Cave is relatively low key, but that is part of its charm. Visitors can camp and picnic there free of charge; the only price is admission to the cave.

Colossal Cave has been a part of Tucson's tourist and recreation scene for more than three decades. The city is fortunate to have it nearby.

The Crystalline Frozen Waterfall.

The Drapery Room.

FARMERS INVESTMENT CO.

Pecans are Farmers Investment Co.'s largest-selling product.

FICO's state-of-the-art processing plant stands just minutes away from the pecan orchards.

The business that became Farmers Investment Co. (FICO) began in Ventura County, California, in 1937 under the leadership of R. Keith Walden, who a half-century later remains its chairman and chief executive officer. In various locations of southern and central California, the company grew agricultural produce. Its first venture, on rented land, was a citrus and avocado tree nursery; from there it began growing citrus fruits and, in the mid-1940s, diversified into the production of cereal grains, vegetable oil crops, cotton, sugar beets, vegetables, melons, potatoes, and alfalfa seed. In 1945 the business became known as FICO.

Feeling that land values were becoming too high in California after World War II, Walden began looking for cheaper farmland. In 1948 he found what he was looking for in Continental, Arizona, 25 miles south of Tucson, and the following year moved FICO's headquarters to Arizona. At that point the Henry Crown family of Chicago became equal co-owners, and they retain their interest today.

To provide a market for its feed crops, FICO entered the cattle-feeding business in 1954, eventually fattening approximately 40,000 head per year in the feedyard at Continental. The firm continued doing this until 1976, when it became apparent that residents of the nearby community of Green Valley found the operation incompatible with their life-style, and the feeding operation was terminated.

During the 1960s FICO farmed essentially all the land in the Santa Cruz Valley south of Tucson. The principal crop was cotton, which was ginned at the company's new and modern gin at Sahuarita, then shipped directly to textile mills in the southeastern United States. At the same time FICO became the nation's largest grower, packer, and shipper of lettuce, raising and processing the crop on its property at Aguila, 90 miles northwest of Phoenix. When the federal government terminated the legal use of contract labor from Mexico, the company converted its produce operation to cotton growing and ginning, and developed markets overseas for the bulk of its expanded production.

In 1965 FICO began converting its cotton farms in Sahuarita, Continental, and Maricopa into the world's largest irrigated pecan orchard. Currently about 6,000 acres in Pima and Pinal counties are given over to pecan production. In 1975 a state-of-the-art freezer warehouse and facility for cracking, shelling, grading, packaging, and shipping the nuts was built and began operating. At the same time the Santa Cruz Valley Pecan Company, a merchandising organization, was created to provide pecans to ingredient users—bakeries, candy makers, and ice cream makers, among others—in the United States, Canada, Europe, and the countries of Southeast Asia. In addition, cellophane-bagged consumer packages and gift products for the consumer trade are marketed under FICO's Green Valley Pecans and Country Estate labels.

In 1977 FICO continued its diversification and expansion when it acquired 28,000 acres of woodland in the Florida Panhandle. This land, of which 15,000 acres has now been cleared of timber, is used in part for growing blueberries,

pecans, and other specialty crops.

FICO began blueberry production in the mid-1980s. In 1985 the firm built its own grading, packaging, and cooling plant, from which its Blue King blueberries are sold in major East Coast markets.

The 1970s also saw FICO making advances in the vertical integration of production and processing at home, and the development of new markets both within and outside the United States. In the mid-1980s, as American producers and manufacturers were having a harder and harder time marketing abroad, FICO was steadily expanding its overseas sales.

In addition to producing food and cotton, FICO has been part of the development to higher use of some of its land. The company sold all the land on which the town of Green Valley was developed starting in the early 1960s. More recently the firm provided the land for the La Posada Retirement Home being built just east of Green Valley by Tucson Medical Center.

Expressing its community interest and sense of responsibility to act as a good corporate citizen in the communities near its home, FICO was an early benefactor of the University of Arizona College of Medicine. It made a commitment in 1984 to donate a valuable parcel of land as a site for a hospital in Green Valley when the time is appropriate.

In its early years FICO directed its major efforts entirely toward production of food and fiber crops. Since the early 1960s, however, the company has expanded its objectives to include the kind of activities that bring it closer to the consumer: warehousing, processing, packaging, and merchandising. The FICO philosophy is to supply what the user requires on a consistent and timely basis where reliability of supply is important.

FICO is proud to be part of U.S. business in this age of high technology and the growing importance of service industries. The firm believes that quality food production, proper packaging, timely supply, and good service will continue to be of major importance to the future of the United States and to its citizens. American ingenuity and opportunity, and the richness of the land, has produced the world's most nutritious and best-prepared food supply—food that Americans can purchase for a lower percentage of their take-home pay than can people in any other country in the world.

Keith Walden's son, Richard S. Walden, is

now president and chief operating officer of Farmers Investment Co. As the second generation of this family-owned business assumes responsibility, and as the firm moves into its second half-century, the efforts of its 300 loyal employees are dedicated to continuing and improving the quality of the products marketed under the FICO, Green Valley Pecans, Country Estate beans, and Blue King labels.

Pecans are processed in FICO's modern facility in Sahuarita.

The firm's pecan groves cover thousands of acres in the Santa Cruz Valley of southern Arizona.

GREAT AMERICAN
FIRST SAVINGS BANK, F.S.B.

Branching out, Great American First Savings Bank opened this 20-story tower at 32 North Stone Avenue in Tucson in 1966.

The Phoenix Tower at 3200 North Central Avenue is a familiar sight on the Phoenix skyline.

The Arizona root of Great American First Savings Bank was Tucson Federal Savings and Loan Association, founded in 1936 in the midst of the Great Depression, and chartered by the federal government early the next year. At the time Tucson Federal Savings was the only savings and loan association in Tucson. An earlier, state-chartered association had fallen victim to the Depression.

Tucson Federal's first office was at 105 South Scott Street, but a shortage of space soon resulted in a move to 305 East Congress and, in July 1938, to 24 East Broadway. From the beginning the firm grew under the leadership of both Tucson and Phoenix men. During the war years, under the leadership of Alfred E. Kerr, assets grew to $5.651 million, savings share accounts totaled $4.356 million, and net worth amounted to more than $130,000 after all debts had been repaid. At that time loans were being made at an interest rate between 6 percent and 6.6 percent, savings certificates were earning 2 percent annually, and a standard red brick house, with two bedrooms and a bath—a total of 903 square feet—and a carport, was selling for $6,200.

Tucson Federal opened its first branch office, on Jones Boulevard at Speedway, in 1951. Within nine years, under the directon of Gordon D. Paris, the association's first chief operating officer, there were four branches and a new headquarters, at 32 North Stone Avenue. The 1950s also saw the birth of competition in the form of two state-chartered savings and loans—Pima Savings in 1953 and Catalina Savings five years later.

The 1960s and 1970s were decades of rapid growth and change, sometimes hampered and sometimes guided by federal regulations. In 1962, the 25th year of operations, Tucson Federal's assets passed the $100-million mark. Branching continued, with the fifth and sixth new offices opened in 1963. That same year plans were made to build a 20-story tower on the land at 32 North Stone Avenue. This building, for several years the tallest in Tucson, opened in April 1966.

Three years later management began to evaluate the desirability of a statewide branch network. A planned merger with a Phoenix savings and loan, which would have provided offices in the Salt River Valley, was frustrated by the federal bureaucracy and ultimately abandoned. Also blocked by the federal government was a proposed conversion in the early 1970s from mutual ownership to capital stock structure. This change was accomplished later on, however.

After the collapse of the proposed merger, planning had continued for entry into the Phoenix market, and in 1973 Tucson Federal was ready. But expansion outside southern Arizona made a new name necessary, and on January 1, 1974, Home Federal Savings and Loan Association came into being. That same year the association opened six offices in Phoenix.

With extraordinarily high interest rates, business was hard in the 1970s, but Home Federal weathered the storms well and continued to grow. Assets, which had passed $100 million in 1962, passed $200 million nine years later, $300 million in 1973, and $440 million in 1975. Prudent management decisions kept profits growing steadily as well.

In 1985, after changes in federal law permitting interstate banking operations, the stockholders of Home Federal Savings approved a merger with Great American First Savings Bank, a large financial institution with headquarters in San Diego. Great American took over Home Federal in March of the following year, and two months later Home Federal offices got the Great American name. Within the bank, the Arizona properties are collectively known as Great American Arizona.

Great American, founded in 1885, is the oldest savings institution in San Diego. In 1987 it operated in three states: California, Arizona, and Colorado. Not surprisingly, most of its business was in California, where there were 140 branches, while in Arizona the number of branches was expanding rapidly. In less than a year after the merger with Home Federal, Great American opened 20 new, full-service branches at Fry's Food Stores in Arizona, an arrangement entered into because Fry's itself is a statewide chain and is owned by the largest food-marketing chain in the United States. At the end of its first year of operations in Arizona, Great American had more than 600 employees in the state and more than 3,500 in all the company.

Great American is proud not only of its record of growth and profitability, but also of its corporate citizenship. The firm believes in giving both money and effort to the communities where it operates, thereby saying a tangible "thank you" for the welcome and friendship it

Gordon D. Paris, chairman of the board.

receives. Thus, Great American is a significant donor to civic and charitable projects where it does business, and employees are encouraged to give to the charities of their choice. Employees also serve on community boards and as volunteers in numerous charitable activities.

In Arizona, Great American is a principal sponsor of the Miss School, Miss Out program, designed to keep junior high school students in school. The bank offers 15 savings certificates of $1,000 each to students with perfect or near-perfect attendance records, and also provides certificates at the end of marking periods and such classroom prizes as T-shirts and tickets to community attractions. In Tucson, Great American sponsors the Tucson Balloon Fiesta, a winter event that fills the skies with beauty and raises thousands of dollars for charities such as the Arthritis Foundation. The Great American association with this annual fiesta is entirely appropriate—the balloon is the Great American corporate symbol.

Great American First Savings Bank, F.S.B., is proud to be part of Arizona's growth, and looks forward to many more years of fruitful association with the people of the state.

SALT RIVER PROJECT

How many American enterprises can trace their antecedents back to 200 B.C.? The Salt River Project, central Arizona's mammoth water and power provider, can do just that.

It was in that ancient time that the Hohokam Indians dug some 250 miles of irrigation canals, bringing water from the Salt River to irrigate their crops. Those same canals were excavated and used by pioneer farmers in 1868, when the modern Phoenix metropolitan area had its beginnings. In 1903 farmers formed the Salt River Valley Water Users Association to govern water use, and that organization later became called Salt River Project.

The key event in the history of the project—and the launch vehicle for central Arizona's prosperity—was the completion of the Theodore Roosevelt Dam on the Salt River in 1911. That massive structure, still the largest masonry dam in the world, controlled the flow of the capricious river and ensured a water supply to support a Phoenix area population that has now reached 1.5 million.

Other dams were later built on the Salt and Verde rivers, providing additional water storage and hydroelectric generating capacity, and huge oil- and coal-fired generating plants were added to meet Arizona's insatiable demand for new energy sources.

"We use the theme 'Keeping the Spirit Strong' because we believe this reflects the Salt River Project's history and culture," explains A.J. "Jack" Pfister, general manager. "To us, this means a tradition of taking on challenges, facing impediments, and finding ways to overcome them."

Today SRP provides water for the Salt River Valley's 1.5 million residents and electricity for 500,000 customers. It operates a 1,260-mile canal system serving central Arizona agriculture. Behind six of its seven dams are storage lakes that ensure a constant water supply and provide recreation for fishermen and boating enthusiasts.

The Salt River Project has become an enterprise many times larger than its founders could have dreamed. Its assets exceed $4.5 billion, and its annual water and power revenues have reached $849 million. Nearly 6,000 Arizonans are employed by the project.

America's first multipurpose federal reclamation project has proved to be a spectacular success, and Salt River Project personnel have every intention of "Keeping the Spirit Strong."

Theodore Roosevelt Dam, key structure in the reclamation complex administered by the Salt River Project, made possible the modern development of central Arizona.

This artist's rendering depicts the new corporate headquarters complex of the Salt River Project in Papago Park Center, east of Phoenix. The first building should be completed in 1988.

ANDERSON DeBARTOLO PAN, INC.
ARCHITECTURE & ENGINEERING

When William Wilde moved from New Jersey to Tucson in 1946, he brought to Arizona not only an architectural practice, but also a cosmopolitan, modernist vision bred during the turbulence of the Russian Revolution and nurtured by the principles of contemporary architecture. For 20 years he helped turn Tucson into a modern city.

Coming to Tucson in 1967 to work with Wilde and design the new Pima Community College West Campus project were Richard Anderson and Jack DeBartolo, Jr., two young architects from a large Texas firm. In 1971 Anderson returned to Tucson as a partner in the office, and two years later DeBartolo, along with Solomon Pan, another young architect from the same Texas firm, joined him. In 1978 Wilde retired, and the firm since has been known as Anderson DeBartolo Pan, Inc.

Richard "Andy" Anderson of Scottish and German descent, was raised in Illinois and first came to Tucson in 1958 to study at the University of Arizona. He's been an Arizonan since then, except for five years during the late 1960s, when, in Texas, he linked up with his future partners, DeBartolo and Pan.

Jack DeBartolo, Jr., scion of a stonecutter family from southern Italy, grew up in Ohio and Florida. He studied architecture at the University of Houston and received his master's degree at Columbia University in New York. As the designer of Pima Community College, he fell in love with Arizona and came to stay in 1973.

Solomon Pan was born in Shanghai, China, and moved to Taiwan with his family in 1949. Eight years later he came to the "land of opportunity" to study architecture at the University of Houston. The same spirit of adventure that first brought him to the United States eventually led him to Tucson.

The growth of the Tucson firm under its new leadership was dramatic, as the principals set out to establish a progressive practice on a national scale. From a six-person firm in 1971, ADP grew to 16 in 1975 and 28 in 1978. The following year the firm added mechanical and electrical engineering to its architectural capabilities. An office was opened in Phoenix in 1981. The following year the ownership base was expanded to include two new principals, Dale D. Harman and Stephen J. Sawyer. In 1983 structural engineering was added. Two years later three additional principals were named: Robert A. Bracamonte, J. Charles Davis, and

ON BLOCK 193
LAN

Michael E. Harris. And in 1986 Joseph W. Griffin became the ninth principal. Today ADP is a 200-person architecture and engineering firm with a long list of major design awards for its projects.

The firm has developed specialties in programming, planning, architecture, and engineering for health care projects, the advanced technology industry, and institutions of higher education. Clientele is now national—from Boston to San Francisco and from San Diego to Miami. However, Anderson DeBartolo Pan, Inc., retains a special presence in the state of Arizona, where its work has covered a broad range of projects.

In Tucson, Phoenix, Flagstaff, Prescott, Yuma, Casa Grande, and Sierra Vista, the firm's work includes major health care, industrial, educational, commercial, and civic projects, including Anderson DeBartolo Pan, Inc.'s, own headquarters facility in Tucson. These projects have been recognized for their beauty, innovation, and contribution to their communities and the state of Arizona.

The new Main Library in downtown Tucson. Block 193 long-range plan and library building design by Anderson DeBartolo Pan, Inc.

THE ARIZONA REPUBLIC
THE PHOENIX GAZETTE
THE ARIZONA BUSINESS GAZETTE

Phoenix was a dusty territorial village on October 28, 1880, when the *Arizona Gazette* made its debut. Only a decade old, the little community had no railroad, no high school, and not much of anything else to recommend it but a remarkable faith in its own future.

The *Weekly Arizona Gazette,* which evolved into the *Arizona Business Gazette,* was also first published in 1880. Then, on May 18, 1890, just one year after the Arizona Territory capital was moved from Prescott to Phoenix, *The Arizona Republican* burst on the central Arizona scene.

Today Phoenix Newspapers, Inc., publishes all three from its modern plant at 120 East Van

Eugene C. Pulliam built The Arizona Republic *and* Phoenix Gazette *into national prominence during his leadership years, 1946 to 1975.*

This building in central Phoenix housed offices of The Arizona Republican, *forerunner of today's* Arizona Republic, *in 1910.*

Buren Street and a Mesa printing facility. *The Arizona Republic,* a morning publication, has the state's largest circulation. The *Phoenix Gazette,* largest of Arizona's afternoon newspapers, maintains its separate identity and news staff, and is a fierce competitor of its morning sibling. The *Arizona Business Gazette* maintains its proud tradition as the state's major business and legal weekly.

Charles H. McNeil and W.D. Frazee, two enterprising businessmen with an appreciation of Phoenix' possibilities, pooled their resources and energies to found the *Arizona Gazette* and its weekly counterpart in 1880. Like most frontier publishers, they gathered the news, sold the advertising, set the type, and distributed the newspapers themselves.

Weary of the dominance of the Democratic slant of Phoenix journals in 1890, Governor Lewis Wolfley and several of his political supporters launched *The Arizona Republican.* On June 1, 1899, the vigorous *Republican* absorbed a major competitor, the *Phoenix Daily Herald.*

The *Republican* became *The Republic* and merged with *The Phoenix Evening Gazette* on November 18, 1930, under co-publishers Charles Stauffer and Wesley Knorpp. These two giants of Arizona newspapering made their journals two of the most influential in the Southwest before selling them to the late Eugene C. Pulliam of Indianapolis, a founder of The Society of Professional Journalists, Sigma Delta Chi, on October 28, 1946.

In 1947 Pulliam broke ground for The Republic and The Gazette Building on East Van Buren Street, still the home of the newspapers' editorial, advertising, and business offices, together with some production facilities. The company now operates a new satellite printing plant in Mesa, one of the West's finest, along with three branch offices, several circulation offices, and a newsprint warehouse. Additional satellite plants are on the drawing board. The corporation now has more than 2,300 full-time and 500 part-time employees.

Under Pulliam's leadership the newspapers achieved regional and national prominence. After his death in 1975 his son, Eugene S. Pulliam, succeeded him as president and has maintained the newspapers as the state's most widely read publications.

ARIZONA STATE COMPENSATION FUND

William L. Finley, president.

Arizona's concern for the financial woes of workers injured on the job led the legislature to establish workers' compensation laws in 1925. For more than four decades workers' compensation programs were administered by the State Industrial Commission.

Then, in 1967, came the business community's revolt against skyrocketing compensation premiums, which rose by as much as 50 percent that year. To solve the problem, the legislature enacted a law, effective January 1, 1969, that created the Arizona State Compensation Fund.

A happy marriage of government and free enterprise, the Fund is structured to operate as a nonprofit mutual insurance company, with a three-man board of directors appointed by the governor of the state but not undergirded by tax funds. It competes with some 200 private insurance companies in offering compensation insurance programs to Arizona employers.

And the Fund competes very successfully, too. From modest beginnings in 1969, it has become Arizona's largest domestic insurance company, with about 40 percent of all annual premiums paid in the state. Its 1969 premium income of $30.76 million has soared to a 1986 total of more than $150 million.

The Arizona State Compensation Fund currently insures 37,600 employers around the state, many hundreds of which are too small, or for other reasons unable to obtain coverage from other carriers. Half of the Fund's clients pay less than $1,000 annually for coverage. Yet it insures such giants as the Arizona Farm Bureau Federation, almost all of the public school boards in the state, and many major contractors.

President William L. Finley points with justifiable pride to the Arizona State Compensation Fund's spectacular growth, which brought more than 11,000 new employers under its umbrella during 1986 alone. His organization now has its headquarters in a stunning new 14-story building at North Second Street and Earll Drive in Phoenix, and serves the state from nine branch offices.

The Fund has had only two presidents. William K. Foster, who served from 1969 to 1979, rose to the presidency of the American Association of State Compensation Insurance Funds—a notable honor for an executive from a small state. Finley has since followed in Foster's footsteps to the presidency of the national association. And in 1984 the Arizona State Compensation Fund became the first state fund to be granted a seat on the prestigious board of the National Council on Compensation Insurance.

Today the Fund serves Arizona as a full-service mutual insurance company, and all profits are returned to policyholders in the form of dividends and lower rates. Its $500-million investment portfolio currently produces annual income of more than $60 million to help keep premiums stable despite soaring health care costs. And the Arizona State Compensation Fund's effective Loss Prevention Department has made remarkable strides in reducing accident rates in all areas of industry. Says Finley, "We're very proud that we have contributed to Arizona's economic growth, and in so doing have helped provide better protection for working people."

The Arizona State Compensation Fund moved its headquarters into this 14-story building at North Second Street and Earll Drive, Phoenix, in 1987.

SOUTHWEST AMBULANCE, INC.

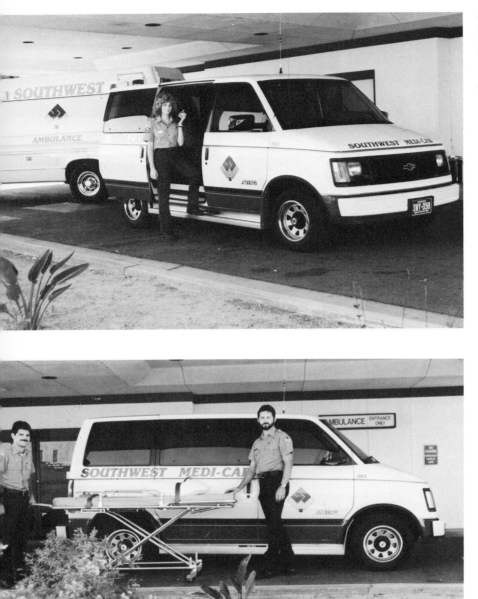

The total medical transportation system developed by Southwest has not been duplicated. From cab to critical care, the one-step program is unique across America.

When Southwest developed the Medi-Coach, it reduced the cost overall of medical transportation.

When Bob Ramsey was a Boy Scout in Phoenix during the mid-1950s, he became so imbued with the importance of emergency medical care that he started the First Response Patrol in his troop. He and his fellow scouts learned first aid techniques and responded to calls for emergency help from anywhere in their neighborhood. *Boys' Life* magazine was impressed by young Ramsey's innovative abilities and published an article about his project.

Although he went on to major in history and Asian Studies at Arizona State University and to work after school in mixed media and advertising, Ramsey never lost his fascination with emergency health care. So it was not surprising

that, in 1982, he founded Southwest Ambulance, Inc., currently Arizona's largest private company in its field.

Ramsey, president and chief operating officer of the corporation, has earned an enviable reputation as an innovator and builder in the several industries with which he has been associated. Because his father was employed in marketing, advertising, and promotion, Ramsey grew up in the world of new ideas and the science of persuasion.

In the mid-1960s he started one of the first mixed-media companies in Arizona, and in 1975 he became vice-president/marketing in the Paddock Pools organization, served as a solar energy consultant, and worked with Arizona's Indians in establishing a newspaper, building a solar school, and organizing emergency medical services. Moving on to EMS (Emergency Medical Services) in the late 1970s, Ramsey advanced rapidly to the executive vice-presidency of KORDS-PMT Ambulance Company in 1981. He broke away to establish the first privately owned nonstop transcontinental air ambulance service, and from there it was an easy move to starting his own emergency ground transportation firm. Bob Ramsey is married to Jenny Norton, state representative, for District 27, Tempe, Arizona.

The impact of Southwest Ambulance and its president on the emergency medical transportation industry in Arizona has been little short of spectacular. Ramsey has brought about exciting changes and established such programs as specialized training for emergency vehicle drivers, less expensive medical transportation for those who do not require all the facilities of an ambulance, courses for paramedics and emergency care technicians, billing preparation for other ambulance services (the City of Phoenix is one), and consulting help for HMOs and other medical organizations.

"This is a sunrise industry," Ramsey declares. "Prehospital services are just emerging as vital components of total health care, and we have only begun to explore the possibilities."

One of those possibilities is in cost containment, a field that has intrigued Ramsey for years. At least a partial solution is Southwest's new Ambulette service, which uses Medi-Cabs and Medi-Coaches to transport patients who do not require full ambulance service.

Another is the innovative Southwest Ambulance instructional program called Evade, which has earned media coverage nationwide. Not only ambulance drivers but also firemen, police officers, and other drivers of emergency vehicles come to Southwest's Mesa, Arizona, school for instruction and to nearby field sites for practical driving problems. The firm's training courses prepare technicians, paramedics, trauma nurses, and others to give emergency care aboard ambulances en route to hospitals.

The company's standard ambulance service is kept at high levels, too. Forty ambulances operate from 21 stations in Phoenix, other Maricopa County cities, and in Pinal County. They average only five minutes in response time, and they are on the scene of an emergency within 10 minutes in 95 to 98 percent of all cases.

Southwest has franchises for exclusive ambulance service in Tempe, Chandler, Glendale, and Casa Grande, and it shares services with other companies in most other communities of central Arizona. Its headquarters is at South 40th and LaSalle streets near the border dividing Phoenix and Tempe.

To respond without delay to calls for help from its broad areas of service, Southwest Ambulance has a staff of 250, including drivers, paramedics, instructors, office personnel, mechanics, and many other specialists. "We are operating a private business," observes Ramsey, "but you can be sure we all consider ourselves in partnership with the public sector. We are on full alert 24 hours a day, seven days a week, and lives hang on the state of our readiness and proficiency."

Ramsey is a leader to establish access to the 911 emergency telephone network that serves central Arizona. He has served on community boards for the establishment and regulation of emergency health services. He may often be seen at the Arizona State Legislature, advocating programs that will improve emergency medical care. As one colleague recently declared, "Bob Ramsey has brought new standards of practice to his industry."

"Ours is a rapidly changing technology," says Ramsey, "and we at Southwest Ambulance, Inc., do our best to keep up with those changes and to take the lead in bringing them about. We play a critical role—literally a life-and-death role—in our community, and we can have enormous impact on the lives of thousands. No wonder we feel challenged every day to do our job a little better than we did the day before."

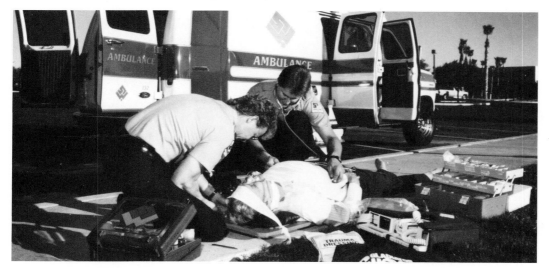

Southwest Medi-Cab was developed by Bob Ramsey to assist health care facilities to reduce transportation expenses.

As the largest private provider of emergency ambulance service in Arizona, Southwest has been selected by many cities to be the sole provider of ambulance service to 911 callers.

ARIZONA PUBLIC SERVICE COMPANY

Keith Turley, chairman of the board.

The three 1.27-million-kilowatt units of the Palo Verde Nuclear Generating Station are on a 4,000-acre site about 50 miles west of Phoenix.

The numbers are almost too vast to comprehend: 1.5 million people, in 11 of Arizona's 15 counties, served with electricity every day; 200 communities in Arizona dependent on the company for power; 9,000 employees in an incredible variety of jobs; and a plant and property value of $6 billion. That's Arizona Public Service Company, the state's largest energy company, which has just entered its second century of providing energy to the people of a fast-growing state.

Even more important than size, however, is the commitment of APS people to serve the public. "Arizona People Serving You" is more than a corporate slogan—it's a philosophy that permeates every facet of the firm's activity.

Arizona Public Service produces electrical energy at coal-burning units in three widely dispersed Arizona and New Mexico locations, with APS' share being 2.043 million kilowatts in all; 22 gas- or oil-fueled units producing another 1.226 million kilowatts for APS customers; three units of the Palo Verde nuclear plant, with APS' share being 1.108 million kilowatts; and a small 5,600-kilowatt hydro plant—more than 4 million kilowatts in all. For many years the firm also provided natural gas to southern and central Arizona customers, but that operation of Arizona Public Service Company was sold in 1984.

Because the corporation has such heavy responsibilities to serve the people of Arizona, its officers and staff have always worked as partners in the development of Arizona's economy and in creating a better quality of life. APS people are prominent members of industrial development organizations and business groups. They work to help solve ecological problems. They give time and money to the development of the fine arts and to a host of charitable societies. Company volunteers with construction and repair skills donate time and energy to helping less fortunate neighbors make their homes more livable.

One of the most notable examples of APS participation in Arizona growth efforts is its special interest in the economy of the state's rural areas and smaller communities. Because these areas have not grown as spectacularly as the urban centers, APS works to attract new industry, and to help establish economic development organizations there.

Arizona Public Service Company is a powerful force for good and a willing partner in the building of Arizona today. However, there was a time when the roots of the organization were tiny, indeed.

Phoenix was a small, dusty frontier town in 1886, when a young Japanese immigrant named Hutchlon Ohnick (the Anglicized version of Hachiro Onuki) was granted a franchise by the Phoenix City Council "to supply the said city of Phoenix and its citizens and residents with illuminating gas or electric lights." A few days later Ohnick and his financial backers formed the Phoenix Illuminating Gas and Electric Company—the great-great-great-grandfather of Arizona Public Service Company.

First there were 12 gas streetlights in Phoenix, then electric service to homes and businesses. Pioneer Phoenicians were a bit leery about electricity when it first became available. There were those who feared that electricity would "leak out" of outlets, blacken ceilings, and kill house plants.

Other communities in Arizona Territory were building electric plants—Prescott in 1884, Yuma in 1892, Flagstaff in 1895, among others. In Phoenix, the major power supplier became Phoenix Light and Power Company, and later the Pacific Gas and Electric Company (not the California utility of the same name).

On February 16, 1920, the Central Arizona Light and Power Company was formed, and later that year it took over Pacific Gas and Electric's operations. CALAPCO acquired the small power companies at Chandler, Gilbert, Tempe, Glendale, Peoria, and Scottsdale during the 1920s and 1930s. In 1945 Arizona was being served by The Arizona Power Company in its northern counties, by CALAPCO in much of the central area, and by Arizona Edison in several southern counties. CALAPCO purchased The Arizona Power Company property in 1949 and renamed it the Northern Arizona Light and Power Company, which became part of a soon-to-take-place merger.

It became obvious to forward-looking Arizonans that the state could be best served by merging CALAPCO and Arizona Edison. That momentous consolidation was completed on March 1, 1952, and Arizona Public Service Company was born. Henry B. Sargent served as APS president with great distinction in the first years after the merger. Walter Lucking, who became president in 1955 at age 41, gave vision and strength to the company, as did Bill Reilly, president during the early 1970s.

Today Keith L. Turley, who began his association with APS nearly 40 years ago, serves as chairman of the board. O. Mark De Michele, who joined APS in 1978 as vice-president/corporate relations, is now president and chief executive officer.

In 1985 APS stockholders approved a corporate restructuring that made the firm a wholly owned subsidiary of AZP Group, Inc., which has since been renamed Pinnacle West Capital Corporation.

Today Arizona Public Service Company is Arizona's largest supplier of electric power, providing about 45 percent of the state's total.

Chairman Turley is optimistic about the fu-

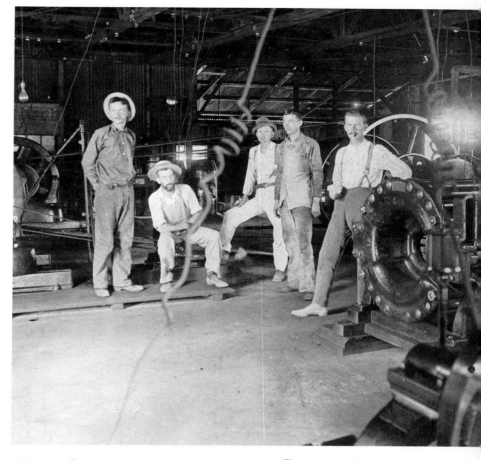

ture of Arizona Public Service. He looks for breakthroughs in such exotic technologies as solar photovoltaics to keep electrical production costs under control, and he believes that Arizona and its energy companies will continue to grow as rapidly as any in America.

But one-on-one human relationships, he feels sure, will always be at the heart of Arizona Public Service Company's success. "We've been successful because we've always recognized that the customer is the beginning and end of our business. I don't believe that will ever change. If it does, or if we forget it, we'll be in trouble!"

This steam electric generator was located in Phoenix at the northwest corner of First Avenue and Buchanan in the 1890s.

An impish gust of wind caused plenty of trouble back in 1903, when it toppled this 90-foot stack being installed at the original power plant of an APS predecessor. The plant, located near Buchanan Street and First Avenue, was operated by Phoenix Light and Fuel Company and had a capacity of 700 kilowatts in 1906.

THE WESTWARD LOOK RESORT

For four decades The Westward Look Resort has been a mecca for tourists seeking sun and relaxation in the clear desert air, and for local social events amid a gracious setting.

The Westward Look Resort traces its lineage back to Arizona's first year of statehood. In the summer of 1912, less than six months after Arizona put the 48th star on the nation's flag, William Watson and his wife, Marie, both Tucson residents, took up 172 acres of homestead land far north of the little city and prepared to build their dream home.

The Watsons hired M.J. Starkweather, Tucson's premier architect, to design for them a spacious house in the traditional regional style. The building included an artist's loft, living quarters, a Spanish-style patio, and a matchless view of the Arizona desert and the Santa Catalina Mountains. But Starkweather improved on the traditionalists, building with steel and concrete dressed up to look like adobe. His foresight was responsible for the excellent state of preservation of the building 75 years later. Guests at the Westward Look will find the original house now used as executive offices and a VIP reception room.

In the 1920s and 1930s Tucson changed gradually. One of the elements of that change was the emerging popularity of guest ranches and the birth of a hospitality industry in the growing

city, now served not only by rail but also by air and by good roads for those who chose to drive. The owners of the Westward Look property added 15 cottages near the original home, and began to invite guests to come from the frozen East to enjoy Tucson's marvelous winter climate.

By the early 1940s the Westward Look property was a full-fledged guest ranch, comfortable but fairly spartan, as such facilities always were. Early in that decade the Nanson family bought the ranch and added 15 rooms. The property got the name Westward Look in 1943. The phrase came from a speech by Winston Churchill, Great Britain's great wartime prime minister, who in turn had borrowed it from a poem by Arthur Hugh Clough. Thus, even the name of this premier hostelry has distinguished antecedents.

In the postwar years the Westward Look grew in popularity, becoming a mainstay not only for Tucson's seasonal visitors but also for local people, who went there for an evening or a weekend of comfort in lovely surroundings. In 1972 a Tucsonan, Jack Hoag, bought the property and immediately set out to enlarge it. Hoag's idea was that each new section should have a distinctive character; thus, for example, the Posada rooms were quite different from the Fiesta rooms. Over the 10 years of his ownership, Hoag expanded the Westward Look to 160 rooms, added the Lookout Lounge, relocated and renovated the Gold Room, added a pool and spa, and expanded meeting room facilities to about 10,000 square feet.

In the 1970s fast-growing Tucson had about 400,000 residents. The Westward Look Resort was one of its three tourist resorts—the other two were the Tanque Verde Guest Ranch and the Arizona Inn. Of these, the Westward Look was the largest. Tucson also had smaller hotels and motels located within the city and on its fringes; these served largely the commercial market. But the Westward Look was the dominant force in the hospitality industry of Tucson and southern Arizona. Its occupancies were healthy year round, and it boasted Mobil four-star ratings both for its lodgings and for its dining room.

Late in 1982 RKO General began negotiating with Hoag for the purchase of The Westward Look Resort. Once the deal was closed, major renovations and further significant expansions took place. Additions included a new lap pool,

making a total of three pools, and 84 new guest suites, increasing the total number of suites and rooms from 160 to 244. Eight tennis courts were resurfaced with Laykold championship surfacing. The lobby, lounge, and Gold Room, the Westward Look's gourmet restaurant, were completely redecorated. The new owners built a tennis clubhouse with complete locker facilities. A recreation center, with full fitness facilities, aerobic classes, and a masseuse, also was added, as was a gift shop. At the same time the nature trail was upgraded and enlarged to include a two-thirds-mile course with nine picnic locations along the trail. Also added was a sports park with a 250-seat barbecue area, two full-size volleyball courts, a full-length basketball court, two horseshoe pits, and shuffleboard and softball facilities.

The 1980s has seen the creation of a number of destination resorts in the Tucson area, as southern Arizona increasingly makes its mark as a year-round vacation destination. However, The Westward Look Resort remains Tucson's preeminent hostelry. It is still characterized by comfort, elegance, and the variety of facilities that its guests have come to expect over the years.

The Westward Look Resort, firmly rooted in the traditions of an earlier Tucson, confidently extends to its guests the most modern facilities and accommodations, backing them up with old-fashioned excellence of service. It is a combination guaranteed to produce success in the future, as it has in more than four decades as Tucson's most distinguished inn.

Guests enjoy the lovely desert evenings overlooking the resort's three swimming pools with the Santa Catalina Mountains in the background.

CITIBANK (ARIZONA)

A. Ray Einsel, chairman and chief executive officer, Citibank (Arizona).

David A. Brooks, division executive, Western Division, U.S. Consumer Banking Group, Citicorp.

Citibank (Arizona), a subsidiary of Citicorp, America's largest bank holding company, is a fascinating blend of old and new, rural and urban, warm humanity and high-tech efficiency.

Its roots go back to the Arizona Territory in 1906, the year 10 Arizona pioneers banded together to charter Yavapai County Savings Bank at Prescott. In 1960 it became Pioneer Bank of Arizona and was moved to Phoenix. Growth and mergers with two other financial institutions created Great Western Bank and Trust in 1969.

Great Western became Citibank (Arizona) on October 1, 1986. Today the resources and know-how of the parent organization are enabling the people of a pioneering Arizona bank to serve its customers even better than before.

Citibank (Arizona), with headquarters in a new high-rise structure at 4041 North Central Avenue in Phoenix, has branches in several communities throughout the state. Citibank provides financial services to every major segment of the Arizona economy, which is one of the fastest growing in the nation.

In addition, Citibankers have demonstrated a healthy concern for the well-being of their fellow Arizonans. The institution and its employees have provided funding and volunteer services to such worthy activities as the YWCA, United Way, Chicanos por la Causa, Arizona Special Olympics, Samaritan Medical Foundation, educational programs, and the fine arts. Through its matching gifts program, the bank doubles employee gifts by matching their contributions dollar for dollar.

Arizona history buffs find the heritage of Citibank (Arizona) and its predecessors a fascinating story. It combines such disparate elements as pioneer entrepreneurs, the Navajo Nation, Kuwaiti entrepreneurs, and even the great Bing Crosby.

The pioneers were the Prescott founders of Yavapai County Savings Bank, which later became Pioneer Bank. Other early investors were the people of Holbrook, who chartered First National Bank of Holbrook in 1922. In 1960 the majority interest in the Holbrook bank was purchased by a group that included Bing Crosby. The famous entertainer even became chairman of the institution's board of directors.

In 1962, after a monumental decision by the Navajo Tribal Council to allow banking on the Arizona portion of the Navajo Reservation, First

National Bank of Holbrook became First Navajo National Bank. The first branch of First Navajo Bank was established at Window Rock, seat of the tribal government.

Meanwhile, the Bank of Tucson was thriving in southern Arizona's major city. That bank merged with First Navajo to form a powerful institution that took the name Great Western Bank. On December 31, 1969, the final merger was completed with Great Western and Pioneer Bank combined resources. Thus, three great Arizona institutions, which had matured in separate corners of the state, were joined as Great Western Bank and Trust, with assets of more than $116 million.

The Kuwaiti chapter of the bank's history started in 1980, when four investors from that Middle-eastern nation purchased Great Western. In September 1985 it was announced that Great Western would become part of Citicorp in October 1986. Citicorp, with a record of success dating back to 1812, is a bank holding company with $203 billion in assets and more than 3,000 offices in 92 nations.

Chairman of the board and chief executive officer of Citibank (Arizona) is A. Ray Einsel, who came to Arizona from First National Bank of Chicago. He played key roles in the development of consumer services at Mountain States Bancard Association in Denver, and with banks in Cleveland and New York.

Einsel succeeded David A. Brooks as Great Western's chairman. Brooks now heads Citicorp's Western Division, U.S. Consumer Banking Group, in San Francisco.

Joining the Citicorp family has proven to be a morale booster for the Arizona employees who had served Great Western Bank. The infusion of new capital, the availability of new technology and ideas, and the satisfaction of being part of a worldwide financial organization have given Citibank (Arizona) people new incentives to serve and to grow with the company.

Chairman Ray Einsel is a firm believer in the value of sharing ideas and improving communication throughout his organization. "Almost anything is possible when we all work together," he states. In a recent goals statement, Einsel expressed his intention for Citibank (Arizona) to be "the premier bank in Arizona by providing a full range of innovative financial services to the consumer and business professional markets, differentiated by an unexcelled level of service."

Workers at a Great Western Bank branch in Phoenix installed new Citibank signs when the financial institution became Citibank (Arizona) on October 1, 1986.

Headquarters offices for Citibank (Arizona) are housed in this building at 4041 North Central Avenue, Phoenix.

On January 28, 1988, Citicorp announced an agreement to acquire United Bank of Arizona, pending regulatory approval. United Bank will be merged with Citibank (Arizona). This merger will combine United's commercial expertise with Citibank's leadership in consumer and commercial banking.

When approved, Citibank (Arizona) will become the fourth-largest bank in the state, with assets of more than $3 billion. The consolidation is expected to result in overall operational efficiencies, as well as added products, services, and convenience for customers.

Citibank is a full-service bank offering a variety of checking, savings, investment, credit, trust, and mortgage products. It has branches in communities throughout Arizona. Citibank also has Mortgage Centers in Phoenix and Tucson.

"Citibank. Because Americans want to succeed, not just survive," boasts the bank's slogan, and Arizonans by the thousands would agree with that claim.

VALLEY NATIONAL BANK OF ARIZONA

I.E. Solomon knew the time-honored formula for business success: Find a need and fill it.

As a small-town storekeeper in remote southeastern Arizona during the late 1880s, he saw a definite need for a bank to serve a scattered but growing population. With support from 14 investors, he gathered $25,000 in capital to launch the Gila Valley Bank. Opening in January 1900, it attracted copper miners, cattlemen, and farmers who handed hard-earned dollars to a clerk behind a desk set up at the rear of Solomon's store. Thus was born the financial institution that became Arizona's largest—Valley National Bank of Arizona.

From this promising beginning the new institution grew quickly, expanding to nearby towns and establishing the first trust department in the state. By 1914 it was profitable enough to rescue the ailing Valley Bank of Phoenix, although eight years would pass before the two were combined as Valley Bank and Trust, with $10 million in deposits.

Like other financial institutions in the United States, Valley Bank prospered during the 1920s. But from 1929 to 1933 deposit balances dwindled from $17.7 million to $6.7 million. The bank president, under the strain of those early Depression years, resigned. The directors asked Walter Reed Bimson of Chicago's Harris Trust to assume the helm.

On January 1, 1933, Bimson met with Valley Bank employees and made a historic declaration: "Make loans! Plain people need to borrow small sums for all kinds of purposes. Those peo-

(Top, right) Serving southern Arizona's fast-growing population is Valley National Bank of Arizona's Southern Division in Tucson, with headquarters in this building.

ple will pour into our bank if we convince them we're here to help them."

"Make loans" and "help plain people" were to be Bimson's guidelines for nearly 40 years. The bank recovered and began to grow again. In 1935 it acquired Consolidated National Bank of Tucson, the first financial institution in the nation to sign up with the Federal Deposit Insurance Corporation.

Recent Chairmen of the Board Valley National Bank (now Valley National Corporation)	
Walter R. Bimson	1954-1970
James E. Patrick	1971-1972
James B. Mayer	1972-1976
Gilbert F. Bradley	1976-1982
Roger A. Lyon	1982-1983
Howard C. McCrady	1983-

At the same time Bimson enlisted the bank in the FHA home loan program, boosting Valley Bank to fifth in FHA loans in the nation—a major reason for Arizona's economic recovery. His staff designed several other unprecedented programs: installment loans, car loans, education loans, loans for medical bills, and others. By the late 1940s this innovative bank had become the 75th largest in America, with deposits of more than $200 million.

During the following decades the institution took an active role in building Arizona by providing funds for agribusiness, manufacturing, construction, and tourism. Before Bimson retired in 1970, Valley Bank introduced direct deposit of Social Security checks and the first plastic charge cards.

A holding company, Valley National Corporation, was formed in 1981, with Valley National Bank of Arizona as principal subsidiary. Under the leadership of Howard C. McCrady, chairman of the board since 1983, the corporation has grown to more than $10 billion in assets. It now employs more than 7,000 people and ranks 22nd in deposits in the nation.

Corporate offices of Arizona's largest bank, Valley National Bank of Arizona, are in the Valley Center in downtown Phoenix.

MICROAGE, INC.

Jeffrey McKeever and Alan Hald were rising young executives of First Interstate Bank of Arizona in 1976, but they had the courage to leave their comfortable positions, borrow money, and start a microcomputer store called The Byte Shop in a low-rent district of Tempe.

In little more than a decade their computer reselling business has enjoyed spectacular growth and has become MicroAge Computer Stores, Inc., one of the largest franchise organizations in the industry, with more than 200 stores in the United States, Canada, Europe, and Japan.

Today MicroAge, Inc., the parent company, encompasses not only the international store chain, but also a franchising organization, a private-label distributor, a value-added wholesaling group, and other related enterprises. MicroAge is headquartered in a modernistic building at 2308 South 55th Street in Tempe.

McKeever and Hald, who use as their company slogan, "Where Vision Becomes Reality," have exhibited both extraordinary vision and a firm grasp on reality in developing their far-flung organization. They have been pioneers and innovators, leading the way in finding solutions to their clients' business problems and avoiding the pitfalls that caused so many competitors to go out of business in their rapidly changing industry.

By 1979 the two partners owned six stores and had the largest company-owned microcomputer chain in the nation. The following year the organization moved into franchising. By 1984 annual corporate revenues had reached the $42-million mark, a figure that grew to $203 million only three years later.

Much of MicroAge's success is attributable to its philosophy of providing a complete package of hardware, software, services, and training to its franchisees and their clients. Personnel in each of the individually owned franchise stores employ "outbound selling" techniques, going out into their communities, calling on clients, and working to find solutions to their unique problems.

MicroAge conducts a training school for franchise owners at its Tempe headquarters, holds annual conferences to share the latest knowledge and product information, and publishes a magazine, *MicroAge Quarterly,* which has a circulation of more than 250,000 copies.

The founding partners make a highly effective team. McKeever is president and chief

Jeffrey D. McKeever (left), president, and Alan P. Hald, chairman of the board, are co-founders of MicroAge, Inc.

executive officer of MicroAge and Hald is chairman of the board. Citing their company slogan, it might well be said that McKeever, the entrepreneur, is "Mr. Reality" and Hald, the futurist, is "Mr. Vision."

Considering the amazing growth of their organization in its first decade, the future of MicroAge, Inc., seems unlimited, indeed.

The Byte Shop (top right), Arizona's first computer store, marked the beginning of Micro-Age International, currently headquartered at 2308 South 55th Street, Tempe (above).

BLUE CIRCLE WEST

Blue Circle West construction materials are being used in major projects across Arizona. Among the firm's production facilities are a cement terminal (right), concrete plant (below), and an aggregate plant (bottom).

Arizona's fast-growing construction industry has an almost insatiable appetite for ready-mix concrete, cement, sand and rock, aggregate, and cement blocks. Since February 1983 a major supplier of those materials has been Blue Circle

West, which has its corporate headquarters at 2625 South 19th Avenue in Phoenix.

Before Blue Circle's entry into the Arizona market, building contractors and other consumers had for many years depended primarily on one major supplier for these materials. It's a more competitive and a healthier situation today.

Blue Circle West's operational area extends from West Texas to the West Coast. In Phoenix and Tucson, Blue Circle has ready-mix concrete plants, cement distribution facilities, aggregate extraction operations, and cement block sales outlets. In California, the company has cement distribution facilities in San Diego and Richmond.

Rapid growth, much of it through acquisition of smaller businesses, has been the hallmark of Blue Circle's history ever since the establishment of Arizona operations. From 1983 sales volume of less than $15 million, the corporation has sent the yearly sales totals skyrocketing to $150 million—a tenfold increase in a little more than four years.

Blue Circle West is ultimately owned by Blue Circle Industries Group PLC, an international parent company based in the United Kingdom. "The Group," as it is familiarly known, is primarily engaged in the manufacture and distribution of cement and allied products, decorative finishes, industrial minerals, ceramic and acrylic sanitary and plumbing products, engineering supplies, quarry restoration, and building materials.

Long established in the British Isles, the company has extended its operations to Mexico, South America, Australia, Africa, Asia, and now to the United States. Blue Circle is not only the largest cement manufacturer in the United Kingdom, but also is one of the leading cement suppliers worldwide.

It was in late May 1983 that Blue Circle completed the acquisition of three cement plants and a lime plant in the United States—installations with a combined annual capacity of more than 2 million tons of cement and 300,000 tons of lime. Thus was born Blue Circle, Inc., in America. The Group had acquired Tucson Sand and Soil's concrete division two months earlier, along with Century Materials' concrete division and the Fast Way ready-mix company. From that consolidation was born Blue Circle West, which first established its headquarters in Tucson.

Expansion soon began, and by the end of 1983 the firm had obtained three concrete batching plants in Tucson and four in Phoenix. In addition, Melwire, Inc., a cement distribution facility, was acquired as a wholly owned subsidiary of Blue Circle West that same year.

During 1984 the corporation added cement distribution terminals in Phoenix and Tucson. Through the acquisition of Standard Concrete, another Phoenix concrete batching plant was added. Then an aggregate operation was purchased from Columbia Materials, Inc. In the fall of 1985 Blue Circle West joined with Cemento de Chihuahua to establish a cement distribution terminal in El Paso. The acquisition of Columbia Materials aggregate and block divisions was completed in January 1986.

There seems to be no end in sight to Blue Circle's growth. In July 1986 the corporation made its largest acquisition yet—the purchase of Johnson-Stewart-Johnson Company, a firm employing 475 people in ready-mix and aggregate operations.

In early 1986 Blue Circle West moved into spacious office, maintenance, and warehousing facilities just south of Interstate 10 at 2625 South 19th Avenue in Phoenix.

Today Blue Circle West employs about 880 people in its diverse building materials operations. It operates more than 225 ready-mix trucks in Arizona and has assets of some $75 million.

John Bourdeaux, a former Martin Marietta executive, is chief operating officer of Blue Circle, Inc., and is officed in Atlanta. Heading Blue Circle West is president Steve Story, who directs the firm from its Phoenix headquarters.

Blue Circle West has had a major impact on the growth of the Arizona construction industry. Because it acquired several firms that might have been forced out of the highly competitive market, it has preserved jobs and enhanced employment opportunities.

Construction has become one of the major industries of fast-growing Arizona, with new office complexes, high-rise corporate towers, freeways, apartment houses, and single-family homes rising on almost every available plot of land in the metropolitan areas. Without such materials suppliers as Blue Circle West, with its worldwide resources, the construction industry in the state would be unable to meet the needs of Arizona's people.

THE PENSUS GROUP

Richard C. Shaw (top) and David Maule-ffinch (bottom) are the founders and principal officers of The Pensus Group, a real estate development and management firm.

Founded in 1978 as Community Development Corporation, the Phoenix-based Pensus Group is changing the face of urban Arizona. This organization has built its reputation as one of the state's most skilled real estate investment and development companies, and has improved the quality of life for many Arizonans.

Named for the Latin word for "thought," The Pensus Group has as its symbol Rodin's sculpture of *The Thinker.* It's a most appropriate symbol, too, because the company has insisted on thoughtful development designed for the people and environment. The firm has established itself as a leader in the analysis, structuring, and completion of a wide variety of highly complex projects, including major planning and zoning cases, large vertical and horizontal assemblies, and distressed properties.

The Pensus Group specializes in multiuse developments—major projects combining space for living, working, shopping, and recreation. One of the foremost of its projects is the new Portales in Scottsdale, the first master-planned, urban-density, mixed-use development in Scottsdale. On the 40 acres of Portales will be a 200-room hotel, 160 luxury condominiums, executive offices, "festival shopping" facilities, restaurants, and theaters. The 1.7-million-square-foot development will be completed in the early 1990s.

The company's two principals, Richard C. Shaw and David Maule-ffinch, are held in high regard by Arizona's real estate development community.

Shaw, a Phoenix native and grandson of an Arizona pioneer, is experienced as a lawyer, mortgage banker, real estate broker, and professional consultant. He has directed the development of more than 2 million square feet of income properties, 6,000 acres of agricultural projects, and a varied list of joint ventures with major financial institutions and management companies. Shaw co-founded the Community Financial Corporation in Phoenix in 1975 as a mortgage banking firm that grew into the Community Development Corporation three years later.

Maule-ffinch was born and educated in England and moved to Phoenix in 1976. From 1978 to 1982 he served as vice-president of the Gosnell Development Corporation, owner and developer of the popular five-star Pointe Resort Communities. There he was responsible for all real estate management, development, and leasing. His experience includes the acquisition and master planning of land holdings worth more than $250 million, and the acquisition, development, and leasing of more than 1.4 million square feet of office, industrial, and retail space.

Both men are prominent in professional associations. Shaw is president of the Maricopa County Industrial Development Authority and is a member of the American Bar Association, the International Council of Shopping Centers, the American Planning Association, and the Urban Land Institute. He is also a lecturer in real estate and finance at Arizona State University. In addition, Maule-ffinch is a bank director and an associate member of the Royal Institution of Chartered Surveyors, the highest professional real estate designation in the United Kingdom.

Shaw and Maule-ffinch became professionally acquainted in Phoenix and joined forces in

1981; the company's efforts were redirected from retail development toward real estate marketing, management, and consulting. The firm reached agreement in 1984 with Arizona-based Anchor National Life Insurance Company to form an investment partnership with assets well over $150 million, representing a large portion of the firm's portfolio.

The Pensus Group is headquartered in the new Anchor Centre at 2201 East Camelback Road, Phoenix.

In the early years the firm's predecessors developed a number of commercial developments throughout Arizona and New Mexico, ranging from 150,000-square-foot shopping centers in Prescott and Gallup to an office building for Peabody Coal Company in Flagstaff. Other projects followed, and it became clear that sound principles of value creation could be applied to the ownership, development, and management of large real estate projects.

The scope of the company's investment/development activity shifted dramatically in 1983, when it broadened its retail emphasis to encompass major land assemblies for mixed-use office, industrial, hotel, and residential development. The Pensus Group's investment portfolio grew rapidly in the mid-1980s to include a broad selection of properties, primarily centered in the greater Phoenix area.

The Portales project is one of the largest land assemblies ever accomplished in Arizona. Fifty-eight different parcels were acquired for the mammoth development.

Although the incorporation of diverse uses into a single large real estate development is a relatively new concept in Arizona, The Pensus Group has established itself as a leader in the field. Shaw and Maule-ffinch have proven themselves to be innovators of remarkable versatility and wisdom.

"The Pensus Group's major area of expertise," explains Shaw, "is identifying opportunity where others see only problems. To see beauty where blight exists, order in the chaos of multiple ownership, diplomacy and compromise in the face of politics and emotion requires a broad knowledge of business, finance, the law, and a little psychology. In all our projects, we strive to create a better, more attractive place in which to live and work."

Shaw and Maule-ffinch have every intention of building solidly on their successes, and already are exploring other large mixed-use projects throughout the Southwest. The Pensus Group will be around for a long time, helping to build Arizona and the Greater Southwest in the next century, and perhaps beyond.

Scottsdale's Portales project, developed by The Pensus Group, is expected to be completed in the late 1980s or early 1990s. It will consist of a 40-acre, master-planned multiuse development combining facilities for living, working, and playing.

ASTRO BLUEPRINT
AND SUPPLY COMPANY, INC.

Joe Castillo, president of Astro Blueprint and Supply Company, has gained prominence in Arizona business, political, and civic affairs.

fers advanced hi-tech reproduction services and technical expertise, and is a distributor for drafting equipment and supplies, and computerized automated drafting supplies.

Astro has a Tucson branch at Stone and Drachman streets and a store at 2401 North 24th Street in Phoenix. Two other Phoenix branches are in the planning stages. The firm does reproduction work for such major clients as the University of Arizona Medical Center in Tucson, the Esplanade and Renaissance Center in Phoenix, Motorola Inc. and Hughes Aircraft, and projects in Las Vegas, Nevada.

Castillo's success story is an inspirational one. The son of a laborer, he studied architectural drawing at Tucson High School and gained practical experience with Southwestern Technical Services in Tucson. He was married and had four small children when he quit his job in 1958 and launched his partnership. To make ends meet that first year, he designed and drafted house plans at home after hours.

Soon he was persuaded to run for the South Tucson City Council, and in 1966 he became the first Hispanic to be elected to the Arizona State Senate in modern times. Castillo distinguished himself during three senate terms and then was elected to the Pima County Board of Supervisors.

It was in 1977 that he decided to invade the Phoenix market, which was already saturated with 26 blueprint shops. To give his business a new and more universal image, he changed the name of the company to Astro Blueprint and Supply Company. Castillo has built his firm in a single decade into one of the largest and most prestigious in Arizona.

Dick Augustson, who joined Castillo in 1967, serves as executive vice-president of the corporation. Castillo, who operates the Phoenix division, is president; his eldest son, Steven, is vice-president and Phoenix manager; his youngest son, Eric, is vice-president and director of sales; and his wife, Dorothy, is secretary/treasurer.

Castillo has earned high positions in Arizona business, politics, and civic affairs. He serves as vice-president of the Better Business Bureau of Arizona, sits on the Executive Committee of the Arizona Republican Party, is chairman of the shareholders' association of Pinnacle West Capital Corporation (the state's largest holding company), and was chairman of the Arizona delegation to the 1986 White House Conference on Small Business.

Joe Castillo was earning only $1.54 per hour as manager of a Tucson blueprint shop in 1958, so he convinced a fellow employee that they should start their own company. They were able to invest only $300 apiece, but that was enough to launch Pima Blueprint on the corner of Speedway and Swan in Tucson. From that humble beginning, with first-year sales of $13,000, grew the forerunner of Astro Blueprint and Supply Company, Inc., which today has stores in Tucson and Phoenix and does an annual business of well in excess of $2 million.

Castillo bought his partner's interest in 1967, and he has made his organization a working partnership of architects, engineers, contractors, and the electronics industry in Arizona's booming economy. Astro Blueprint, with headquarters at 4870 East 22nd Street in Tucson, of-

RUSS LYON REALTY COMPANY

Russ Lyon Realty Company, the Valley of the Sun's oldest family-owned brokerage, was founded in 1947 by the late Russell A. Lyon, Sr. It has grown from a one-man enterprise to a multifaceted commercial, industrial, and residential firm projecting more than $300 million in sales during 1987.

The founder's youngest son, Dennis H. Lyon, president and chairman of the board, has directed the company's expansion since 1968. Russ Lyon Realty has a sales force approaching 300 sales associates working out of six valley offices.

Russ Lyon, Sr., already had two successful careers to his credit when he and his wife, Janis, and their two young sons—Russ Jr., now a prominent shopping center developer, and Dennis, a dynamic salesman who has advanced through the ranks of the agency—arrived in the valley on March 28, 1947, during orange blossom season. Lyon then proceeded to purchase a home on 2.5 acres in Scottsdale so his sons could horseback ride and explore the desert.

Lyon had been a big-band musician with Phil Spitalny's Orchestra, followed by the start of his own Russ Lyon and His Band in 1932; then he held a position with Music Corporation of America; and finally, in 1945, he formed the Russ Lyon Agency, a talent company, which he sold to a group of former MCA agents prior to moving west.

Six months after arriving in Scottsdale, he launched himself in the real estate business. Because of his personal attitudes and integrity, the venture enjoyed a healthy, rapid growth. Lyon established an organization known for quality service, total professionalism, fair play, and extreme thoroughness. Now, under the guidance of Dennis Lyon, the firm has expanded to meet the needs of the community and to maintain leadership in the real estate industry.

Russ Lyon Realty was primarily a two-office company until 1976, when expansion began with branch offices in Carefree and North Scottsdale. The expansion kept pace with the tremendous growth in the northeast valley. In 1980-1982 the firm expanded the Phoenix office at 2036 East Camelback Road; the Paradise Valley branch, at 4707 East Cactus Drive; the Carefree office, on Sundial Circle; and the Scottsdale office, at Lincoln and Scottsdale Road.

A new branch at 23350 North Pima Road was added to the Lyon family in 1982. A separate

Russell A. Lyon, Sr., founder.

Dennis H. Lyon, president and chairman of the board.

corporate headquarters is located at 7377 East Doubletree Ranch Road at the new Gainey Ranch Financial Center, which was opened in 1985.

The Russ Lyon Realty Company has continued to grow, creating and strengthening new departments in property management and leasing, and relocation and syndication. More significantly, in 1986 its commercial division broke off into a separate firm, Lyon Commercial Brokerage Company, with Tom Richardson as president and chief operating officer.

Despite the changes in management and markets, company philosophy has remained the same.

W.A. KRUEGER CO.

A sampling of the magazines, books, and brochures printed by the W.A. Krueger Co. reveals the high standard of quality and the versatility of this organization.

The W.A. Krueger Co. has its corporate headquarters in this building at 7301 East Helm Drive, Scottsdale.

Jack W. Fowler, Krueger chairman, president, and chief executive officer, guides a building-block growth policy, which maintains personal service to customers by keeping plants moderately sized, product focused, and independently managed.

W.A. Krueger Co., one of the nation's largest and most respected printing firms, moved its corporate headquarters to Scottsdale in 1974 and today is recognized as Arizona's preeminent printer.

Krueger is a multidivision printer of magazines, books, and commercial products, employing 3,400 skilled people in eight manufacturing centers across the United States. Its plants are located in Wisconsin, where the company was founded, as well as in Arizona, Arkansas, Kansas, California, Mississippi, and Illinois.

The firm was established in Milwaukee in 1934 by William A. Krueger, a man of rare vision and technical expertise. He was joined in the venture by a German immigrant, Robert A. Klaus, who later served as company chairman in Arizona until his retirement in 1978.

In its infant period the W.A. Krueger Co. employed traditional letterpress printing, but Bill Krueger had his eye on the future. He became fascinated with what he called "this new-fangled planography," the printing technology we now know as offset lithography. He and his partners were among the pioneer developers of the process, which makes possible the most exquisite reproductions of color photography and has revolutionized the printing industry.

The W.A. Krueger Co. plant in Milwaukee established an enviable reputation in the Midwest, and after World War II the firm accepted bigger and grander challenges to spread its fame across America and around the world.

The company expanded its operations, always careful to keep its manufacturing centers small enough to maintain the high standard of quality that fueled its growth.

It was in 1950 that Krueger made its first major penetration into Arizona, a step made possible when Klaus won a coveted contract to print *Arizona Highways* magazine, which already had established itself as the premier state promotional magazine in America.

Krueger established its Arizona printing plant in 1962 at 2802 West Palm Lane, Phoenix. That plant has been expanded and equipped with state-of-the-art presses and associated equipment as new technology was developed. It is there that *Arizona Highways* magazine, along with many of its books and special products, is printed today. The magazine was the first major publication of its kind in the nation to go to four-color process photography reproduction on every page, from cover to cover.

The Krueger plant in Phoenix has won acclaim for its beautiful color catalog printing, and for its computerized preparatory services in the production of fine books and other printed materials.

The W.A. Krueger Co. grew rapidly after 1962, establishing new manufacturing centers in several states, and in 1974 decided to move its corporate headquarters from Wisconsin to Scottsdale. The firm is now administered from offices at 7301 East Helm Drive, in the Scottsdale Industrial Airpark. Jack W. Fowler is chairman, president, and chief executive officer of the corporation.

The W.A. Krueger Co. continues its careful plan for both physical and technological expansion. In 1984 Krueger and the Swiss printing company, Ringier AG, bought W.F. Hall Printing Company in a 50-50 joint venture. Now renamed Krueger Ringier Inc., the subsidiary itself is one of America's 10 largest printers. Krueger Ringier specializes in top-quality rotogravure work, and is the largest American printer of mass-market paperback books.

Long a dominant force in the industry, Krueger has continued to expand and to be a leader in printing technology. However, the company prides itself on maintaining the personal touch in serving more than 500 customers at any given time. This personal relationship is preserved because the firm keeps each manufacturing center relatively small and manageable.

Each plant specializes in books, magazines, or commercial products. Thus, this large organization is able to give small-company attention to each customer's unique service needs, whether that customer is planning a press run of 10,000 or 10 million. Because technological advancements have given more printers the ability to achieve high quality, Krueger depends on its management expertise and customer service strategy to remain an industry leader well into the next century.

The W.A. Krueger Co. has made Arizona a major name on the national printing map, and is playing an important role in the technological and business development of the state.

A color-imaging operator at Krueger's 50-percent-owned subsidiary, Krueger Ringier Inc., uses rapidly evolving prepress technology to electronically enhance and manipulate photos for a Spiegel catalog.

Futuristic technology is replacing this professional's brush, but not the need for his trained eye and judgment.

HALL OF FLAME

George F. Getz, Jr., knows that an idle wish can change one's life.

It was in the fall of 1955 that Getz noticed an antique fire engine in a used car lot near Chicago and casually mentioned that "it would be kind of fun to have one of those to drive kids around on." So Mrs. Getz bought the engine for $750, wrapped a ribbon around it, and presented it to him on Christmas morning. Her gift sparked an interest in vintage fire-fighting equipment that soon became a passion in Getz' life, and he has been collecting antique engines and associated equipment ever since.

His passion has resulted in the creation of the Hall of Flame antique fire engine museum, now housed at 6101 East Van Buren Street, Phoenix. This fascinating collection is the largest in the world, comprising approximately 135 vehicles and thousands of other fire-fighting memorabilia. It attracts more than 20,000 visitors from around the globe each year. The Hall of Flame is operated by the National Historical Fire Foundation, a nonprofit foundation formed by Getz, a Chicago industrialist, in 1961.

One of Getz' most cherished acquisitions, an

This hand-drawn fire vehicle was built about 1860 and was used in fighting the Great Chicago Fire of 1871. It is on display at the Hall of Flame museum.

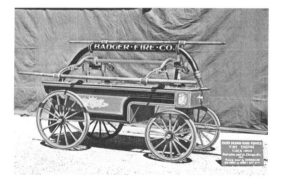

George F. Getz, Jr., founder of the Hall of Flame, at the wheel of an Ahrens-Fox engine built in 1930. It is one of 138 vintage fire engines in the collection.

1860s Rumsey hand-pumper that helped fight the Great Chicago Fire of 1871, is on display in the museum. So are hand-drawn vehicles used in eighteenth-century Europe and colonial America.

Visitors are drawn to the vast assemblage of firemen's helmets, bells, horns, badges, axes, hose carts, and much more. Serious researchers into the history of man's ancient war against fire pore over the 4,000 books and documents in the Richard S. Fowler Memorial Library housed at the Hall of Flame.

Getz' devotion to preserving this important facet of American history, which had been virtually neglected until the 1950s, has made him known to leaders in the fire service nationwide and around the world. Largely as a result of his work, there are now more than 200 other collections of antique fire-fighting equipment in existence.

The Hall of Flame collection was first housed in an old automobile agency in Lake Geneva, Wisconsin. There it attracted much national publicity that resulted in scores of gifts of antique fire equipment. When Getz moved his permanent home to the Phoenix area, he set up the museum in a building adjoining his Scottsdale office. Margaret Hance, then a member of the Phoenix Parks Board and later mayor of Phoenix, became interested in the museum and was instrumental in obtaining 12 acres of land in the Papago Park Recreation Complex. The Hall of Flame was opened in a new building at that location in 1974, and it has since developed into a major resource for the people of Arizona and all America.

SNELL AND WILMER

Frank Snell

Mark Wilmer

The law firm of Snell and Wilmer, one of the oldest, largest, and most influential in the Southwest, has played a vital role in the development of modern Arizona.

Superlatives abound in any description of Snell and Wilmer. Arizona's largest law firm embraces more than 160 attorneys, 50 of whom are partners, and there are 240 other employees in this diverse organization. Its offices occupy 7.5 floors of Arizona's tallest building, the Valley Center in downtown Phoenix. Among its Arizona clients are Arizona Public Service Company, the state's largest utility; Valley National Bank of Arizona, its largest bank; and Merabank, the state's largest thrift institution. National and international clients include Household International, Inc., Ramada Inns, Safeway Stores, Del E. Webb Corporation, American Motors, Ford Motor Company, Montgomery Ward, and a host of other major companies. The firm prides itself, however, on the number and diversity of small corporate and individual clients it is privileged to serve.

Snell and Wilmer partners sit on the boards of many corporations and civic organizations in Arizona, and the firm is well known as a contributor of expertise and funding to such Arizona cultural institutions as the Phoenix Art Museum, the Heard Museum, the Phoenix Symphony, the Arizona Opera, and the state's universities and colleges.

The firm has always worked for the advancement of the legal profession in Arizona, devoting substantial funds and effort to the organized bar and pro bono activities.

Snell and Wilmer's antecedents go back to 1924, when young Frank Snell started practicing law in Miami, Arizona. A graduate of the University of Kansas Law School, he moved his practice to Phoenix in 1927, joining an older attorney, Fred J. Elliott. When Elliott entered semiretirement in 1934, Snell took over the practice.

Mark Wilmer, a Wisconsin native who took his law degree at Georgetown University, started practice in Texas. He joined Jim Walsh and Frank Beer in practice in Mesa, Arizona, and then joined Snell in 1938. Wilmer has earned renown as the dean of Arizona's trial attorneys, and as a specialist in water and Indian law. He and Snell have been building their successful practice ever since joining forces.

Joe Melczer, Jr., joined the firm in 1946 and has been a key partner for four decades. By 1950 the partnership was known as Snell, Wilmer, Walsh, Melczer and Beauchamp. For simplicity's sake it was decided that the firm would thereafter be called Snell and Wilmer. Both Frank Snell and Mark Wilmer, now in their eighties, are still active in the firm, as is Joe Melczer, Jr.

Today Snell and Wilmer attorneys are organized into several practice areas: corporate and municipal finance, real estate, taxes, utilities, trusts and estates, litigation, administrative, and labor. Partners and associates are active in community leadership roles, and are known throughout the state as architects of Arizona progress.

VISIONQUEST

The highly structured and challenging schedules of Vision-Quest's high-impact programs help withdrawn youths develop healthy relationships with peers and staff members. The shared experiences of the trail build a strong rapport among all participants.

Bob Burton, chairman of the board of VisionQuest (right), and Steve Rogers, executive vice-president, founded the program for troubled adolescents in 1973 along with Sandy Eggleston. The three had worked in the traditional juvenile corrections systems they found frustrating and ineffective, and they conceived Vision-Quest as an alternative.

is using the heritage of the pioneers to demonstrate to troubled youngsters that disadvantageous circumstances need not impede positive achievements in life.

VisionQuest was founded in 1973 by R. Ledger "Bob" Burton and Steve R. Rogers, former corrections professionals who had become frustrated with the apparent ineffectiveness of traditional youth-rehabilitation programs. Continually they saw troubled youths progress to criminal adulthood. The traditional corrections approach, Burton and Rogers believe, offers youths punishment, rejection, and self-inflicted pain. A locked cell, they believe, teaches a child that he is no better than an animal. The use of mind-altering drugs to control behavior tells a child that what he thinks is unimportant. Life in an overcrowded, understaffed juvenile facility demonstrates to a child that society sees no value in him.

VisionQuest has developed a range of programs designed to help young offenders learn self-discipline, independence, and respect for others in an atmosphere without cells, barred windows, or controlling drugs. Beginning with six youngsters in a group home in Tucson, Burton and Rogers drew upon the atmosphere of innovation that characterized juvenile corrections in that city during the late 1960s and early 1970s. In collaboration with Judge John P. Collins, a leader in alternative approaches to corrections, VisionQuest created programs that were forerunners of current practice among many of today's more progressive juvenile-treatment specialists.

Early experiences with wilderness survival training for group-home residents suggested that troubled youths respond well to the challenge of outdoor activities. This finding was the origin of several successful VisonQuest programs designed to help youngsters gain confidence, control anger, face fears, acquire practical skills, and cooperate with others.

VisionQuest was one of the first treatment programs in the nation to develop the use of special wilderness camps as a focus for juvenile treatment. VisionQuest's impact camps differ from traditional child-care formats by relying less on facility structures than on outdoor-activity programming to reorient youths toward productive endeavors. What is demanded of the child is not to "do time," but instead to meet challenges, gain physical strength and stamina, learn skills that are transferrable to a real-life

In Arizona today, many of the traditions that tamed the Old West are again being used to build a better America. VisionQuest, a Tucson-based, private-sector company dedicated to helping troubled youths and young offenders,

situation, and assemble a record of positive achievement.

Another innovative VisionQuest program is the Wagon Train. In 1976 a VisionQuest group home participated in a five-month-long bicentennial Wagon Train to Valley Forge, Pennsylvania. VisionQuest counselors immediately recognized that the culture that had evolved on the trail—a culture based upon cooperation, self-discipline, and the work ethic—helped kids to gain maturity, self-control, and confidence. Today four VisionQuest Wagon Trains operate across the country at all times of the year. Some 2,000 youngsters have traveled more than 150,000 miles through 48 states since the program began.

The OceanQuest program shares similar goals with the Wagon Train, but it uses the sea to provide the challenging environment that motivates change in young attitudes. Youngsters assigned to OceanQuest help to operate two schooners that sail along the seaboards of North America under the direction of professional sailors on VisionQuest's staff. VisionQuest pioneered the use of ocean sailing as a format for youth treatment, and today it operates the only year-round program of its kind in the nation.

For selected—and primarily minority—youths who have achieved success in Vision-Quest's basic regimen, the Buffalo Soldiers program provides an opportunity to develop a special pride. Named in honor of the historic, all-black 9th and 10th Cavalry regiments of the U.S. Army, these elite troops of young people perform a special outreach function. They demonstrate to other, especially minority, youths that difficult circumstances can be overcome through positive attitudes, self-control, and self-application in pursuit of a goal. VisionQuest's Buffalo Soldiers fulfill a busy annual schedule of public appearances, in which they perform a series of original and complex precision drills and marches on foot or horseback. Their skill and pride have been admired by crowds as diverse as observers of Tucson's annual rodeo parade and members of Congress watching from the steps of the U.S. Capitol in Washington, D.C.

From modest beginnings VisionQuest has grown into one of the largest programs of its kind in the United States. It has served as a catalyst for change in the way many state authorities view the treatment of troubled youths. Its nontraditional techniques, as well as the success it has enjoyed in turning young people toward positive lives, have gained media attention in nations as distant as Germany and Japan. VisionQuest has inspired similar programs in Great Britain and Australia. In the United States, meanwhile, the prestigious Rand Corporation has issued a report, "One More Chance: The Pursuit of Promising Intervention Strategies for Chronic Juvenile Offenders," in which VisionQuest is described as "the kind of people that most of us would trust our own kids with."

As this mule-drawn Wagon Train creaks across Arizona's high desert country, it is opening new frontiers in the field of juvenile justice.

The Buffalo Soldiers instill youngsters with a sense of history and personal pride. Membership in the elite group is a goal that stimulates VisionQuest participants to strive for excellence.

KNOELL HOMES

Thomas E. Knoell (left), president of Knoell Homes, and Frank Knoell, founder and chairman of the board, on the company grounds with Camelback Mountain in the background.

The new headquarters building of Knoell Homes at 4040 East Camelback Road, Phoenix, is located on the Knoell homestead, owned by the family since 1920.

World War II veterans were streaming into the Phoenix area in 1947, planning for a bright future in homes of their own. Frank Knoell, himself recently discharged from the Army Air Corps, decided to devote his future to building those homes.

He bought lots at 23rd and Luke avenues in Phoenix and started building homes that young families could afford—two-bedroom homes with one bath, on a large lot—and the price was only $5,950. Knoell built quality into his homes, and people appreciated that.

Today, more than 15,000 homes and 40 years

later, Knoell Homes is still building affordable residences, 800 or more each year, in 16 different central Arizona residential communities. Moreover, Frank Knoell is still active in the family-owned corporation, serving as chairman of the board. His son Tom, who grew up with the company, started as a laborer in 1965; he earned a degree in construction engineering from Arizona State University, and has been president of Knoell Homes since 1981.

The Knoell homes have changed with the times and the tastes of Arizona home buyers. Still Knoell, one of the state's most diversified builders, offers a home for almost every budget, ranging in price from $60,000 to $230,000. The Knoell quality that has been so appreciated over a span of four decades is still being built into every one of its homes.

Knoell Homes has its executive offices at 4040 East Camelback Road, on a piece of the land Frank's father planted in citrus trees when he migrated from central Nebraska in 1922. The home where Frank and his brother, Hugh, grew up was here, and Phoenix gradually came out to meet and surround it. The firm moved into its beautiful new building in 1986.

Even before he returned home from Air Corps duty in World War II, Frank knew what the future had in store for him. His father-in-law, Bert Cavanagh, telephoned him at a Mississippi air base and offered him a place in a real estate firm, which was also to include his brother-in-law, Harry Cavanagh. Frank was to head the company's construction department, but that side of the business never really developed. In 1946 Frank, on his own, started building homes. Two years later Frank bought into Casa Linda Builders with his brother Hugh and changed the name to Knoell Bros. Construction, Inc.

Within a few years Frank bought Hugh's interest, and in the late 1950s he branched out into neighboring Tempe and gave the company the name it has had ever since: Knoell Homes.

"That first Tempe subdivision at Mill and Alameda was a big gamble," Frank recalls. "One Sunday morning in 1959 my wife, Peggy, and I were having coffee in a Tempe restaurant, waiting for the grand opening events to begin. I counted the automobiles that passed the corner of Mill and University during two hours, and there were no more than 20 of them. We both started to wonder if we had made a terrible mistake by making the big move to the small com-

munity of Tempe."

Their fears were unfounded. People did come in large numbers and bought homes, just as they did in every future Knoell development in the valley. Knoell established its headquarters in Tempe for a decade before moving to 2401 South 24th Street, Phoenix, in 1976. Then, in 1986, came the move to the new headquarters building on East Camelback Road. Thus the firm that had its beginnings on the family homestead 40 years before made the full circle back to where it started.

Knoell Homes now faces a vastly different competitive situation than that of four decades ago. From a new industry with an uncertain future and a handful of builders, the Phoenix area has developed into a burgeoning metropolis where some 600 home builders—many of them national in scope—are battling for a place in the sun. Only a couple of the builders of 1947 are still building among the major competitors. It is a tribute to Knoell Homes' foresight and adaptability that the firm still holds on to its place among the top five Phoenix-area builders.

"We determined long ago that our established reputation as a quality builder was not enough," Tom Knoell declares. "We have to keep building that reputation every day to remain a dominant force."

Knoell's widely dispersed housing developments pose a challenge for supervisors and planners. On Sunday afternoons the sales manager travels by helicopter between Knoell subdivisions, some as much as 60 miles apart. From the air he can see which subdivisions are getting the most traffic. If competitors are drawing heavily, he finds out why.

The firm keeps changing the designs of its homes as customers' tastes change. Any miscalculation can be costly. Knoell has enjoyed consistent success in predicting what Arizona tastes will be, however, and its new Diamond Ridge development at Mountain Park Ranch in the southeast valley is currently rated the most active sales generator in the state. Diamond Ridge homes are priced from $160,000 to the low $200,000s, and they offer custom design characteristics. Buyers get a choice of stone fireplaces, along with dual-paned windows, Signature Series tile roofing, lush landscaping, and more. They are a far cry from the primitive 1947 Knoell offerings, with water heaters outside the house and evaporative coolers on the roof.

Today the firm, officially known as Knoell

Homes, has two areas of business: home building and land development. Priding itself on its reputation as a family-operated hometown builder, it has maintained a low profile in the booming central Arizona community. But directors of charitable organizations, fine arts groups, educational institutions, and a host of other community groups will testify that Knoell has been a dependable financial supporter during all its 40 years.

"Discover the Beauty of Knoell" says the well-known corporate slogan. Arizonans who appreciate quiet efficiency and solid quality know that this kind of beauty is far more than skin-deep.

Since 1947 Knoell Homes has been building to meet the needs of a variety of home buyers. Quality has been a constant mainstay of homes, whether for low budgets or for luxury seekers. Photo circa 1960

Today a sales associate shows a family the Seville home at Diamond Ridge. This more than $200,000 home is one of the newest in the ever-changing designs offered by the firm.

LINCOLN LASER COMPANY

Polygonal scanning mirrors are manufactured in a wide variety of sizes and shapes depending upon customer requirements. These are representative of the mirrors produced by Lincoln Laser Company.

Inspector/Verifier machines on the plant floor ready for shipment. These machines perform automatic optical inspection of printed wiring boards.

The first phase of the Lincoln Laser Company plant was completed in 1981.

During a brief encounter at church in 1973, David C. Lincoln mentioned to his friend Randy Sherman that he just couldn't find good wooden jigsaw puzzles anymore. Sherman replied that the old production techniques had perhaps become too expensive, and that maybe they should try cutting out the puzzles with lasers.

That conversation was the beginning of a new industrial enterprise, the Lincoln Laser Company. The firm, established in Phoenix the following year, never has made jigsaw puzzles. But it has become the world's leading independent supplier of laser scanning equipment, and its innovative research and development department is devising new products and applica-

tions every year.

Lincoln, whose father, John C. Lincoln, founded Lincoln Electric Company and a Phoenix hospital named in his honor, is the chairman and guiding force behind this fast-growing operation. A graduate of California Institute of Technology with a master's degree in electrical engineering, he and Randy Sherman have built Lincoln Laser into an internationally recognized corporation.

Sherman, an experienced manufacturing executive, is president of Lincoln Laser. Vice-presidents Derald Hanson and Dwight Smith are other executives who have been with the firm almost from its founding.

Lincoln Laser Company began its manufacturing operations at 625 South Fifth Street, Phoenix, in January 1975, devoting its energies primarily to the production of laser scanning equipment and components. The firm moved to its present building at 234 East Mohave Street in Phoenix in 1981, and three years later doubled its floor space to more than 26,000 square feet.

That increase in operating capacity was necessitated by the company's expansion into systems production—primarily the assembly of complex equipment for automatic optical inspection of printed circuit boards. The device, known as the Inspector/Verifier, is assembled under a license from AT&T. It has the potential of saving millions for large-scale manufacturers of printed electronic circuit boards.

Lincoln Laser sales have increased an average of 30 percent per year and now top the $6-million mark annually. The firm manufactures metal mirrors for scanning and optical equipment, and produces exotic components of many kinds for sophisticated industrial applications. The company employs nearly 125 people, many of whom it trains in-house.

Among the products that use Lincoln Laser components are laser printers, increasingly used in the publishing and copying industries; bar code readers, commonly seen at supermarket checkout stations; quality-control devices, more accurate and less costly than human technicians; and many others. New applications for laser products are being developed constantly.

Lincoln Laser Company currently sells about 20 percent of its output overseas, principally in Japan and Europe. Among its American customers are some of the nation's most prominent high-technology corporations.

GENERAL MOTORS DESERT PROVING GROUND

Because dedicated technicians put automobiles and trucks through torturous tests in blistering heat at the General Motors Desert Proving Ground, GM customers can be certain they are driving safer, more efficient vehicles.

More than 400 full-time employees and another 200 affiliated workers conduct tests on engine performance, fuel efficiency, air conditioning, brakes, and noise. They measure the durability of tires, paint, plastics, fabrics, and countless other components. Each year more than 12.5 million test miles are driven and recorded at this amazing facility.

General Motors established its first Arizona testing operation in Phoenix in 1937 with only six employees on a five-acre site at 20th Street and East Roosevelt. Known as the Phoenix Laboratory, it used city streets and desert roads for most of its testing programs. That first year 67,000 miles of test driving were logged. During World War II the Phoenix Laboratory teamed with the U.S. Army Ordnance Department to test tanks and other military vehicles on the south face of South Mountain Park.

Today, a half-century after the establishment of the first General Motors testing laboratory in central Arizona, the Desert Proving Ground has become one of the largest and most diversified testing facilities in the world, covering 5,000 acres of land 15 miles southeast of downtown Mesa.

Ingenious test roads—73 miles of them—simulate every kind of driving surface, from banked freeways to rutted backroads and "Belgian block" surfaces guaranteed to shake cars and drivers almost beyond endurance. In addition, 350,000 square feet of building space is devoted to the quest for better, safer motor vehicles.

General Motors places the highest priority on rigorous testing of products in all its many divisions. In addition to the Desert Proving Ground, the corporation maintains a cold-weather testing operation in Kapuskasing, Ontario; a high-altitude site in the Colorado Rockies; and a multipurpose proving ground some 40 miles north of Detroit, Michigan.

The Desert Proving Ground was dedicated at its present site on April 22, 1953, and was at that time managed by M.J. Muzzy, with a staff of 18 people. Manager Don Briggs, the eighth in the half-century of GM proving ground operation in Arizona, took over direction of the facility in 1986.*

Arizona has been a beneficiary of technical expertise and community service provided by Desert Proving Ground personnel over the decades. GM people are involved in scores of civic and charitable projects, one of the most prominent of which is the Child Crisis Center support provided by Desert Proving Ground employees.

Everyone who depends on the safe performance of an automobile, bus, or truck owes the General Motors Desert Proving Ground team a debt of gratitude as well.

*Interview was conducted prior to Don Briggs' untimely death in an airplane crash in Detroit, Michigan, in August 1987.

The General Motors Desert Proving Ground near Mesa, Arizona, now covers 5,000 acres. The present site was dedicated in 1953.

A.J. Foyt is shown driving the Aerotech, a high-speed developmental vehicle, over the GM Desert Proving Ground track in November 1986. Foyt averaged 218.44 m.p.h. in four laps.

MARINE CORPS AIR STATION

Aircraft at the front gate welcome visitors to Marine Corps Air Station Yuma.

Flight line activity is heavy at the air base.

The Marine Corps Air Station in Yuma, with access to 1.5 million acres of aviation training ranges, has been in operation as a Marine Corps facility for more than 25 years, and continues to be the Corps' premier aviation training facility.

It's all here.

Miles and miles of air space above the desert of southwestern Arizona and southeastern California provide Marine Corps aviators the opportunity to sharpen their flying skills in near-combat realism. A Tactical Aircrew Combat Training System, called TACTS for short, gives aircrews instant, live feedback in air-to-air combat and air-to-ground action. A squadron of Israeli-built, F-21 KFIR fighter jets, piloted by specially trained U.S. Marines skilled in enemy tactics, provides other Marine pilots a chance to go against combat-proven aggressor aircraft in air-to-air dogfights.

A Weapons and Tactics Instructor course, held semiannually, provides graduate-level training to top Marine aircrews, who take what

they learn back to their home bases and teach it to their fellow aviators. Almost ideal weather (flyable 98 percent of the time) allows units to get more training accomplished in two weeks in Yuma than they could in many more weeks at their home bases. In short, Yuma's Marine Corps Air Station has all the assets aviators need to enhance their skills and maintain readiness to support the national defense.

Located near the California border and approximately 25 miles from Mexico, MCAS Yuma became home in 1987 to Marine Aircraft Group-13, a tactical air combat unit that eventually will have 80 of the Corps' more advanced attack aircraft: the AV-8B Harrier II. MAG-13 moved to Yuma October 1, 1987, from MCAS El Toro, California. It will have four Harrier squadrons. MAG-13 replaced two training squadrons at Yuma that trained aircrews for the F-4 Phantom, a fighter/attack aircraft, and the A-4 Skyhawk, a light attack bomber. These two squadrons left, one assuming a new role at El Toro and the other being decommissioned.

Being home for MAG-13 isn't MCAS Yuma's only mission. Squadrons from throughout the Marine Corps, as well as other services, deploy here to take advantage of the expanse of ranges and the fine weather. Each year approximately 70 units bring 11,500 service members and 1,100 aircraft to Yuma for an average stay of two weeks or more. In addition, 21,200 other transient aircrewmen stop at the air station annually.

MCAS Yuma has more than 210,000 annual airfield operations, making it among the most active stations in the Navy Department. More than 85,000 of that total are civilian air operations; the air base is a joint-use airport with Yuma County.

In 1987 other units inhabited MCAS Yuma in addition to MAG-13's squadrons. Marine Wing Support Squadron-371, whose mission is to support the MAG in a field or combat environment, was a newcomer. So was Headquarters and Maintenance Squadron-13, whose mission includes providing maintenance, supply and administrative support to the MAG. The Second Light Antiaircraft Missile Battalion, which provides air defense with its HAWK missiles, and Marine Air Control Squadron-7, the radar "eyes and ears" for the flying squadrons, also were there.

By 1991, when MAG-13 completes its transition to Yuma, approximately 5,000 Marines and sailors will be aboard MCAS Yuma on any given day. Presently that total hovers around 4,400. Permanent civilian employees number about 940. In 1987 MCAS Yuma had an approximate annual payroll of $68 million, and a total economic impact on the local community of $115 million.

However, the base hasn't always been "Marine green." The site's history as a federal installation stretches back to February 21, 1928, when President Calvin Coolidge authorized the federal government to lease 640 acres of desert land near Yuma for use as a flying field. Three weeks later, on March 16, a 20-year lease was signed, with an option for another 20 years at one dollar per year. Thus, the present site began its long relationship with aviation.

The land, covered with cactus, brush, and desert wildlife, was soon to become an air facility, Fly Field. Aviation was still in its infancy, and Fly Field soon became the center of attention in Yuma, particularly during the summer of 1928, when it served as a stopover point for 25 planes participating in an air race from New York to Los Angeles.

The installation achieved new importance with the outbreak of World War II. Taken over by the Army Air Corps and renamed Yuma Army Airfield, it became the site of one of the nation's busiest flying schools, graduating pilots by the hundreds. But flight activity ceased after the war, and the area was partially reclaimed by the desert.

On July 7, 1951, the Air Force reactivated the base and established a weapons proficiency center for fighter interceptor units. The airfield

was named Yuma Air Base, but five years later was renamed Vincent Air Force Base, in memory of Brigadier General Clinton D. Vincent, who had died the previous year.

Soon it became necessary to transfer the training of these fliers to overwater ranges. As a result, the 4750th Air Defense Wing at Yuma was relocated to MacDill Air Force Base, Florida.

In anticipation of the move, the facility was signed over to the Navy on January 1, 1959, and on January 10 the Marine Corps' Colonel L.K. Davis became the first commanding officer of the newly designated Marine Corps Auxiliary Air Station. On July 20, 1962, the designation of Marine Corps Auxiliary Air Station was changed to Marine Corps Air Station, its present name. The year 1987 marked the silver anniversary of the base adopting its present name.

Marines have called Yuma home for a quarter-century and look forward to a promising future in this fast-growing city that anchors southwestern Arizona.

An aerial photo of Marine Corps Air Station Yuma.

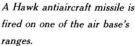

A Hawk antiaircraft missile is fired on one of the air base's ranges.

NORTHERN ARIZONA UNIVERSITY

The Old Main building at the institution now known as Northern Arizona University is pictured in 1913. Note boardwalks and fence.

Dr. Eugene M. Hughes has been president of Northern Arizona University since 1979.

From the first visit to Northern Arizona University a visitor senses that this is an institution of special character and educational mission.

There is breathtaking beauty in this forested campus 7,000 feet above sea level, nestled near the foot of the snow-capped San Francisco Peaks. The sky is an unblemished blue, and the crisp mountain air is a tonic to the spirit. There is a dedication to excellence that can be felt on every hand, and an infectious friendliness and intimacy that was lost years ago on many of the giant urban campuses of our nation.

Northern Arizona University is special because it dares to explore new paths, while at the same time reaffirming time-tested principles of educating young people. It is a university that stresses excellence in teaching above all else, and it has the courage to map out its own areas of expertise, refusing to try to be all things to all people.

This is Northern Arizona University, a fully accredited four-year institution of higher education in Flagstaff, supported by the State of Arizona and governed by the Arizona Board of Regents. With an enrollment just exceeding 13,000 students, it is the smallest of Arizona's three state universities, and the only one that houses most of its students on, or very near, the campus. Such a residential intellectual community enjoys a close-knit character and commonality of purpose that is highly conducive to the pursuit of excellence.

NAU is comprised of nine academic divisions offering 111 baccalaureate, 39 master, and 7 doctoral degree majors. Its diversity is evident in its academic organization: College of Arts and Science, College of Business Administration, College of Creative and Communication Arts, Center for Excellence in Education, College of Engineering and Technology, School of Forestry, School of Health Professions, College of Social and Behavioral Sciences, and School of Hotel and Restaurant Management.

Worthy of special note are the forestry school, the only one in a state boasting thousands of square miles of national forests; the hotel and restaurant school, Arizona's only academic unit preparing leaders for the burgeoning tourism industry; the health professions school, unique as a trainer of medical support personnel; and the Center for Excellence in Education, a bold new concept in the interdisciplinary preparation of future teachers.

The history of Northern Arizona University goes back to the early 1890s, when Flagstaff political leaders resolved to lobby the legislature for some sort of territorial agency in their small town. When they succeeded in obtaining funds for that agency—a reform school for boys—they started construction of an imposing stone structure, known today as Old Main. Funding and enthusiasm for the project waned, however, and the building stood unfinished until the territorial legislature, on March 11, 1899, authorized the creation of the Northern Arizona Normal School at Flagstaff. Dr. Almon N. Taylor was appointed the first principal (now called president) of the new teacher-training school, and he served through the entire first decade of the school's history.

Thus, the future Northern Arizona University took its place along with territorial institutions of higher learning at Tucson and Tempe, and gave Arizona a northland college it could call its own. It functioned as a teachers' college for almost a half-century, growing slowly and fighting off periodic attempts by the legislature to close its doors to save money.

Then, on July 1, 1945, as Arizona began its spectacular period of post-World War II growth, the institution was given broad new educational responsibilities and renamed Arizona State College at Flagstaff. The college expanded its academic offerings, its campus (now 719 acres), and its dreams of the future. On May 1, 1966, it was granted the present name of Northern Arizona University in recognition of the fact that it had become a comprehensive institution with diversity, quality, and national reputation.

Of the many great presidents who have led Northern Arizona University in the past, one who has had a great impact on the institution—and on Arizona higher education—is Dr. J. Lawrence Walkup, whose tenure covered the critical growth years of 1957 to 1979. He was succeeded on July 1, 1979, by Dr. Eugene M. Hughes, the current president, who has led NAU to new academic heights and has made the university's presence felt in positive ways in every county of Arizona.

Northern Arizona University's Lumberjack athletic teams, both men's and women's, compete in the Big Sky Conference of the National Collegiate Athletic Association's Division I. NAU's excellent sports facilities include the J. Lawrence Walkup Skydome, seating 15,300 for football, basketball, indoor track, and many other sports and public events. The NAU Natatorium, opened in 1983, is one of the finest aquatic facilities in the West. Winter sports, hiking, and camping are enjoyed by thousands of enthusiastic participants.

This university wisely insists that its student athletes be students first and foremost, and it has kept intercollegiate athletics from assuming a dominant role in NAU affairs. Just as important in the NAU student activity picture are music, drama, and the visual arts.

The university faculty, now numbering 450 full-time teachers and researchers, have advanced degrees from many of the nation's most prestigious academic institutions. Three-quarters of the full-time faculty have earned doctorates, and some two-thirds have achieved tenure at NAU. Although teaching excellence is NAU's primary goal, its faculty win national prominence each year in research, publication, academic awards, and community service.

Proud of its nine decades of service to the people of Arizona and the nation, Northern Arizona University looks ahead with justifiable optimism to a future in which its goal—the pursuit of excellence—will continue to challenge both faculty and students.

The snow-covered San Francisco Peaks make a dramatic backdrop for the campus of Northern Arizona University.

The arts and sciences are the core of undergraduate study at Northern Arizona University. Dr. John M. DeKorte is shown supervising a chemistry lab exercise.

CANNON & ASSOCIATES, INC.
CONSULTING ENGINEERS

Cannon & Associates has performed engineering work on some of southern Arizona's most important historic buildings, among them the old Cochise County Courthouse in Tombstone as well as the Hiram Stevens house and the Charles O. Brown house, both in Tucson. The Stevens house is part of the Tucson Museum of Art complex, and the Brown house, originally the Congress all Saloon, is the property of the Arizona Historical Society, which leases it to the Old Adobe restaurant.

The firm also does engineering work for large public projects and specializes in bridge design. It was involved in the multimillion-dollar expansion of the Tucson International Airport and designed the Kino Parkway Overpass (recently renamed Murphy's Overpass) over the Southern Pacific Railroad tracks.

But Jerry Cannon says the most important project his company has undertaken was its study of Navajo Bridge in northeastern Arizona. The structure, a steel-arch bridge 616 feet clear span and built in 1927-1928, replaced Lee's Ferry as the main northern crossing point over the Colorado River. The Arizona Department of Transportation hired Cannon & Associates as the prime consultant on the job, with the objective of examining the bridge and recommending ways in which its traffic capacity could be expanded.

In the course of a year's work, engineers from Cannon & Associates worked with about 30 agencies, including the Navajo Nation, the Bureau of Indian Affairs, the National Parks Service, and other federal agencies, as well as with private landowners. The firm concluded by recommending that a new bridge be built near the existing one, and that the historic span be kept as a footbridge.

Neither Jerry nor Dolores Cannon is a native Arizonan; he came from California, she from Idaho. He, however, took his first degree from Arizona State University, and, after moving back to California, the couple came to settle in Tucson in 1973. They founded the firm six years later, with Jerry the engineer, Dolores the bookkeeper and office manager, and one draftsman. The first payroll was $300.

In its first eight years Cannon & Associates, Inc., has grown from being a three-person firm to one that employs 15, and it has a branch office in Phoenix. As Arizona continues its vigorous growth, the organization appears destined to grow right along with it.

Kino Parkway Overpass (Murphy's Overpass), Tucson. Cannon & Associates staff, November 16, 1987.

The Navajo Bridge at the Colorado River. Courtesy, Special Collections Library, Northern Arizona University, Flagstaff

If a person went looking for a Tucson engineering firm with real expertise in historic renovation and restoration, he would have to look no farther than Cannon & Associates.

Situated in the Armory Park Historic Neighborhood, just south of Tucson's downtown, Cannon & Associates occupies a house built in 1904. Jerry and Dolores Cannon, who founded the firm in 1979, live across the street and, therefore, probably have the shortest commute to work of any couple in Tucson.

It wasn't always that way. The firm's first offices were on Factory Avenue in Tucson, and the Cannons lived on the city's east side. Then came a move to an office in the Herder Building near the University of Arizona. Finally, in the early 1980s, Cannon & Associates came to roost in Armory Park. But the firm is now outgrowing the 1904 house, so a new headquarters building is planned—in the same historic section of the city.

JOHNSON-BRITTAIN & ASSOCIATES

Johnson-Brittain & Associates, a civil engineering firm, has its roots in Tucson, and most of its energies have been devoted to improving the city where the company was born.

Michael Johnson, a Tucson native and graduate of the University of Arizona, was one of the founders of the firm in 1980. Johnson's father was a Tucson contractor of bridges and precast concrete since the 1940s. The company began with six employees and an office on East First Street, near Himmel Park. Robert Brittain, a native of New Mexico, came from Las Cruces to Tucson in 1979, and joined Johnson-Brittain two years later.

Johnson-Brittain & Associates has concentrated on public-sector work, designing projects largely, although not entirely, for governmental entities in the Tucson area and for the Arizona Department of Transportation. This focus sets the firm apart from many other civil engineers, who tend to work mainly for developers and architects that operate in the private sector. Only about 20 percent of Johnson-Brittain's volume is derived from private entities.

In the area of its specialization, Johnson-Brittain has accomplished a number of major road and drainage projects. The firm designed the widening of major arterials throughout the Tucson area, including portions of the Kolb and Palo Verde corridors, and a section of the Aviation Parkway. The design of Speedway from Alvernon to Tucson Boulevard required consideration of sensitive neighborhood issues as well as cost and technical factors. Johnson-Brittain designed the storm drainage at Tucson Boulevard and Grant Road, an intersection long plagued by flooding during the city's rainy season. The company also designed the widening

of a section of the Tucson-Ajo Highway, and has performed site-selection studies for the Central Arizona Project water-treatment plant in Tucson.

One of Johnson-Brittain's most interesting jobs came as an adjunct to a project on South Camino Seco. The challenge was to harvest water that otherwise would run off the street and use it to irrigate landscaping nearby. The solution was both innovative and effective.

Outside Tucson, Johnson-Brittain designed a mall crossing in Scottsdale, part of the Papago Freeway's inner loop, and the Buffalo Soldiers Trail in Sierra Vista. The firm has also provided engineering for Davis-Monthan Air Force Base and Fort Huachuca, working on roads, drainage, and surveying.

Like other civil engineering firms, Johnson-Brittain works in a highly competitive market, where an average of 20 companies apply for each major job. It is a tribute to Johnson-Brittain & Associates that governmental officials rank it among the top civil engineering companies in southern Arizona.

Civic Center Plaza. Part of the City of Scottsdale's plan to revitalize the central business district included a "couplet" roadway system to carry traffic around the downtown area and reduce congestion on Scottsdale Road. Johnson-Brittain provided the civil engineering work for the first couplet segment.

Johnson-Brittain staff, August 1987. The emphasis on major roadway projects has resulted in a group of individuals with specialized experience and expertise called for by that work.

H.C.A. SONORA DESERT HOSPITAL

A special kind of caring.

Sonora Desert Hospital, located in beautiful northwest Tucson, opened in July 1986.

Sonora Desert Hospital, one of 50 psychiatric hospitals in the United States that is owned by Hospital Corporation of America, opened in Tucson in July 1986. The opening culminated years of study concerning the necessity of providing a psychiatric facility on Tucson's northwest side, for a long time the fastest-growing section of the city.

City demographics indicated the need for more psychiatric services of all kinds. The need for additional beds was especially acute in northwestern Tucson, clear across the city from the two other psychiatric hospitals. Similarly, there was need for outpatient services of all types, and for educational programs both for interested citizens and professionals. Sonora Desert Hospital now is contributing to the fulfillment of all these needs, as well as to others in the community at large.

The hospital offers a number of special programs, including one for adolescents with chemical dependencies, another for children requiring psychiatric care, and still another for the elderly and aged. In addition to these specially targeted programs, the facility offers general psychiatric care for adults, adolescents, and women on both an inpatient and an outpatient basis.

At Sonora Desert Hospital, school-age patients can attend school on site, so that their hospitalization does not mean they lose academic credit. The school has its own staff of teachers, and mental health professionals and community members also are involved.

In addition, Sonora Desert Hospital has launched a bilingual-bicultural program in coordination with the treatment it offers. In a community less than 75 miles north of the Mexican border, all services can be provided in Spanish, whether the patient and his family are bilingual or speak Spanish only. In conjunction with its bilingual-bicultural approach, the hospital actively recruits Hispanic staff members.

Sonora Desert Hospital is part of a medical complex in northwest Tucson that includes Northwest Hospital, Desert Life Nursing Home, and the Fountains at La Cholla, a congregate care facility completed in 1987. As part of this complex, Sonora Desert plans gradual growth in harmony with the area. A year after it opened, the hospital had brought in modules to be used by some of its programs, and construction of a new medical office building was about to begin.

Sonora Desert Hospital is committed to serve the community to the limits of its abilities, both as a clinical facility and as a good corporate citizen. In its first year of operation, for example, it was the largest donor among psychiatric hospitals to the United Way of Tucson. Education programs open to the community deal with a variety of subjects and constitute a public resource.

Sonora Desert Hospital is busy fulfilling its philosophy that mental health is everyone's birthright, and it looks forward to years of leadership in Tucson's healing community.

ARIZONA FARM BUREAU FEDERATION

Arizona farmers and ranchers are a breed of rugged individualists, but in 1921 they decided to band together to achieve their mutual goals. They called their family-based organization the Arizona Farm Bureau Federation.

C.S. "Farmer" Brown of Mesa was the founding father and first president of the association. Often to the detriment of his own farm, Brown volunteered his time to travel throughout the state over primitive roads to make the organization a cohesive and effective one. Because of the dedication of this human dynamo, the Arizona Farm Bureau Federation soon was serving Arizona agriculture in vital ways.

It continues to do so today.

Three Arizona counties, Maricopa, Graham, and Cochise, created "farm bureaus," which recruited Brown. He persuaded farm leaders of other counties to establish farm bureaus, and to band together in a statewide effort to support agriculture and advocate its programs in the state legislature.

Brown's successor as president in 1924 was J.J. Gould, Phoenix. Those who have served as president since that time are (in order) Walter Strong, Phoenix; George Bridge, Yuma; Sam Wallace, Phoenix; Hollis Gray, Tempe; Nat Dysart, Peoria; A.M. Ward, Casa Grande; L.G. Vinson, Phoenix; Cecil Miller, Sr., Phoenix; Clyde Neely, Gilbert; Dr. A.J. Height, Tempe; A.J. Fram, Tempe; Floyd Hawkins, Chino Valley; Jess Watt, Litchfield Park; Marvin Morrison, Gilbert; Floyd Hawkins, Phoenix; and Cecil Miller, Jr., Litchfield Park.

Today's Arizona Farm Bureau Federation is the largest agricultural organization with 13 county farm bureaus in the state. It numbers nearly 4,000 farm families in its membership, and promotes their interests every day of the year.

Those interests are compelling ones. They include preserving agriculture's water rights in an increasingly urban state, helping Arizona's people understand the need for using agriculture, and working for more than 160 ideas of its members.

The Arizona Farm Bureau Federation is fortunate to have the leadership of a nationally prominent agricultural spokesman, Cecil Miller, Jr., of Litchfield Park, who has been elected to 17 consecutive one-year terms as president. Andy Kurtz, executive secretary, and the Farm Bureau staff have offices at the state headquarters, 2618 South 21st Street, Phoenix.

C.S. "Farmer" Brown, of Mesa, was the founder and first president of the Arizona Farm Bureau Federation.

Cecil Miller, Jr., Litchfield Park, has been president of the federation since 1971.

Agriculture continues to be a vital part of Arizona's economy, with production values increasing each year. Cattle, cotton, vegetables, and citrus rank as the most important of the 32 major agricultural commodities produced in the state. Cultivation of landscaping plants is becoming increasingly important as well.

Family operation is still the norm on Arizona's 8,500 farms, so the family approach taken by the Arizona Farm Bureau Federation when it was founded nearly seven decades ago is still as valid as ever.

CHEYNE OWEN, LTD.

Back row (left to right): Jonathan Parker, CAD operator; Mark Richards, environmental planner; and Alvin Ross, CAD operator/manager. Center row (left to right): Rafael Pivaral, drafter; Jeffrey Vasquez, engineer in training; Christina Bell, administrative assistant; Patricia Owen, clerk; Deborah Anderson, drafter; Richard Furgeson, engineering technician/designer; Jeanne Judd, assistant engineer; Fred Brinker, chemical engineer; Marsha Kelly, marketing manager; and David Kraman, drafter. Seated (left to right): Dennis McCarthy, registered civil engineer; Allan Marshick, senior vice-president, registered civil engineer/land surveyor; Michael C.R. Owen, president, registered civil engineer/land surveyor; Ray Murray, vice-president, registered civil engineer; and Stephen Chansley, vice-president, registered mechanical engineer. Not shown: Charles Davis, CAD operator.

Cheyne Owen, Ltd., is a young and aggressive multidisciplinary consulting engineering firm providing civil, environmental, land planning, and subdivision design; hydrology, drainage, and highways; and mechanical and process design in water, wastewater, and industrial waste. It was founded in 1983, with two main objectives in mind—to share in the economic growth of Arizona, and to provide the highest-quality engineering services available at an affordable cost to the client.

Since the firm's inception, it has enjoyed steady, successful growth, doubling the dollar volume each year, says founder and president, Michael C.R. Owen. Owen, a native of New Zealand, received his bachelor of engineering degree in 1967, and later earned an M.S. in environmental engineering from Loyola University in Los Angeles. He attributes the firm's success to a highly trained and skilled staff, effective management and cost-control principles, and state-of-the-art procedures.

"Engineering can and should be fun," is the philosophy at Cheyne Owen, and the successful completion of a diversity of projects reflects the pride that comes from enjoying one's work. Owen believes that a project can only be successful when the people performing the work enjoy the challenges.

To meet the changing needs of its clients, the firm has streamlined procedures by developing an efficient and innovative computer-automated drafting system, with specifically tailored software developed by the firm's engineers. This system is used for almost all of its projects, including difficult topographical and civil drawings, and particularly for land plan-

ning and design. Vice-president Ray Murray explains that as of February 1988, the firm is working on numerous land planning projects incorporating the computerized design and drafting system.

Fred Brinker, the firm's process engineer and computer manager, reports that Cheyne Owen is currently under contract with the City of Tucson to provide CAD training for its personnel. In addition, the firm has created computer models for master planning of municipal utilities, Dbase programs for tracking of drawings, provision of instrument indexes, and to create CPM schedules.

In 1984 the firm was commissioned to provide a $50-million, comprehensive wastewater master plan for the City of Sierra Vista, which included development of a computer software system for land zoning, demographics, and wastewater conveyance, and has used this master planning model for Willcox and Marana.

In 1987 the firm completed a multimillion-dollar upgrade renovation, and design of an industrial waste treatment plant for IBM-Tucson, which included development of a computerized control system, and an innovative 8-million-gallon waste storage handling and disposal system.

Cheyne Owen is an equal opportunity employer and is dedicated to the advancement and development of minorities. Alvin Ross, a Navajo Indian who joined the firm in 1985, was trained on CAD and is now the firm's CAD manager and chief CAD operator.

Cheyne Owen's staff of 19 includes six engineers, two of which are registered land surveyors.

Patrons

The following individuals, companies, and organizations have made a valuable commitment to the quality of this publication. Windsor Publications and the Arizona Historical Society gratefully acknowledge their participation in *Arizona: An Illustrated History of the Grand Canyon State.*

Anchor National Companies*
Anderson DeBartolo Pan, Inc./
    Architecture & Engineers*
The Arizona Biltmore*
Arizona Farm Bureau Federation*
Arizona Public Service Company*
The Arizona Republic/
    The Phoenix Gazette/
    The Arizona Business Gazette*
Arizona State Compensation Fund*
Arizona State Savings and Credit Union*
Astro Blueprint and Supply Company, Inc.*
John E. Bergeson
Blue Circle West*
Bill Brodersen
Michael J. Byrne
Cannon & Associates, Inc./
    Consulting Engineers*
Carroll & Associates, Inc.
Carole and Fred Carroll
Cheyne Owen, Ltd.*
Citibank (Arizona)*
Colossal Cave*
Desert Schools Federal Credit Union*
Eagle Milling Company*
The Estes Co.*
Evergreen Air Center*
Fairfield Homes*
Farmers Investment Co.*
Garrett Turbine Engine Company
General Motors Desert Proving Ground*
Glen-Mar Door Manufacturing Company
Golden Eagle Distributors Inc.*

W.L. Gore & Associates, Inc.*
Great American/
    First Savings Bank, F.S.B.*
Lillian H. Hall
Hall of Flame*
Houston International, Ltd.
Johnson-Brittain & Associates*
KCEE Radio*
Knoell Homes*
W.A. Krueger Co.*
Lincoln Laser Company*
Loews Ventana Canyon Resort*
Russ Lyon Realty Company*
McDonnell Douglas Helicopter Company
Marine Corps Air Station*
Messinger Mortuary & Chapel, Inc.*
MicroAge, Inc.*
Martha White Nelson
Northern Arizona University*
Palo Verde Hospital*
PCS, Inc.*
The Pensus Group*
Ralph's Transfer, Inc.*
Salt River Project*
Shamrock Foods Company*
Snell and Wilmer*
Sonora Desert Hospital, H.C.A.*
Southwest Ambulance, Inc.*
Mr. and Mrs. Robert Sundt
Thomas-Davis Medical Centers, P.C.*
Trailside Galleries*
Tucson Medical Center*
Valley National Bank of Arizona*
VisionQuest*
The Westward Look Resort*

*Partners in Progress of *Arizona: An Illustrated History of the Grand Canyon State.* The histories of these companies and organizations appear in Chapter 9, beginning on page 145.

Bibliography

SUGGESTIONS FOR FURTHER READING

General History

The oldest of the general histories of Arizona is Hubert Howe Bancroft's *History of Arizona and New Mexico* (San Francisco, 1889) which, despite its age, is still of considerable value. The best of the multivolume histories is James H. McClintock's *Arizona: Prehistoric, Aboriginal, Pioneer and Modern* (3 volumes, Chicago, 1916), but unfortunately it ends with the time of statehood. Most massive is Thomas E. Farish's *History of Arizona* (8 volumes, San Francisco, 1915-1918). Also deserving of attention are Richard E. Sloan and Ward R. Adam's *History of Arizona* (4 volumes, Phoenix, 1930) and Editor Edward H. Peplow's *History of Arizona* (3 volumes, Phoenix, 1958).

In fairly recent times some interesting one-volume histories have appeared, including: Rufus K. Wyllys' *Arizona: The History of a Frontier State* (Phoenix, 1950); Anne Merriman Peck's *The March of Arizona History* (Tucson, 1962); Odie B. Faulk's *Arizona: A Short History* (Norman, Oklahoma, 1970); Marshall Trimble's *Arizona: A Panoramic History of a Frontier State* (New York, 1977); and Bert M. Fireman's *Arizona: Historic Land* (New York, 1982). Jay J. Wagoner's *Early Arizona: Prehistory to Civil War* (Tucson, 1975) covers several periods of the Arizona story.

Useful reference works on particular subjects include: Will C. Barnes' *Arizona Place Names* (Tucson, 1935), which has been expanded and enlarged upon by Byrd H. Granger (Tucson, 1960); Joseph Miller's *Arizona: A State Guide* (New York, 1956), which was originally a part of the WPA series; Henry P. Walker and Don Bufkin's *Historical Atlas of Arizona* (Norman, 1979); and John S. Goff's *Arizona Biographical Dictionary* (Cave Creek, 1983), which contains sketches of the lives of 300 Arizonans of all eras. John O. and Lillian Theobald's *Arizona Territory: Post Offices and Postmasters* (Phoenix, 1961) is the definitive work on the subject. The University of Arizona's *Arizona: Its People and Resources* (Tucson, 1972) approaches the economy and sociology of the state, while Bruce Mason and Heinz Hink's *Constitutional Government in Arizona* (Tempe, 1982) explores the government. Editor Andrew Wallace's *Sources and Readings in Arizona History* (Tucson, 1965) gives excellent direction to the historical reader.

The Ancient Past and Native Americans

Harold S. Gladwin's *A History of the Ancient Southwest* (Portland, Maine, 1957) serves as an introduction to the area prior to the coming of the Europeans. Studies of Arizona Indian tribes include Frank C. Lockwood's *The Apache Indians* (New York, 1938), a classic; John Upton Terrell's *The Navajos* (New York, 1970); and Jack D. Forbes' *Warriors of the Colorado* (Norman, 1965). For study of the Navajos, Lynn R. Bailey's *Bosque Redondo* (Pasadena, California, 1970) and the writings of Dan L. Thrapp, especially *The Conquest of Apacheria* (Norman, 1967), are of great value. Geronimo's story is told in *Geronimo's Story of His Life,* edited by S.M. Barrett (New York, 1906), Britton Davis' *The Truth About Geronimo* (New Haven, Connecticut, 1929), and Angie Debo's *Geronimo* (Norman, 1976).

The Spanish Empire and Settlements

The works of the late Herbert E. Bolton are important classics. Especially significant are *Coronado: Knight of Pueblos and Plains* (New York, 1949), *Kino's Historical Memoir of Pimeria Alta* (2 volumes, Berkeley, California, 1948), and the *Rim of Christendom* (New York, 1936). Elliott Coues, who was in Arizona in the 1860s, was the translator and editor of *On the Trail of a Spanish Pioneer: The Diary and Itinerary of Francisco Garces* (2 volumes, New York, 1900). A volume in the New American Nation Series, Charles Gibson's *Spain in America* (New York, 1966) gives an overview of the great empire. Peter Masten Dunne was the translator of *Jacobo Sadelmayr* (Tucson, 1955), the story of one of the lesser known padres and John L. Kessell wrote the worthy *Mission of Sorrows: Jesuit Guevavi and the Pimas, 1691-1767* (Tucson, 1970), which tells of the troubles of a lesser mission. For a view of military matters in the Spanish New World see Sidney B. Brinckerhoff and Odie B. Faulk's *Lancers for the King* (Phoenix, 1965) and for government in general Marc Simmons' *Spanish Government in New Mexico* (Albuquerque, 1968). A significant figure of the late Spanish period is the subject of *Anza and the Northwest Frontier of New Spain* by J.N. Bowman and Robert F. Heizer (Los Angeles, 1967).

Mexico and the Mountain Men

The full story of the years of Mexican rule over Arizona is yet to be told but helpful are Odie B. Faulk's *Constitution of the State of Occidente* (Tucson, 1967). Sidney B. Brinckerhoff's "The Last Years of Spanish Arizona, 1786-1821" *(Arizona and the West,* Spring 1967) deals with an earlier era. The highly regarded *Old Bill Williams: Mountain Man* (Chapel Hill, North Carolina, 1936) by Alpheus H. Favor, Sharlot Hall's *First Citizen of Prescott: Pauline Weaver; Trapper and Mountain Man* (Prescott, 1932), Bernice Blackwelder's *Great Westerner: The Story of Kit Carson* (Caldwell, Idaho, 1962), M.M. Estergreen's *Kit Carson, a Portrait in Courage* (Norman, 1962), and Forbes Parkhill's *The Blazed Trail of Antoine Leroux* (Los Angeles, 1964) recount the adventures of fur traders, guides, and scouts.

The Mexican War, Guadalupe Hidalgo, and the 1850s

This period, one of the most interesting in Arizona's history, has produced a wealth of materials. Bernard De Voto's *The Year of Decision, 1846* (Boston, 1943) is very popular; Seymour V. Connor and Odie B. Faulk's *North America Divided: The Mexican War, 1846-1848* (New York, 1971) is also useful. Otis E. Young's *The West of Philip St. George Cooke, 1809-1895* (Glendale, California, 1955) and Dwight L.

Clarke's Stephen Watts Kearny: Soldier of the West (Norman, 1961) are accounts of two important figures of the era. Editor Henry L. Dobyns' *Hepah California: The Journal of Cave Johnson Couts . . .* (Tucson, 1961) chronicles the adventures of a less important but an equally interesting character.

Robert V. Hine's *Bartlett's West: Drawing the Mexican Boundary* (New Haven, 1968) recounts the aftermath of the war. Of considerable interest is Edward S. Wallace's *The Great Reconnaissance: Soldiers, Artists and Scientists on the Frontier, 1848-1861* (Boston, 1955). Harlan D. Fowler's *Camels to California* (Palo Alto, California, 1950) tells of that famous adventure. Lieutenant Beale's life is told in Gerald Thompson's *Edward F. Beale and the American West* (Albuquerque, 1983) and in Carl Briggs and Clyde Francis Trudell's *Quarterdeck and Saddlehorn: The Story of Edward F. Beale* (Glendale, 1983). Paul D. Bailey presents a rather different individual in *Jacob Hamblin: Buckskin Apostle* (Los Angeles, 1948). Roscoe P. and Margaret P. Conkling produced a major work in *The Butterfield Overland Mail, 1857-1869* (2 volumes, Glendale, 1947), but one ought not to overlook Gerald T. Ahnert's *Retracing the Butterfield Overland Trail Through Arizona* (Los Angeles, 1973). Ray Brandes' *Frontier Military Posts of Arizona* (Globe, 1960) is indispensable on that subject. The same may be said for Richard E. Lingenfelter's *Steamboats on the Colorado River, 1852-1916* (Tucson, 1978). Frank C. Lockwood's *Life in Old Tucson, 1854-1861* (Los Angeles, 1943) is well known for telling stories of the people of that time and place. A volume entitled *Latest From Arizona: The Hesperian Letters, 1859-1861,* edited by Constance Wynn Altshuler (Tucson, 1969), is important for details of the time just before the start of the great conflict.

The Civil War and Early Territorial Period

Ray C. Colton's *The Civil War in the Western Territories* (Norman, 1959) gives an overall view of the period while Aurora Hunt's *Major General James Henry Carleton, 1814-1873* (Glendale, 1955) focuses on Arizona's part of the story. George W. Baylor's *John Robert Baylor: Confederate Governor of Arizona* (Tucson, 1966) is the biography of a Confederate figure, while A.M. Gressinger's *Charles D. Poston: Sunland Seer* (Globe, 1961) presents the "Father of Arizona Territory." Benjamin Sacks' *Be It Enacted: The Creation of the Territory of Ari-*

zona (Phoenix, 1964) is a major modern work on the birth of Arizona Territory. Pauline Henson's *Founding a Wilderness Capital* (Flagstaff, 1965) is the well-told tale of establishing Prescott in the wilderness.

Travel in the 1860s is described in J. Ross Browne's *Adventures in the Apache Country* (Tucson, 1974) and Martha Summerhays' *Vanished Arizona* (Philadelphia, 1908) is the classic account of an army wife in the Southwest. *Powell of the Colorado* (Princeton, 1951) by William C. Darrah tells of the great expeditions and James H. McClintock's *The Mormon Settlement in Arizona* (Phoenix, 1921) is the classic account of some of those who settled the land. Jay Wagoner's *Arizona Territory, 1863-1912: A Political History* (Tucson, 1970) covers politics during this period and John S. Goff's *Richard C. McCormick* (Cave Creek, 1983) is the biography of an important early governor. Economic history has been dealt with in its several aspects: Robert G. Cleland's *A History of Phelps Dodge* (New York, 1952) is a good account of mining; Allen A. Erwin's *The Southwest of John H. Slaughter* (Glendale, 1965) is a story of a cattleman; and Donald M. Powell's *The Peralta Grant* (Norman, 1960) is a well-researched account of the fabulous "Baron of Arizona."

Later Territorial Days and the Search for Statehood

Earl R. Forrest's *Arizona's Dark and Bloody Ground* (Caldwell, Idaho, 1950) covers the Pleasant Valley War, while Don Dedera's *A Little War of Our Own: The Pleasant Valley Feud Revisited* (Flagstaff, 1987) is a more recent account of the same. Frances M. Quebbeman's *Medicine in Territorial Arizona* (Phoenix, 1966) is an excellent account of the physicians of the era while Editor A. Gustafson's *John Spring's Arizona* (Tucson, 1966) tells of a teacher, and Douglas D. Martin's *The Lamp in the Desert* (Tucson, 1960) tells of the university. Arizona's part in the Spanish American War, at least one colorful portion, is chronicled in Charles Herner's *The Arizona Rough Riders* (Tucson, 1970). Joseph Miller's *The Arizona Rangers* (New York, 1972) does the same for a little-known group of lawmen, and Richard E. Sloan's *Memories of an Arizona Judge* (Palo Alto, 1932) looks at life from the standpoint of one who served 16 years on the bench.

Biographies are important for the history of any period and some which are representative of this time are: George E. Webb's *Tree*

Rings and Telescopes: The Scientific Career of Andrew E. Douglass (Tucson, 1983); Dean Smith's *The Goldwaters of Arizona* (Flagstaff, 1986); C.L. Sonnichsen's *Colonel Greene and the Copper Skyrocket* (Tucson, 1974); Margaret F. Maxwell's *A Passion for Freedom: The Life of Sharlot Hall* (Tucson, 1982); and Dale L. Walker's *Death Was the Black Horse* (Austin, Texas, 1975; later reissued under the title *Buckey O'Neill: The Story of a Rough Rider*). In both words and pictures Editor Dean Smith's *Arizona Highways Album: The Road to Statehood* (Phoenix, 1987) portrays Arizona at the turn of the century.

The Last 75 Years

Historians often take the view that anything which has been happening in the last half century is a "current event" and therefore not yet ready to be written as history. That view is not unknown in Arizona and consequently recent decades are in need of documentation. J. Morris Richards' *The Birth of Arizona* (Phoenix, 1940) remains the only account of the creation of the new state. *George W.P. Hunt and His Arizona* (Pasadena, 1973) is the account of the long-time first state governor, while Editor George F. Sparks' *A Many Colored Toga: The Diary of Henry Fountain Ashurst* (Tucson, 1961), Robert Paul Browder and Thomas Q. Smith's *Independent: A Biography of Lewis W. Douglas* (New York, 1986), and Ernest W. McFarland's *Mac: The Autobiography of Ernest W. McFarland* (Phoenix, 1979) deals with some other political figures. Frank Gruber's *Zane Grey: A Biography* (New York, 1970) and Candace C. Kant's *Zane Grey's Arizona* (Flagstaff, 1984) are also worthy volumes.

The water issue is the subject of Norris Hundley, Jr.'s, *Dividing the Waters: A Century of the Controversy Between the United States and Mexico* (Berkeley, 1965) and John H. Terrell's *The War for the Colorado* (2 volumes, Glendale, 1966). One aspect of labor unrest during World War I is told in James R. Kluger's *The Clifton-Morenci Strike* (Tucson, 1970).

Much more remains to be written on recent Arizona.

Index